I CAN'T BELIEVE I'M NOT DEAD

Escaping Abuse, a Cult,
Attempted Murder, and Other Insanities ...
A Story That Cannot Be True, But Is

KENDRA PETTY

O'LEARY
PUBLISHING
The Influencer's Press

NAPLES, FL

ISBN: 978-1-952491-50-4 (print)
ISBN: 978-1-952491-51-1 (ebook)
ISBN: 978-1-952491-55-9 (hardcover)
Library of Congress Control Number: 2023902444

Editing by Jessica Jones and Heather Davis Desrocher
Line Editing and Proofreading by Boris Boland and Kat
Langenheim
Cover and interior design by Jessica Angerstein

Printed in the United States of America

This book is dedicated to my brother, Kent Jr.;
my protector.

The names of the guilty
have been changed
to protect the innocent.

CONTENTS

A STORY WORTH TELLING

I am not famous. I may not even be a semi-demi-pseudo-celebrity, about to experience her 15 minutes of fame. I am like you. I grew up someplace unfabulous, moved away, built a successful career, fell in love, got married, and did all the things that contributing members of society are likely to do. What do I possibly have to say that merits your attention? Why would I have the audacity to write a book about myself?

Well, every time I have shared a story from my life experiences with my friends, they would stare at me, slack-jawed, while shaking their heads in bewilderment. They would say, "You know, you really have to write this down. Write a book!" Invariably, my response to them was, "I am not a writer, and who would care, anyway? You are only listening because you are a captive audience!" They would insist that was not the case; I would insist it was, and that was the end of that.

Admittedly, most of my life's events and stories are pretty lurid and colorful, but I am not an exhibitionist. I knew that if I were to tell my stories to anyone beyond my circle of friends, it would have to be for a damned good reason.

The element that turned me in the direction of writing was time. There is no way to process and understand the significance of the events of your life – much less write about them in a way that might actually benefit a reader – until you have a little perspective. In other words, the phrase, "Tragedy plus time equals comedy," is absolutely correct. My amendment to that is: "Tragedy, plus time, plus comedy, plus attempted murder, plus incredible feats of survival, equals a story of redemption worth telling."

The passage of time has allowed me to reflect on how – despite my life having been a repeated cycle of trauma – I have risen above those experiences. I now lead a happy, successful life. Trauma did not define me. While it has been **interesting** to catalog everything that has happened to me, it is truly **meaningful** for me to see how I was able to move forward after each experience. I began to realize that my story is less about the details of the catastrophes that I lived through and more about the way I chose to respond. I dealt with them; I questioned, reflected and healed. And, good God, there was a lot to deal with and heal from.

All of which brings me back to my response to friends who insisted that I write about my life: "Who would care, anyway?" The answer to that is – possibly – you, dear reader. I believe that any time you experience something that has enhanced your life, or has made you stronger, or just made you reflect on who you are in an interesting way, it is important to share it. Storytelling is how we learn, teach, grow and connect with one another – and my hope in sharing some of my story is that it will touch, inspire, motivate and help you.

Now that I am strong enough, and far enough away from all the tragedy to write about it, I am sharing my stories because I want to show that it is possible to move past adversity, illness, violence, poison, madness and loss – tremendous loss. I was able to move past – and to let go, heal and forgive – those who have hurt me and wronged me. Just as important, I was also able to forgive myself.

The way I did that followed just one of many paths I could have chosen, but I hope that my story will inspire **you** to find what will keep you going and allow you to live in happiness and joy. I hope that you will learn, as I have, how to not just survive – but how to **thrive**. And just maybe, you will write about what **you** experience, and you will become the next in a long line of storytellers, because our stories need to be told.

PROLOGUE

here is the deepest secret nobody knows
(here is the root of the root and the bud of the bud
and the sky of the sky of a tree called life...)
—E.E. CUMMINGS

Each of us has someone who shaped our childhood experience and ultimately who we have become as adults. For me, that person was my older brother, Kent Jr., who was two years older. He was the storybook, made-for-TV-movie, perfect version of a big brother. He was my first playmate, my best friend, and my protector. It was as if one of his assignments in life was to be my protector. And in the end, he paid the ultimate price for protecting me.

He watched over me, loved me, and always played with me – even when his friends complained about having a younger child (and a girl) hang out with them. He was strong, athletic, fun and loving. I looked up to him; I worshiped him. We were so close and loved each other tremendously. Whenever I talk about my childhood with Kent Jr., I know that the way I describe the intensity of our connection sounds nearly impossible to some people. But that really is how we were.

In every photograph of us, we were touching – holding hands, arms around each other, a hand on the other's leg, leaning on each other. We were like a unit, connected at the hip, and always laughing together. We learned to be silly from our father, and we both developed a sense of humor that – when my mother was not trying to stifle it – made life fun and funny. My dad was – and is – a really entertaining and funny guy, and was the saving grace in our mother's household. The negativity in my house came from my mother – Jeannie; but Dad and Kent Jr. mitigated my mother's toxicity with their love and naturally high spirits.

Kent Jr. and I played together all the time, and our dad, when he was home, played with us too. We loved to wrestle and roughhouse or play ball. It was usually rambunctious and rowdy, which my mother hated. She was always yelling at us to quiet down or take it outside, which we often did. My life was split into two modes: being inside (and feeling miserably anxious because of my mother) and being outside (and feeling free and unfettered, like children should).

I loved being around my brother. We shared a bedroom sometimes, and would talk into the night, giggling about something funny that happened that day, until we fell asleep. He was the best brother anyone could ask for: kind, gentle, and such a good soul.

One of the best mornings I ever spent with Kent Jr. was on Friday, June 13, 1975. It was the summer before third grade, and I was sup-posed to go to my last day of BlueBird summer day camp for an award ceremony. My mother wasn't going to the ceremony, and my dad was working, so I planned to go alone – even though I really didn't want to. But then, I heard that my brother was going fishing at Craig's Pond across the highway, with Terrie our babysitter (who ended up being a horrific human being). Well, if my brother was going fishing, I wanted to go with him! So, I begged my mother to let me skip the award ceremony. She agreed, and told my brother that it would be his job to make sure I got back and forth across the highway safely.

I was 8 years old, and Kent Jr. was 10 years old. Looking back, I realize how insane it was to let children cross two highways on foot. But Terrie was 15 years old, so I am sure my mother thought we would be OK. Little did my mother know that the babysitter she left us with was irresponsible, reckless, selfish and dangerous. I had a birthday party to go to that afternoon, so my mother instructed my brother to make sure they brought me back across the highway from Craig's Pond in time for the party. As my protector, my brother wholeheartedly agreed.

Those were the last words my mother ever spoke to my brother.

Off we went, across the highways to fish in Craig's Pond. I was beside myself with excitement to be with my brother and do something fun outside. I had never been to Craig's Pond, but I had heard a lot about it from friends, which added to my excitement. The pond was large, with a pedestrian bridge across it that was built with chains. As we walked across the bridge, it moved up and down, which was a fun experience.

Mr. and Mrs. Craig owned the pond and would let people fish from the bridge or the water's edge. Their house was set back from the highway, to the left and behind the pond. On the other side of the pond was a guest house that looked like a lighthouse. It was a beautiful property, and it was going to be a great morning for fishing!

The morning seemed to fly by as we fished from the bridge. I was having so much fun that I lost track of time. Several hours later, Terrie reminded us that it was time for us to head back for the birthday party. She was going to continue to fish, and said that my brother could take me back to the party by himself.

I begged her to go with us. I don't know why I thought it was so important that she come back with us – probably because I had never crossed those highways on foot, and it scared me. But she refused to go with us.

Kent Jr. and I headed across the bridge, and Terrie's words that we would be fine played in my head. Those were the last words that Terrie ever spoke to my brother.

CHAPTER ONE

THE BEGINNING AND THE END

You may wonder how my mother could let young children cross a busy highway all alone, or allow her children to be in the care of a terrible babysitter. The answer is that my mother was mentally ill. Like many in her generation with mental illness, she went undiagnosed for much of her life. But those of us who lived with her could have provided a diagnosis in keeping with the DSM (Diagnostic and Statistical Manual of Mental Disorders) any day of the week. We know now that she is a manic bipolar narcissist with sociopathic tendencies.

I do not believe in blaming others for what has happened in my life, and I know that it would be simplistic to blame the misfortunes and trials of life on my mother. As adults, we are solely responsible for our happiness and success, regardless of the challenges we have faced. Yet, my mother and her illness shaped my childhood and my life in a very profound way.

Kent Jr. was the saving grace of my childhood. He and I happily played together for hours, staying as far out of our mother's line of vision – and hearing range – as possible. We were not the type of children who played board games. We were the "Let's see what happens if I throw myself down this hill or jump off of this rooftop" kind, which meant that we could not stay under her radar.

When we were forced to play inside, we found activities that would allow us to monkey around as much as possible. Once it was too dark (in my mother's opinion) for us to be running around outside, we would often play the "chair game." The game was played on a round, gold, velvet chair in the living room that could spin 360 degrees without stopping. It would keep spinning as long as there was at least one of us to push it. We spun and spun and laughed and laughed until we were close to wetting our pants. We would laugh hysterically not only because of the physical sensation of the spinning, but also because of the ridiculousness of watching the other child holding on, helpless and terrified.

The chair game was a brilliant example of how to fly above the radar and make my mother angry. Our laughter annoyed the hell out of her. It wasn't just that we might get hurt and that she might have to deal with the consequences. No, what pushed her to the edge was our loud laughter. It never occurred to us that it was the **laughter** that irritated her, until one night when she expressed her feelings about it by covering our mouths with duct tape so she could not hear us. By my mother's standards, that wasn't an extraordinary measure – it was just practical.

Despite our mouths being covered in duct tape, Kent Jr. and I continued spinning in the chair/rocket ship/carousel/race car, confident that everything now would be OK, since we had been muzzled. If noise had been the problem, that problem had been solved; there wasn't anything to be concerned about anymore. On that particular evening, our mother was in the kitchen, blissfully oblivious to whatever we were up to – and numb to the responsibilities of child-rearing.

Just as we were losing ourselves in the fun of the chair game, and forgetting that we were perpetually on thin ice with our mother, Kent Jr. spun the chair so hard that I flew out of the chair. I landed on the floor headfirst. The pain was so shocking to me that it took my 6-year-old senses a minute before I burst into tears. I started wailing silently behind the duct tape.

My nose started running and then it stopped up. Then, panic set in, because there was no way I could breathe. Between the stuffy nose and duct tape, my airways were totally blocked; there wasn't a single decent breathing option available to me.

I was too scared to ask my mother for help. I would not take off the duct tape, because that would mean a terrifying level of trouble. That thought totally escaped me. My brother clearly had the same thought, because he would not take the tape off either.

I have no idea how Mother figured out that something was wrong, but she finally came out of the kitchen into the living room. She ripped the tape off my face, screaming at me for getting hurt after she told us to knock it off. To add injury to insult, she gave both of us a whoopin'.

My brother and I were the ones who got the spankings, but our father often received the same kind of hysteria and rage. Mother was always over the top, screaming and yelling at all of us on a daily basis. Remembering the level of hysteria and violence that was a daily part of my childhood only reinforces my certainty that Mother had a deep mental illness.

The chair and duct tape episode is one of my early memories of my mother's abuse, but there were other incidents before that. Not only was my mother abusive, but she was also not a good mother. Instead of being thoughtful, loving, or nurturing like most mothers, she was a mean, angry, screaming and throwing machine. When I was only a few months old, she put my carrier down on the kitchen table in such a way that it flipped over, and I landed face-down on the kitchen floor. She did not have any motherly instincts.

I know that there are many awful parents who live by the rule of, "Never in front of the neighbors," effectively keeping the family disaster a secret. While my mother usually practiced that rule and knew not to reveal her dark side to people outside of our home, there were a few occasions where she did not control herself and allowed someone other than family a peek into her madness.

When I was 7, I invited my friend Angie to my house for a sleepover. Unfortunately, she witnessed one of my mother's outbursts, which I am sure scared the life out of her. Angie and I woke up early, when the sun came up. With no clock in my room, we were unaware of what time it was. We were lying in bed talking and laughing our heads off about some silly little kid stuff. Out of nowhere, my mother burst through the door and started spanking and slapping me with both arms and hands flying. She said it was too early for us to be awake and to be so loud.

I don't remember how that sleepover ended or how Angie reacted, but I also do not recall Angie sleeping over at my house again after that. I did continue to sleep over at Angie's house – because her parents were normal.

My mother did not work outside the home, so there was little to divert her attention from whatever my siblings or I were doing. One of the few things that distracted her was social time with our neighbors, especially Don and Noreen from across the street. Noreen didn't work outside the home either, and so she and Mother spent time together and became close friends. Occasionally, Noreen babysat us children.

Don got along with my dad too, and sometimes the four of them spent evenings together. But I never forged a friendship with Don and Noreen's daughters. One daughter, Cary, was younger than I was and very shy and timid. The older daughter, Taylor, was several years older and not interested in hanging out with me. So, not much time was spent with them, even though they lived right across the street and our mothers were best friends.

Living with my mother was absolutely no picnic for any of us. However, the worst was yet to come.

As I said at the beginning, Friday, June 13, 1975, was one of the best days I spent with my brother. It also turned out to be the absolute worst day of my life. Kent Jr. and I left Terrie on the bridge, fishing, and we headed back across the pond to the highway. At the first highway, Kent Jr. held my hand and waited for the right opportunity to cross. When there were no cars, he ran, pulling me along.

I said, "No, we can't go yet."

He said, "It's fine. Let's go." pulling me along with him.

We were halfway across when I broke free from his hand and ran back to where we had been standing on the side of the highway. He continued to run to the other side; he turned around and waved me to come, yelling that it was safe.

Just then, I saw a large black car barreling down the highway toward him. I yelled at him to move, pointing to the car. But he continued to stand on the edge of the highway and wave for me to come. My yells got louder as the car approached. Our eyes were locked. He never took his eyes off me, as I yelled at him to move.

The last thing my brother saw was me. He never saw the car that hit him. The only thing on his mind was his responsibility to protect me. I watched in horror as the car barreled into him, flipping him up onto the hood and then into the windshield. As the car slammed on its brakes, my brother flew off the front of the car and landed headfirst onto the asphalt.

I screamed and screamed in terror. I ran across the highway without looking, straight to my brother. He was lying in a crumbled, broken, bloody mess. I saw that a huge piece of his scalp was completely missing where he had landed on his head – it was just a bloody skull.

I screamed at him to get up; I begged him to get up. I was in absolute hysterics, jumping up and down, screaming and begging for someone to help him.

A woman who had been in a car behind the car that hit my brother stopped and got out of her car. She came up to me and asked if the boy was my brother. I cried, "Yes, please help him."

She immediately took control; she told me to go find my mother. I guess that she wanted me away from the horrific scene of my bloody brother, laying on the highway dying. I did as I was told, and ran across the other highway into our neighborhood.

It was four blocks to our house. I ran, crying and sobbing, into our house. I ran through the house trying to find my mother. The only person in the house was my 1-year-old brother Frankie; he was napping on my parents' bed. But my mother was nowhere to be found. To this day, I do not know where my mother was. I ran out of the house and across the street to Don and Noreen's house. I was banging on the door and screaming. Noreen answered the door, and I screamed that Kent Jr. had been hit by a car on the highway.

Everything became a blur at that point for a brief time. I remember Terrie showing up at some point before we went to the hospital. She was in hysterics and crying, and had bloody hands. I don't know if her hands were bloody from fishing or from my brother, but I suspect the latter.

I remember that Terrie's mother, Faye, drove me to the hospital. My memory from that point on – once we arrived at the ER – was crystal clear again. Faye and I walked into the ER and walked by a room where a doctor and my parents were. I saw the doctor was giving my parents shots presumably to help calm them down. My parents did not look up and seemed unaware that I was there.

Instead of taking me to my parents, Faye escorted me into the ER waiting room next to the surgery room. Doctors and nurses were rushing in and out of the two large swinging doors, bringing in more equipment and supplies. I knew that my brother was in there. I prayed that he would be OK. *Please God, let my brother be OK*, I kept saying in my head, over and over. I cried, rocked in my seat, and shook profusely. I felt sick to my stomach and wanted to throw up. A police officer came over and started questioning me; I answered his questions as best I could. When he was done, I went to the restroom to throw up. But relief would not come, ever.

After my interview with the police, I was carted off to the house of a schoolmate, Eric. Eric was a class friend who had two other brothers and a sweet mother who took me in that afternoon. I tried to play with the boys, but I was just too distraught. I kept wondering what was going on with my brother. I settled in to watch TV, but as I lay on the floor, all I could think of was my brother. I replayed the entire accident over and over in my head, and kept praying that he would be OK.

Night fell, and someone finally came to get me from Eric's house. They drove me to my house, where there were lots of cars parked outside. When I walked in, the house was jammed with people. I knew many of them, but some I had never seen before. My grandparents, who lived eight hours away, were there also.

My mother was sitting next to my dad, who was laying down on the couch. They were both crying, as was everyone else. At that moment, I knew that my brother was dead, even though I hoped that I was wrong. I went over to my parents and sat with them on the couch, touching my dad's arm as he wept.

Eventually, they got up and asked me to come into my bedroom with them. We all sat on the bed, and they told me that Kent Jr. had gone to be with the Lord. We cried together; we prayed for my brother. Once again, I broke down into hysterics. My best friend, my protector, my brother, had died while protecting me. He had died violently, grotesquely, and horrifically – and I immediately thought about the huge part I had played in this death.

Why didn't I run with my brother when he told me to? Why did I get scared and turn back?! If I had not turned back, he would not have gotten hit. It was my fault; it was my fault, I thought, but I was too scared to tell my parents.

If I had not skipped my BlueBirds award ceremony, my brother would not have been hit. If I didn't insist on going to the birthday party, he wouldn't have died. If I had run across the highway when he told me to, he would be alive. My brother ultimately lost his life protecting me.

His death, and my part in it, is the biggest regret of my life. It is the one thing I would undo, if I could. Losing my best friend, my brother, changed my life and my family's life forever. How would I live without my brother?

The guilt that comes with killing someone – especially someone you love so deeply – will never, ever leave me. To this day, I carry it with me. I killed my brother; there are no two ways about it. Yes, one can blame my mother for letting us go in the first place, and one can blame Terrie for not going back with us, and one can blame the woman who hit my brother, but ultimately the real blame lay with me. If I had just run when my brother did, he would be alive today.

To this day, decades later, I still see the accident in detail on a very regular basis. It is a very vivid memory – from him waving at me to cross the highway and telling me it was OK, to him confidently looking into my eyes, protecting me, to the car hitting him and tossing him about, and then ultimately to him landing on his head. It is a vision I have replayed in my mind thousands of times; it is something that never leaves me.

The days following Kent Jr.'s death were filled with people stopping by the house. At one point, I was laying in my parents' bed to be away from the crowds, and a woman poked her head through the bedroom doorway. It turned out to be the woman who had sent me to find my mother when my brother had been hit. She wanted to stop by and check on me; her concern was touching. She did not stay long – I am sure she was at a loss for words – but even at my young age, it meant a lot to me that she came.

We visited the funeral home several times to see my brother. He was in a viewing room, in a casket, dressed in a suit and bow tie that he had worn a few months earlier for our last family photograph. I remember dressing for that family picture and having been upset that I had to stop playing to put on a dress and brush my hair. I had questioned my mother about why we had to go take a picture, and I remember her words so clearly: "Because we may not all be here one day, and we want to remember what we all looked like."

I look at that family picture now and think of my mother's words. I see my brother in the suit that he would be buried in just a few months later. Death is the cruelest trick of life – period.

On one visit to the funeral home, my paternal grandmother was with us. As I looked at my brother lying still in the casket, hair glued to his head where he had none after losing his scalp, my grandmother reached under the part of the casket that covered his legs. She said, "His legs are crushed." Why would she do that? It was just another horrifying thing to add to the already horrifying situation. I honestly do not understand people sometimes.

We had his first funeral at our Baptist church in Lawton where we lived. Then, we drove two hours to Kingfisher – the town where my brother and I were born – for another funeral in the Methodist church that my father had attended.

The two-hour drive was agonizing. My parents drove in the town car ahead, and I had to drive in a car with my maternal grandparents. I cried the whole way because I couldn't ride with my parents. I had not spent any time with my parents throughout the entire ordeal. I had been shuffled around from house to house with relatives and friends. I can't imagine the pain of losing a child, but I do know the pain of losing my brother. The fact that we couldn't be together as a family was heartbreaking. And I wondered if they knew that it was my fault that my brother died, and if that was why they separated themselves from me.

After the funeral at the Methodist church, we drove to the cemetery in town where we were to bury Kent Jr. We waited while they lowered the casket into the ground. My mother was wailing and crying, and it was so very terrible. The casket would not fit, so they set it aside and dug the hole wider. We left my brother alone to be buried in the ground. My poor brother – I did not want to leave him, but it was time to drive to the nearby family farm.

We had both always loved spending time with our cousins on the farm and getting into all kinds of mischief with them. As an adult, those relationships that I still have with my cousins are some of the truly amazing things that came from my childhood. I am very grateful that my cousins and my aunt are still very important in my life.

In the days, months and years that followed, I missed my brother so much. The devastation, guilt, and loneliness that I felt was crushing. The trauma of the whole experience brought on a succession of horrible night terrors, in which I saw myself about to be killed. Sometimes, I would scream in my sleep; but more often, I would jump out of bed and run around the house. Sometimes I even ran out of the house. I was running from whatever was trying to kill me until I eventually woke up, out of breath, shaking, sweating and scared to death. These night terrors lasted for decades – into my 40s, when they finally started to slow down to a dull roar. Now I only have one every few weeks or once a month instead of nightly, which is a big relief.

For some reason, my mother decided that we needed to befriend Maria, the woman who drove the car that hit my brother. She would come over to the house to visit, and we would go to her house to see her. I do not think that was a good decision, because every visit brought up more pain from my brother's death. As I understood it, she never drove again after the accident.

As we all tried to put our lives back together, my mother's mental illness only worsened. The death of my brother made her even more mad – both in the literal and figurative sense. She became more violent and broke down constantly. She became angrier and angrier, and over the years she beat me more and more. I always felt that it was because she blamed me for my brother's death, and so I accepted the abuse as my punishment for what I did.

I understand that losing a child brings incredible pain and can overwhelm one's mental state. However, my mother was not right from the start. Kent Jr.'s death was horrible, tragic and devastating – it changed

my family forever. My parents lost their firstborn – the "good" child –
and were now left with the little hellion (me) and Frankie, who was only
1 year old when Kent Jr. died.

CHAPTER TWO

THE MADNESS DEEPENS

When my brother was alive, Mother punished me regularly with yelling and spankings. After he died, the spankings escalated to beatings – hellacious, cruel, severely painful beatings. They were the kind of beatings that left marks (bruises, cuts, scratches and welts).

Mother liked using a paddle, her hands, a belt (even the buckle end), or any object she could find. She also shoved, pushed and slapped me, and pulled my hair out. She even choked me frequently – usually to the point where my eyesight would get dark, and I would see sparkles of light. As I got older, and bigger, the violence toward me worsened. Mother stopped choking me, but she stepped up the beatings and cruelty considerably.

Sometimes I had to explain the marks on me when I was at school. I have no idea if anyone believed the lies I told to cover for my mother, but they were just one indication of the cult of secrecy that she created in our house.

Mother never choked my little brother Frankie, except once when he was about 2 years old. It freaked me out so badly that I jumped on her back and screamed, "Stop choking him! Stop choking him!" My mother turned around and lit into me, hitting and choking me. But it was the last time that I remember her putting a hand on Frankie like that.

The night terrors that started right after Kent Jr. died became progressively worse. They would often cause me to run out of my bedroom; and as I got older, I would even run out of my house and hotel rooms (when I was traveling). Running from death in my sleep with my eyes wide open meant that I would wake up in strange, unfamiliar places. It was frightening.

Eventually, after some embarrassing experiences waking up naked outside, I learned to sleep with my clothes on. I have done a lot of work to heal and minimize the night terrors.

After the death of Kent Jr., my mother took a part-time job (maybe to get out of the house and take her mind off of things), and so I spent more time with Terrie the babysitter. Terrie lived next door to us with her mother, Faye, and her stepdad Wayne when I was in "Kendragarten." My mother would send me over to Terrie's to get me out of the house. I liked Terrie at first, but she soon started to show her true colors and had a mean streak.

One time, when Kent Jr. and I were younger, we were roughhousing in the pool. He accidently pushed me underwater and I struggled to get up, choking on the water. It was an accident for sure, but Terrie hit him hard several times until he cried. She was a big girl, so I know it hurt, and I felt bad for him.

Another time, I was over at her house drinking a Coke out of a glass bottle. She tipped the bottle up while I was drinking and held it on my mouth. I was not old enough to know to just stop drinking and breathe through my nose, or to pull away and let the Coke spill out. So instead, I kept drinking until I ran out of breath. She only pulled the bottle away when I choked, and I spit Coke everywhere. She thought it was the funniest thing.

Once when we were baking cookies, I told her that I loved vanilla. She said, "Oh, you do? Well, try a spoonful." She shoved the pure vanilla in my mouth and laughed so hard, knowing that it would taste disgusting.

Eventually her cruelty transitioned into something more perverse. One time, when she was babysitting me and her female friend was over, she grabbed me and threw me across her lap. She said, "Let's see what color panties Kendra has on today." She pulled my pants down; I begged her to stop and started crying. I had on white panties with yellow and green polka dots. She thought it was hysterical and made so much fun of them. I was mortified and crushed.

One night when I was 6, Terrie was babysitting Kent Jr. and me at our house. After she sent him to bed, she pulled out the sofa bed and told me to sleep there. I crawled into the bed, and she lay down next to me and said, "Let's play a game. I will pretend to be the husband and you be the wife." She rolled over on top of me (she was a large girl who was much older than me, and I was a skinny, petite girl); then, she began touching me aggressively through my pajamas and made me touch her. It scared me and it hurt – I did not understand what was happening.

Over time, this role play of hers became more and more aggressive. Ultimately, one night at her house, when I was 7, she raped me. She penetrated me very aggressively with multiple fingers and it hurt so much that I cried.

She did the same thing on other nights after that, and it always hurt. I struggled with UTIs because of it. She was abusive before my brother died, but spending more time with me alone gave her the opportunity to do more terrible things to me. When I look back at the horrible abuse and rape, I become so angry. What kind of a teenage girl gets off on that? I also worry and wonder if she ever did anything to my brother. I hope not, and because she spent most of her time alone with me, I try to believe she didn't. I never told my parents about what Terrie was doing to me. It was something else to hide and feel shame from for many years.

My father, who is an extremely smart and driven man, worked at a radio station as a DJ for many years. At one point he took on the role of sales manager for the station, while still doing some shows on the radio. But he wanted more, and maybe he also wanted out of the house away from my mother, and to take his mind off our tragedy.

He also wanted to earn more money – and so, after my brother passed, he took some classes and started building homes. With my father doing double-duty at the radio station and trying to grow his homebuilding business, I was left with my younger brother and my mother all of the time. That was no fun at all – because of my mother.

When my dad was home, my parents fought so fiercely that often I ran from the house. I would dash down the street, trying to find someone to call the police so they would keep my parents from killing each other. Nobody was ever arrested or removed from the house, though, because by the time I reached the end of the street, I would think, *Do I really want the police to come? How embarrassing would that be? My parents will be furious with me.* Still, every time those fights happened, I would run out of the house in fear, thinking that maybe that time I would find someone to help.

There were times when I got caught in the middle of their fights. They would do this crazy tug-of-war with me – my mother would try to leave and take me with her, dragging me by the arm; and my dad would hang onto my other arm, pulling me. He would yell that there was no way she was going to take me. On two occasions, my mother used her car as a weapon – driving it into my father's car, with her children in it, because she was so angry with him.

My mother also turned her violence on herself. She had a flair for the dramatic, and if we were riding in the car while she was fighting with my dad, she would open the door to jump. My dad would grab her arm and slam on the brakes, putting all of us in danger.

One night, we were on a two-hour drive to Kingfisher to see my dad's mother. There had been a light snowfall that evening, and my mother was angry about something. Her voice got louder and louder and then she finally flung open the door to jump out of the car while we were going at least 60 miles an hour. My dad slammed on the brakes and pulled off to the side of the highway; Jeannie jumped out and ran into a pasture in the dark, snowy night.

My father, Frankie and I sat in the warm car, waiting for her to return. When she did not come back, my dad went to find her. He too disappeared into the dark, snow-covered pasture. He eventually came back to the car with my mother, and we continued our journey.

There was no rhyme nor reason to her behavior. At any moment, she could have a meltdown, which invariably led to her screaming at the top of her lungs for what seemed like an eternity. Then, she would get physically violent with me. Mother could never just scream about something once and be done with it; she would go on and on and on, screaming and throwing things, slamming doors, and breaking things.

There was no way for me to relax or ever let my guard down at home. I had to stay hyper-aware and vigilant. Almost every day, my childhood was like a 911 trauma center.

Again, my brother's death greatly affected us all. It was something none of us would ever get past. My guilt over his death – and the vision of him being killed – haunted me day and night for decades. I suppose it was the same for my mother. Although she had not been there when Kent Jr. was hit, I am sure she always felt guilty for letting us cross a highway alone. I know she blamed herself – but she also blamed me. Because he had died and I had lived, my mother's anger and violence were always focused on me.

I played outside, away from Mother, as much as I could. I played with friends in the creek, climbed trees, fished for crawdads, rode my bicycle, and raced my friends. We made jumps for our bicycles and skateboards, built forts, and went exploring or go-kart racing. As long as it was outside and physical and fast, I wanted to do it. I kept my energetic little body on the move.

After my brother died and Dad started building houses, we moved away from the neighborhood where the tragedy happened, into a house that Dad had built. I would visit his construction sites that were close by, and play and climb on anything and everything there. There were so many things I did to entertain myself in a house that was under construction: I swung from the rafters, walked a balance beam of 2-by-4s, or climbed over piles of pink insulation (big mistake, by the way). There was always something fun to do or always some form of trouble to find.

One day my friend Stephanie and I were playing at one of my dad's houses and happened to be on opposite sides of the house for a short time. There were boards spread out on the ground in the area where I was playing. I was wearing cheap sneakers that had thin rubber soles, and I was jumping from board to board. I happened to jump onto a board that had a huge nail sticking up out of the end; it went all the way into the middle of my foot. It hurt so bad, but instead of screaming and falling down, I remember analyzing the situation (as I often do, especially in emergencies): *I've got to get this nail out of my foot! What's the best way to do that?*

So, instead of just screaming for help, I reasoned that I could pry myself off the board if I used my free foot to step on the other end of the board, hold it in place, and then lift my stuck foot off the nail. That was a perfect plan, or so I thought.

What I could not realize is that there was an equally large nail sticking out of the other end of the board as well! As I quickly slammed my foot onto the other side of the board, the other nail went all the way into my other foot. Now I was completely stuck to the board, as if I was attached to a snowboard! I fell hard and fast to my knees, and screamed at the top of my lungs, which brought Stephanie running. I have no idea how we got the board off and the nails out of my shoes and feet, but we did. As I pulled my shoes off, I saw that both my white tube socks were filled with blood. It was gruesome and very painful. (Later in the ER, the doctor said if the nails had been just a little longer, both nails would have come out of the tops of my feet.)

After removing my shoes and socks, I realized how badly I was injured. I crawled all the way home, past three or four houses; Stephanie walked behind me, holding my bloody socks and shoes. I crawled up my driveway and Stephanie opened the front door for me.

My mother was in the entryway, vacuuming the carpet in the brand-new home that my dad had just built for us. I was on all fours. I looked up at my mother and screamed that I had just stepped on nails. Jeannie saw the blood and yelled at me, "Well, don't get blood on my new carpet!" Parenting at its finest.

I have no idea how I avoided getting blood inside the house. I had bled the whole way home; there were thin trails of blood on the street for weeks, until a hard rain washed it all away. During that time, whenever we drove down the street and saw the bloody tracks, we would laugh, and say, "There's Kendra!" I had literally painted the town red.

People always talk about how resilient children are, which conjures up an image of brave youngsters keeping their chins up in the face of total horror. That's accurate, but not always the whole story. Children's resilience is also evident by the way that they will play, explore, and do crazy things to have fun – no matter what else is going on around them. In the midst of my mother's reign of terror, I still had fun with my friends, even if I was experimenting with simulated stigmata. Before Kent Jr. died, I had fun with him, running around and doing dumb stuff like climbing a formation of rocks that made up the outer wall of the house. Yes, I had to go to the emergency room because I got a small piece of the rock stuck in my eye, but it was still fun!

Over the years, my adventures – and some misfortunes – have resulted in over 80 injuries that required visits to a doctor, an emergency room, or a hospital. I have had many stitches, broken bones, and even concussions. My friends think my stories of peril and injury are funny, and so did I for a long time. But as I have aged, I have found such escapades too physically painful, and the healing process too long, and therefore not so funny anymore because of their frequency.

Still, if something bizarre was going to happen to someone in my circle of friends or family, it was going to happen to me. My ability to escape death and endure physical injury always seemed nothing short of incredible, not only for me as a child, but also for my entire adulthood as well.

While I was growing up, my mother would nag and bitch about what an awful child I was to subject her to the inconveniences that my adventures brought her. She was wildly uninformed about what it took to actually nurture children through a crisis. And, of course, she immediately would transform any crisis of mine into her crisis. So, she saw no need to comfort me – in her mind, she was the one who was suffering.

The person who Mother felt needed the most hugs was apparently her – because she would force me to hug her and tell her I loved her after every violent beating. That always disgusted me. It was certainly a bizarre, sick way to get affection and to hear that you are loved. Expressing affection became a minefield, one that I navigate to this day.

Jeannie's modus operandi muddied the emotional waters for me, to say the least. And like a lot of abusers, Mother was careful not to do her worst in front of her husbands, so my dad – and later, my stepdad – were somewhat clueless about the severity of the situation. How clueless? Who knows? All I can recall is that I did not want to tell my dad (or later, my stepdad) about the abuse, because there was no telling whether I would get in trouble for speaking up. I knew that secrecy was essential to my mother's way of behaving, and I was scared to death of her, so breaking the seal was not an option.

The death of my brother and my parents' constant fighting took a toll on their marriage, and eventually my dad left. I was in fifth grade when I found out they were splitting up, and I was so relieved at first. I thought, *No more fighting, no more running down the street while second-guessing my instinct to call the cops, no more of my mother trying to jump out of moving cars – and maybe, just maybe, fewer beatings for me.*

Boy was I wrong! Her anger at me ramped up considerably since I was now her only focus. And the fact that my dad left her only gave her more reason to be angry. Even though the divorce was tougher than expected, I was glad that one of us – my dad – got out. It meant that we would have a safe place to go when it was his weekend with us. There would be "dad time" without my mom, which meant more fun.

My dad is a very funny guy, and he always made us laugh. Time spent with him was a way to find some relief. Dad was always up to play, build and race go-karts, wrestle, and roughhouse (lots of that), play ball (even in the house), run around, and just do whatever we wanted to make us laugh and be happy.

Several months after my parents split, Dad announced that we were going to Disneyland. I went out of my mind with joy. Then, immediately after that announcement, he started talking about how it was best for children to be raised by both a man and a woman. So, I thought he was talking about getting back together with my mother, which I thought would be great – he could protect me. Disneyland, and my parents getting back together? That would be too good to be true!

After his speech, we went and picked up a woman named Carol, who – much to my surprise – would be going to Disneyland with us. *Who the hell is this?* I knew nothing about her, and I knew that her presence definitely meant that my parents were not getting back together.

The four of us went to Disneyland and had a great time. I do recall that Dad spent a lot of time in her hotel room in the evenings. When I asked him what they were doing in there, the answer was invariably, "Reading the Bible." OK, whatever.

After a fun-filled time at Disneyland, we headed back to Oklahoma and Dad deposited Frankie and me at home with Mother. When we walked in, she was lying on the couch with our previous neighbor Don (yes, Noreen's Don). It was so bizarre. But then she giggled and announced, "We're getting married!" *What the hell?! I was only gone for a few days! How did this happen?* My world was getting crazier by the minute.

It all came about when – shortly before my parents' divorce – Noreen had died. She had cancer, and sadly, she passed away. Don lost his wife; their two daughters lost their mom, and my mother lost her best friend. It was horrible, especially coming right after the death of my brother. But the sheer convenience of having each other as friends – both suddenly available, and in close proximity – was enough for Jeannie and Don to get together.

So, Don married my mother, and the two girls who were never really my friends became my stepsisters. We moved into Don's house, which was across the street from our old house. It was weird, to say the least, and very hard to be back in that neighborhood. Every time I walked out of the house, I would see the house that we used to live in with my dad and my brother, who were both now gone. It was a daily reminder of the tragedy that befell my family.

As part of his residential real estate development company – building beautiful homes – Dad had started to build Don a house. This was before Don got together with my mother. So, when the house was finished, we (Don, his girls, Mom, Frankie and I) all moved from the small, cramped house that was across from my old house into the house that Dad built. Awkward.

Equally awkward was that when we first moved into the house that Dad built for Don, I shared a room with Taylor, my older stepsister – even though there were enough rooms for us to have our own. Taylor had sustained some brain damage at birth from a critical lack of oxygen, due to the umbilical cord being wrapped around her neck. Because of that, she could be very angry and violent. She was older and larger than I was and would often beat me up when the spirit moved her. The only times that I remember my mother coming to my rescue were when Taylor would beat me up or push me down the stairs.

I am grateful that Mother would interfere in those incidents, any one of which could have been the end of me. I knew my mother was capable of dealing a death blow, and it was good to be less of a participant and more of an audience in those events. However, I could not help being mildly suspicious that she was just pissed at Taylor for edging in on her turf.

What was even more awkward about the living arrangement was that our room shared a vent duct with Mother and Don's room, and we could hear them during their "intimate time." If I was not already sexually scarred for life, that would have done the trick all on its own.

My dad married a woman named Paula, who had a toddler son, and they then had another son together. So, there were lots of siblings in my life. One time in junior high, it was my dad's weekend to have my brother Frankie and me with him. We went with my dad, my stepmom, my stepbrother and half-brother to Kingfisher to visit his mother. We children were all packed in together in a large guest bedroom there. In the middle of the night, I was awakened by my dad running into the bedroom, dressed only in his tighty-whitey underwear, shouting, "Who's screaming? Who's screaming?"

Like me, all three of my little brothers were asleep, and Dad couldn't figure out which of the boys was screaming. Checking on them one by one in their bed, he was confused; but finally, he was confident everything was OK. He turned out the light and shut the door behind him, still trying to figure it out. I was lying there and also wondering what was going on. Then I suddenly realized it had been me screaming, because I had had a night terror. I was so embarrassed; I never told my dad it was me.

There was so much violent trauma in my childhood that was emotionally buried because my mother's emotions and behavior took center stage. Night terrors continued to be how my fears and trauma revealed themselves.

Unfortunately, even after my mother remarried, and almost into my adulthood, she continued to abuse me. When I was 17, I was driving with her and my siblings in the car. My mother thought that I cut too close to an approaching car to cross a highway. It was the exact spot on the highway where my brother had been killed, so I am sure that added to what happened next. She started screaming at me and poured a full glass of iced tea over my head and began beating me over the head with the hard plastic cup and her fist. I didn't dare disagree with her; I was frantically trying to wipe the iced tea out of my eyes so I could see where I was going. But her actions easily could have caused me to crash and injure all of the children in the car. It was just another example of my mother's insanity.

For years after my brother died, we all continued to grieve, and it definitely contributed to my parents' split. But while my dad found solace in dating new women and remarrying a few times, and my mother found solace in Don, I was on my own. My little brother Frankie was too young to remember my brother or the events surrounding his death, but he became someone for me to love and protect, as Kent Jr. had done for me.

Grieving people look for meaning in life and ways to heal, which frequently leads them to religion for answers, guidance and structure.

Don was grieving the loss of Noreen and trying to meet the challenge of raising his daughters on his own. My mother had a chorus of demons in her head, but she also had experienced the genuine horror of losing her firstborn child. Soon after they married, mother and Don – who had always been churchgoers – tumbled headfirst into religious fanaticism. They started their own church. I can't say what the exact ingredients were that led to that decision, but I can only imagine that my mother's insanity and megalomania – as well as a heavy dose of grief for both of them – contributed to it.

The questions that circled around the events of the day that my brother died have stayed with me throughout my life, as has the guilt I have felt. It was all part of the psychic burden I carried as I entered the next phase of my childhood. I would feel like I was always in the wrong place at the wrong time. The physical and verbal abuse would get worse, as my mother would become immersed in a cult-like religion.

CHAPTER THREE

THE CULT

The religion that my mother and Don subscribed to was classified as non-denominational Christianity – with a twist – their twist (or I should say, "twisted"). It was, if nothing else, terrifying to the outside observer.

In my young adulthood, after I left Oklahoma and moved to New York City, I dated a Catholic girl from the Bronx. I took this girl, Anna, to visit my family, and she experienced their over-the-top religion at a Sunday morning church service. On full display was shouting, dancing, running around, convulsing, speaking in tongues, and the laying on of hands (so one could fall to the ground in a spasm of "healing"). Seeing several hundred people clapping and waving their arms in the air and speaking in tongues while deacons put their hands on believers' heads to "heal" them as they writhed on the ground, was too much for Anna. During the service, she burst into tears, terrified, and vowed to never return.

I wholeheartedly agreed with her. A person can watch all that madness and ruckus on television; it is entirely another thing to experience it in person. I could not blame her for being shocked. The whole scene was undeniably alarming.

While the spirit of the Lord never quite entered my body, it definitely entered my house. My mother and stepdad's religious enthusiasm graduated to complete and utter mania, and they decided to found their own church in our living room when I was 13. In one fell swoop, we went from relatively normal, observant, conservative Baptists, to all-church, all-Bible, all-God, **all** the time. Everything centered around their God and their religion, and I mean **everything:** every conversation, every activity, every breath, every thought. Every minute of every day was about their religion, their church, and their God.

In reality, it was a cult. There was no room for independent thought or action. They were extremists with an us-against-the-world mentality. If I tried to function as an individual, or if I reacted to something emotionally or intellectually, I was shut down with prayer and punishment – mostly in the form of beatings.

Everything was black and white – the church was totally draconian. If you did not pray in tongues, you were going to hell. If you did not engage in the laying on of hands to be healed for what ailed you, you were going to hell. If you did not do exactly what everyone else in their church was doing, you were going to hell. That basically meant that the entire rest of the world – billions of people – were all going to hell.

Like people in other cults, we were isolated from anyone who was not a part of our core group. In the world that my parents created, you were "saved" if you were a member of their church/cult, partly because they believed that you probably did not have the devil in you. My family's church believed that the devil could and would take hold of people's souls, and that demons could and would live within people's bodies and minds. If you were not a non-denominational Christian, with the same exact beliefs as my parents, you were absolutely, unquestionably, evil, and damned. And you could contaminate those who lived within the bubble of the cult.

My mother and her husband even went so far as to believe that God would heal our illnesses or injuries if a believer would lay their hands on us and pray in tongues. That meant there was no need for a doctor unless the situation was absolutely catastrophic. As an athlete and as a very adventurous girl who had energy, speed and strength, I often needed doctors and ER visits in my childhood, as well as in my adulthood. However, my access to proper care became very spotty once we entered the cult. I found that I would have to beg to go to the emergency room when badly injured. In my parents' minds, the only thing to do in the insane modern world of godlessness was to stay isolated from others to avoid exposure to sinners, demons and the devil. So, I often found myself being prayed over for sickness or injury – because, they said, "God will heal."

There was a time in eighth grade, when I was still in public school, that my mother and stepdad went to a religious retreat for several days. Since my mother was out of town, I rode to school with my good friend, Miriam, and her siblings. Miriam's mother drove us in a huge van because there were so many siblings. When we arrived at the junior high, I started to leave the van, but I decided to let everyone else get out first. Children piled out of the van, one after another. As I was finally leaving the van as the last one out, Miriam – out of habit – slammed the large sliding van door closed.

My head was smashed in the sliding door. The impact was so great that everything immediately went dark, and I once again saw sparkles. I stumbled out of the van, not knowing which way was up or down. I could barely stand. Both of my ears started bleeding badly. One had been cut completely through, and the other was quite mangled. When I finally got my vision back, everyone was standing around me, staring in disbelief.

Miriam's mother rushed me back into the van and to the emergency room. Her father was a doctor, and he came in and stitched me up. Listening to him run the thread through the cartilage of my ear was enough to make me want to throw up. There were multiple large bumps all over my head where the pressure of the van's door basically blew out the back of my head. I was severely concussed. When the doctor finished stitching me up, he wrapped my head up with bandages. I had a raging headache for a week.

When my mother returned home and saw me lying on the couch bandaged up, she started screaming at me, "I can't go out of town for even just a few days without you getting hurt!"

There was never, ever a time that my mother comforted me or tried to make me feel better. Nurture was not in her nature. I cried and called my dad, saying, "She is yelling at me for getting my head slammed in a van door."

And – if my mother had been home when it happened, I would not have been taken to the hospital; instead, she would have prayed over me, saying, "God will heal it." Who knows what would have happened to my bleeding, mangled ears?

Another perfect example of the "God will heal" philosophy happened when I was 17. I was allowed to attend a Valentine's party that a classmate was having at her home in the country. I was so excited, because I never got to do anything like that. We were not allowed to associate with people from outside the church, but since these kids went to my Christian school with me, my mother finally made an exception.

At the party, we were playing a game of hide-and-seek tag outside in the dark. I was always athletic and fast, and I **loved** competition – so, that game was a lot of fun for me. As I was trying not to be found or tagged, I heard a branch crack behind me and knew someone was close by. I took off running at breakneck speed in the dark. Just as I was thinking that I could slow down because I had outrun whoever had been behind me, I ran directly into a barbed-wire fence. The top half of me bent completely over the fence as the bottom half of me got tangled. I snapped back up rather than flipping over the fence, because the bottom half of me was stuck in the barbed wire. I literally had to pull myself off the fence.

I could tell from the pain that I was hurt pretty badly, but it was dark, so I could not see just how bad. I limped back to my friend's house and into the bathroom, legs bleeding. The new jeans that my dad had given me for Christmas were in shreds. And on one of my thighs, I had cut a long, wide, deep, bloody gash all the way across my leg that looked like a check mark. It was like I had been trademarked by Nike. It was hideous and disgusting; I saw things under the skin of my leg that I never knew existed, including my torn muscle.

I was in a bit of shock, and I lay down on the couch. My friend's parents then came in to check on me – and they freaked out. They called my mom and told her that they could take me to the hospital, but she told them to bring me home. She was not going to come and get me, and it was clear that she was not going to take me to the ER.

I lay in the back seat in terrible pain on the drive home. When I arrived, I had to be carried inside. My mother was very angry, because I was always getting injured in extreme ways, mostly through no fault of my own.

When my mother finally calmed down after reacting to the barbed-wire incident, she and my stepdad prayed over my leg. They asked God to heal it and to alleviate my pain; then, she sent me to bed. We could not clean it because of the pain, so I just lay in bed all night, unable to sleep. I couldn't go to school the next day – the wound was gruesome and only getting worse.

Finally, about 24 hours after the accident, my mother agreed to take me to the emergency room. The emergency room doctor looked at my huge gash in dismay and said, "We can't stitch this up. It has been open too long and the tissue around it is dying." They cleaned it up really well, bandaged it, gave me a tetanus shot and pain killers, and sent me home with instructions on how to keep the wound clean and change the bandages.

I have no doubt that today there are more advanced ways to deal with a large open wound like that one, but that was the mid-1980s in Oklahoma (a state not known then for stellar medical care). Because my wound was not stitched up immediately and was so deep, it took a very long time to heal. I missed a lot of school; and when I returned to school, I was unable to participate in basketball practice or games, which was very disappointing. Even after the wound closed, I had a massive, bright red scar that looked like a checkmark on my thigh for many years. I was so embarrassed about the scar that I rarely wore shorts.

It is funny how – when you are young – your perspective on something like a scar is determined by what others might think. The scars on my ears were so bad that I never pulled my hair back to expose them. But I have added many, many other scars since those days, and I have learned to wear them with pride. They are a testament to my internal and external strength, not to mention my keen survival skills.

The checkmark on my leg eventually shrank some and faded to the color of my skin. Today, it is not as noticeable. The point of telling these stories is that my mother's insanity and her cult never allowed room for normal things in life, like proper medical care. They believed that God would heal. If God healed that wound, it sure took Him a long time to do it.

In another incident, after a choir performance, my stepsister shut my hand in the car door – and locked it. That episode ended with a trip to the ER; my music teacher took me because my mother was not there. Several of my fingers were fractured, and I had to wear a splint for a month. Again, my mother was very upset when I got home from the ER. She had to help me wash my hair and do other things that I could not accomplish with one hand, which made her even more angry.

I have broken my right hand three other times, too. The last time – the result of a bar fight in San Antonio that I did not start – ended with surgery to put titanium in my hand. I have become quite adept at managing with one hand, although my handwriting is now impossible to read, since I am right-handed.

My mother found a Christian school for her children and stepchildren to attend. Although not a part of our cult, it was a radical, hard-core religious institution. If a student participated in activities that were not school-sanctioned and church-sanctioned, he or she could be expelled.

This strict approach aligned with my mother's beliefs, so it worked perfectly for her. She was so controlling and domineering that we did not even contemplate breathing without her permission. Jeannie's fire and brimstone were infinitely more terrifying than anything God could summon, so no matter how messed up I thought the program was – both at home and in school – I always followed it.

At that school, if you listened to the radio or any secular music, you could be kicked out. If you read any books or magazines that were not on their "approved list," you would be punished or kicked out. In my house, there was no music other than Christian music; no dancing outside of religious ceremonies; no magazines, books, or media unless it was religious. Only G-rated shows and movies on TV were allowed, and only on very rare occasions. That basically left us with cartoons and the mildest of Disneyesque content, and even that was limited to two hours per week, max.

After a full day of Christian school, which included Bible reading, we would come home and read the Bible some more. And we would memorize scripture for at least an hour. Then, we prayed for half an hour before moving on to homework. We were in church or in Bible study, outside of school, at least four times a week; and we also did Bible study with my stepdad at home in the evenings.

Anything that was considered secular was forbidden, so there was no exposure to the real world at all. Once, I was punished when my friend Nikki left her *Teen Beat* magazines in my car. Even though I insisted they were not mine and that I had not read them, they were shredded in front of me – and then I was beaten.

My mother and stepfather used religion and the insular stability of their cult to get them through their day. They got what they needed out of their religion, which is not that unusual. People find whatever they need to help them get through life, because life can be pretty damn hard. Many people find things to get them through their day, whether it is their spouse, children, work, a hobby, working out, their pet, substances, or religion.

My parents were the center of the world they had created. Eventually, their non-denominational church's following grew large enough for my parents to move it out of our living room into a real church building. Eventually, they would hire a pastor, too – but for a long time, my stepfather Don was the pastor. After we moved to a real church and hired a pastor, I began to play the drums for our church music services. It was the only thing I enjoyed about that oppressive religious time.

Even though all that religion was part of every waking moment of my life from sixth grade on, it never clicked with me on the inside. When teachings are accompanied by the "wrath of God" – physical and verbal abuse – they are not very appealing. The church and its associated activities were all that I knew, so I spent a lot of time involved in it. But I had no emotional or spiritual connection to the religion that my mother and Don lived. I could not accept their doctrines of fear, damnation, punishment, and what amounted to a denial of basic humanity.

I was not sophisticated enough in my thinking as a child or teenager to break it down; but my inability to get on board with the religion was probably because I knew deep inside that my mother was a horrible person. She simply justified her behavior with her religion. Everything she said was framed in the context of the Bible, and about how God would provide, and how He had anointed her to carry out His retribution.

I saw no sense in it. Even in my naive youth, I thought, *Mom, you're a horrible person. There's no way that God wants me to be like that.* How could God approve of you choking your child until everything goes dark? How does God sanction beating your child to the point that when they go to school, they have to explain away the marks and bruises on their body?

Still, rejection of the church, or rebellion of any kind, was unthinkable. I knew that if I rebelled, the punishment that I would suffer would be extreme. The thought of that was enough to prevent any resistance from taking root.

Mother kept a steady supply of wooden paddles on hand; my stepfather made them from pallets that came into his grocery store. He drilled holes in the paddles to reduce air resistance as Mother swung them, which made it easier for her to beat us children. There were always four paddles lined up along the fireplace, large to small, one for each child. The two younger children were rarely paddled, but Taylor was sometimes, since her issues caused her to lash out in anger.

As for my paddle, it was broken frequently from so much use on me. When my paddle would break, Mother would use the other paddles on me. They all ended up breaking, one after another. My stepdad would then make more wooden paddles from the pallets, always drilling holes in them.

If all of the paddles happened to be broken, she would grab the belt and start beating me with that, often with the buckle side. She would use the belt on my body, on my head – anywhere she felt like it.

While beating me, my mother would quote scripture, scream prayers, and yell in tongues. She would be praying over me and casting the devil out of me, as though religion was her defense for having to beat me.

Because of the behavior of my mother and stepfather, my respect for religion began a long process of erosion. I was not a bad child, nor was I disobedient. I was scared to death of my mother and always did my best to fly under the radar of her anger, but I would just never know what would set her off.

Later in our lives, my younger stepsister told me that she remembered how I would always step in if one of the younger children was in trouble. She said that I would try to take the blame to protect them. I don't particularly remember that, but it could be, since I tried to take on the role of protector after my brother died. I could not bear the sight or sound of any of the younger children getting hit.

Another issue in my childhood was that I liked girls. As I am sure that you can imagine, a little girl who liked other little girls **that way** was not in Jeannie's program. I had a teacher when I was in kindergarten who I thought was the prettiest woman on earth. So, one evening, I piped up at the dinner table that if I were a boy, I would marry my teacher.

My mother blew up in a frenzy of shock and horror. The subject was dropped immediately, but I was so confused! Why should she be angry if I loved someone or if I thought they were pretty? Maybe she had a sense of what was going on with me, or maybe it just confused and scared her. I have no idea. But in my mother's world, girls were girls and boys were boys. All of the conventional social rules and contracts were to be respected and maintained.

Jeannie made us girls wear dresses and slacks to school in late elementary and junior high, when everyone else was wearing jeans, Tuff Skins or Wranglers. Once or twice a week, we girls were allowed to wear jeans to school.

When I started attending Christian school, the dress issue was less appalling because all the girls had to wear dresses, so I blended in. Even though I hated wearing dresses and pantyhose, at least I could surrender my crown and sash as Queen Dork as I was no longer the odd girl out.

Mother upped the ante when I hit seventh grade by making my stepsisters and me wear makeup and get our hair done. This was mandatory. In Lawton, Oklahoma, where I grew up, the usual path for girls was high school, marriage, then babies. Jeannie probably thought she was setting us up for success with the boys of Lawton by making us focus on our looks; but it was equally possible that her twisted sense of femininity simply included looking a particular way.

I often compare my mother to Joan Crawford in *Mommy Dearest*. My mother was an evil mother on steroids. My mother demanded order, obedience, compliance and silence. She also demanded a spotless house, for which we four children became completely responsible after she married my stepfather.

Every Friday we came home from school to pages and pages of handwritten lists for cleaning the house. We children cleaned everything in the house, and I mean everything. We also did our own laundry, including her and my stepfathers' sheets and towels, and cleaned their bedroom and bathroom. The level of detail on these lists was equal to an extreme deep-cleaning of the entire house every week.

She inspected our work and made us do it over if her extreme expectations were not met, literally running her fingers over the hardest to reach places to ensure there was no dust. And she reviewed our work on all the mirrors in the house from different angles and lighting to ensure there were no smudges.

For a very brief time when we moved into the house that dad built, we had a cleaning lady, but that was very short lived. She quickly figured out she could save that money (probably to give to the church) by making us children do everything.

We also each had our own night to cook, and the other children did the dishes. My stepdad cooked several times a week and we had leftovers as well for some meals, so my mother cooked maybe once a week. We usually made our own breakfast, always made our own lunches to take to school, as well as our snacks. I also mowed the lawn and edged the yard, but that was in addition to my duties in the house.

My stepfather often bought the groceries since he managed grocery stores. I honestly do not know what my mother did all day long while we were at school – probably read the Bible and chanted in tongues all day, and thought of new ways to make our lives a living hell. I eventually figured out that my mother was a housewife raising children and running the household when we were young, and she was married to my father; once she married my stepfather that shifted. Now she had four children old enough to do all the chores – and I mean all the chores – so she shifted from housewife to Queen Bee, sitting on her throne and watching her subjects work tirelessly to cross each thing off the list that she made. I even ironed my stepfather's shirts for work; but I was paid something like twenty-five cents a shirt, so I didn't mind as much.

My older stepsister and I even drove all of us children to and from school once we were old enough to drive. I did not mind that either because I liked to drive and preferred that to riding in a car with my mother. Of course, she refused to participate in any school activities of ours, and never came to any of my athletic games or competitions.

The fact that my mother offloaded everything on everyone else was wrong – so very wrong. You should know that I am a very firm believer that children need to pitch in at home, have responsibilities and chores, and share the load. The key word being *share*. Once the children all left home and Mother no longer had them to do everything for her, a lot of it fell to my stepfather, even though he worked full time, and she still did not work at all.

All of that was the backdrop to my adolescence. Possibly, the only good thing about the Christian school was that I found two very good friends there, Fiona and Nikki. Each of them was instrumental in keeping me sane in high school. They served as the wedge that propped open the door to the rest of the world for me to see what normalcy looked like. Neither Fiona nor Nikki had any idea that they served such an important role in my life – or if they did, they were discreet enough to never acknowledge it.

I grew up thinking that fighting, anger, hysteria and fear was normal. After all, this was life in my house before my parents divorced. I thought it was just how adults behaved and how families operated. When my mother and Don married, the religious mania, continued beatings, and cult environment was just more of the same destabilizing chaos which, while I hated it, seemed like standard practice to me. My life and my siblings' lives were so restricted that we very rarely socialized with friends after school or on weekends and did not participate in anything that was not associated with the church or our Christian school. Even all of my various athletic teams were part of the Christian school system in Oklahoma once I left public school.

In my junior year, I did finally manage to go to Fiona's house occasionally, and even had a few sleepovers. The environment was disorienting. When I was there, I did not feel anxious. It felt good being at Fiona's house; her mom, who was also a teacher at our Christian school, was very sweet, and her dad, a fireman, was calm and quiet. They had never divorced or remarried, and were just a happy, calm, and respectful family unit – something completely unfamiliar to me.

Until Fiona and I had those visits and sleepovers, I thought that everybody was choked or beaten or screamed at every day. I began to see that not everyone had their lives endangered or lived in constant fear. Going to Fiona's showed me that there was an achievable alternative.

My friend Nikki was also a guide out of hell. While Fiona was wholesome, Nikki was a normal teenager who liked music, dancing, misbehaving, laughing, and generally causing a different kind of chaos than what I was used to – the fun kind. Nikki transferred into our school but was not indoctrinated the same way the rest of us were, and she had a pretty mainstream knowledge of the world outside the Christian school and Lawton. Somehow Nikki managed to keep the fact that she listened to secular music and watched General Hospital under the radar at school.

The Christian school was focused on individual study, called self-taught or self-paced, which meant that we had some guidance; but basically, we taught ourselves by reading our textbooks and doing classwork out of workbooks, and then testing ourselves and even scoring our own work. There was a teacher available if we had questions; but they did not guide us through our studies or bring their own perspectives into the curriculum through lectures or typical classroom style teaching. We did work in cubicles so we could not interact with anyone else during school.

It was like working and learning with blinders on, and, for me, it was just more isolation. This type of learning molded me into a visual learner, and to this day when someone is trying to explain something to me at work, I often ask them to put it in writing. This is because I process things so much better through reading rather than listening. This created a huge problem in college because all classes were lectures, so I struggled to learn. I spent a lot of time reading and memorizing on my own throughout college because that is how I learned from eighth through twelfth grades.

In my senior year of high school, somehow I was lucky enough to have Nikki in the cubicle next to mine. That was a life saver for my last year at that ridiculous school. One day I heard her sort of muttering-singing and drumming quietly on her desk. "I would. Die for. You." Over and over again, "I would. Die for. You." Thump, thump, thump, thump. I passed Nikki a note under a small crack in our cubicle and asked, "What are you singing?" She passed a note back, "It's Prince's new song." I passed yet another note to her "Who is Prince?" This was 1985. I was a senior in high school – and I had no idea who Prince was.

Oh my gosh, what *else* was I missing? You know the saying, *you don't know what you don't know?* In that moment I started to know what I didn't know, and it was both unnerving, yet very, very exciting. Leaving my mother's house and leaving Lawton not only was becoming more attractive, but it also was clearly the only option for me. I had to break out of that bubble.

Even though I had Fiona and Nikki at school, I was desperately miserable. There was no way to express how I felt because it was well established that the only person in our household who was allowed to have feelings and show any type of emotion was my mother. If you were sad or mad, she did not allow it – whatsoever. If you were happy or excited, it was in defiance of her, and she hated it. If you had an opinion, it was automatically seen as an oppositional stance, and she would punish you. I did not understand how a God-fearing woman could have so much hate and anger in her; but we children were not allowed to show any negative emotion whatsoever.

The even crazier thing was that in the public's eye my mother was the sweetest person because she was an amazing actress. The way she could turn it on and off for the public baffled and amazed me. My mother's dictatorship and the stranglehold in the name of the cult was so insular that

I had absolutely no understanding that there was a world beyond Lawton that did not operate the same way. I could not know that there might be an infinite number of ways to live my life other than what I knew.

Fiona's household was great; but there was no clear path to how I could be part of a family like that. Nikki's secular world seemed totally cool and freeing; but it was also completely incongruous to the way I lived with the endless rules and regulations that had to be followed. But I always knew there was a happier life out there for me. I just needed to figure out how to attain it.

When you know you have to leave a situation, not only because of the misery, but also because it just might kill you, your brain goes into overdrive trying to find the escape hatch. My friends' lives showed me that there were other, much happier, ways to live. But neither Nikki nor Fiona could provide direction for how to get there because they had no idea of my world.

It was like I was starving, standing in the street in a snowstorm, looking through the window of a warm and glowing restaurant, watching people feast on steak and lobster dinners – but with no clue how to join them (also, I had no idea what steak or lobster were until I was an adult living in NYC).

Living on the wrong side of the window for so many grueling years had ground me down into a debilitating depression. The way the mind works under unimaginable strain is weird. Thought patterns that make total sense at the time can reveal themselves years later to have been truly bizarre. My own thoughts created a warped logic that reasoned the only way to escape from the horrors of my home life was to kill myself. Managing the pain and fear I lived with was nearing the impossible;

and the only thing that would block it out, along with the constant fear of my mother killing me during one of her regular, violent rages, was to leap into the inevitable. The peace I would undoubtedly find on the other side would be worth it.

My bedroom was on the second floor of our house; and I spent countless hours lying in bed calculating the risk of jumping through the window. Would the glass and height be enough to kill me if I leapt out? If it was, would anything on the ground break my fall? There were bushes near the house. If they cushioned the impact, would I be maimed and forced to live the rest of my life as a quadriplegic in my mother's care? The fact that jumping might actually lead to a fate worse than my imagined death, along with the guilt of leaving my little brother in my mother's care, kept me in my bed on the second floor waiting for something else to present itself as an escape plan.

As a side note, I now know as an adult, jumping out of a second story window would not have killed me. But as a child, I was desperate to find relief from the pain.

Shockingly, the plan for escape, at least temporarily, presented itself through religion. Fiona was the one who first heard about the unexpected opportunity and brought it to my attention. There was an organization called Teen Missions International that sent Christian teens on missions all around the world. Fiona thought it sounded interesting and I thought it sounded like a lifeline; we snapped into action to make it happen.

It cost a lot of money. In the mid-eighties, $3,000 was a lot of money and it definitely would not come out of my parents' pockets – so we decided to start fundraising on our own. I was already driven by making money. I had been an expert earner since the age of 10 when I started hustling around the neighborhood washing cars, cleaning houses and dog kennels, mowing lawns, babysitting, shoveling snow, whatever I could manage for a few bucks.

When I was twelve, I started working at my stepfather's grocery store, where I worked every single weekend and many evenings for six years. Knowing how to hustle a buck was my jam; and I jumped into gear to scrape the $3,000 together. Just when I had myself sorted out, Fiona decided not to go. She was risk averse by nature and probably the notion of all that newness overwhelmed her. Also, Fiona did not want to run away from a horrendous family situation; staying at home was a pleasant prospect for her.

While I was very disappointed that Fiona would not join me, her dropping out would not affect my plan at all. The children involved in the program were told to choose countries that interested them. While I knew nothing about other countries, I used our encyclopedias to study the different choices. The encyclopedias were a constant for me from the time I could read. I chose the Philippines as my first choice, and Haiti as my second choice for my mission. The spots for the Philippines filled quickly and I did not get into that group. As it turned out, I had good fortune on my side because the bus that took the group to the airport for the Philippines trip was in a terrible crash, several people died, and many were injured. My innate good fortune to escape death on so many occasions in my life baffles me; but also makes me feel that there must be a higher purpose for me. More on that later.

There was room for me in the Haiti group. Haiti, home of Papa Doc, Baby Doc, a civil war in progress and the escalating AIDS crisis was my destination. At the time it was the poorest country in the world, and AIDS gripped everyone in fear. There was speculation that Haiti is where AIDS started, so I received a fair amount of criticism for my choice; but I did not let that deter me, nor was I scared of contracting a disease. I needed an escape and that was the best choice for me.

Before we all left the United States, the teen missionaries had to go to a boot camp in Merritt Island, Florida. It was a very hardcore experience; we were in tents in a swamp for weeks, without showers or any other normal comforts. I had no idea at the time that bathing from a spigot, or in a snake and alligator infested pond, was a fair representation of what was in store for me, but it was. And it prepared me sufficiently for the surprises Haiti had to offer.

Along with the unpleasantness of a complete lack of modern conveniences like air conditioning, beds, and running water, we had to get up at 4 a.m., in the dark, and hit a grueling obstacle course by 5 a.m. Because I loved athletics, the obstacle course was fun and not a challenge for me – with the exception that it was 5 a.m. in the hot Florida swamps, and I had not had breakfast yet. We started every day like that and spent the rest of our days learning to construct things. We learned how to mix mortar, dig ditches, build structures, put roofs on them, shingle them – the works.

When we were too exhausted to lift another cinder block, we attended Bible lessons and learned how to preach the word and convert people. All of that was, of course, to be expected on a Church sponsored trip. But none of us spoke Haitian Creole or French, the most common languages in Haiti, so once we got to Haiti, we would leave the actual conversion and preaching to the American missionary. Her name was Diane and she had been stationed in Haiti for years, and now our assigned liaison.

After two weeks of boot camp, I arrived in Haiti. We were all bundled into a tap-tap, which looked pretty outrageous to my untraveled eyes. It was a colorfully painted truck with a roof suspended over it that was basically a bus; they were all over the cities in Haiti and a common form of transportation. Our tap-tap ride took all day and got us to the base of a mountain where we spent the night in a hostel before heading out early the next morning for a full day hike up and into the mountains.

Donkeys hauled much of our gear through the mountains to the village of Vallieres; but we also carried packs of supplies on our backs for the long hike as well. For the first time in my life, I saw little naked children running around with pot bellies and hair turning red from malnutrition. Many women were bare-breasted, balancing whatever it was they carried around in baskets on top of their heads. All I could think was, *Holy cow*. I had never seen anything like this in real life – only in books.

Most likely the people in Vallieres were thinking the same thing about us, as they had never seen so many white people clustered in that village before. They came up to me and pulled at my skin, touched my hair, and treated me like the oddity I was. That night, they served us dinner, which was fine; but the strain of the day took its toll on one in our group who threw up right at the table. We had no idea what we were eating – goat, dog, whatever – but we were polite, and we chalked up the vomiting to the exertions of the day.

After dinner we were spent from our days of traveling, so we bunked down in the village's cinderblock church into what was, for me, a dreamless sleep born of total fatigue. I woke several times throughout that first night, only to see all the holes in the cinder blocks filled with the locals' faces. They were watching us sleep all night long. It scared me; although this became a regular occurrence once we pitched our tent on their soccer field. I would often wake in the middle of the night to several faces peering through the vent in my tent, and it continued to scare the bejesus out of me.

Over the next few days, we focused on setting up camp, which consisted of building our own outhouse, pitching tents, cooking over propane stoves, and boiling our drinking water. We did our laundry and bathed in the river and played in waterfalls when we could. We charged head-first into full-on construction of the three-room school we built for the children of the village. We worked every day except Sunday, clearing the land, moving boulders and brush with our hands, leveling the ground, and mixing the mortar by hand for the building. The construction took all summer. It was difficult manual labor; but I enjoyed the challenge and hard physical work.

We also got to know the villagers, particularly the children, by singing songs with them, playing games, performing puppet shows and, of course, going to church multiple times per week. Even though we could not speak Haitian Creole, we all managed to make it work somehow.

As much as we felt that we were making inroads with the people in Vallieres, there was no denying that their culture was ingrained and would not be whitewashed. We were included in their world, but we could not replace the essential parts of it. All of the mission students slept two to a tent; and on Saturday nights the company was particularly welcome as that was when the villagers who practiced Voodoo had their own worship.

Haitian Voodoo is a big part of Haitian culture and on Saturday night while lying in our tent trying to sleep, we could hear the drums beating, the chanting and screaming, and the noises of things we had never seen or heard before, nor could we identify. We were terrified. I tried to sleep; but the combination of the Voodoo practice, and the habit the villagers had of peering into our tents, was nerve wracking.

Almost as nerve wracking as when a hurricane blew through our camp and obliterated everything. Our tents and belongings were blown everywhere, and we spent a whole day walking around and picking up whatever we could find to rebuild. We recovered most of it; but the hurricane was a reminder that there was never a moment during the trip that we could relax and presume everything was safe. I fought off dysentery and a spider bite, but the scariest was yet to come.

Haiti, as the poorest country in the world at the time, was also undergoing serious political upheaval and a civil war. We had, for the most part, been insulated from all of that on the mountain top; but one Sunday, while I was on guard duty watching the tents while everyone else was down in the village at church, a group of armed civilians marched onto the field close to our tents. While their leader shouted orders, they started practicing maneuvers while every man wielded rifles.

Just as the girl who was supposed to relieve me of my shift came along, a fight broke out amongst the troops. The men were yelling and screaming at each other; and we sat and watched while the guy who had started the argument and the leader pulled their rifles on each other, screaming and yelling.

We were very scared. We could only assume they were going to shoot each other. It was pandemonium – all of them screaming at each other, cocking their rifles, and shoving it in the face of the man who started the argument. The other girl and I really freaked out, clutching each other, certain that someone was about to die a mere thirty yards from us.

Should we leave? Do we run? If so, where? Before we had to decide, the guy who had started the fight threw down his rifle and fled down the mountain. Everyone else in the group collected themselves and went back to practicing their maneuvers.

The other girl and I just sat there, frozen, terrified. We had no business in that country when all that was going on; and while I would not trade the Haiti experience for anything, it was an undeniably poor decision on the part of the organizers to take teenagers into a civil war zone.

As the summer wound down, we proudly finished building the school, and had a dedication ceremony with the villagers. We packed our things, hiked back through the mountains to Cap-Haitien to debrief, and prepared to travel back to the United States. We had only been in Haiti for almost three months, but the culture shock of returning to civilization was huge.

When we arrived in Cap-Haitian we loved having ice in our drinks, soda, real food, and coffee, which I had never had before but fell instantly in love with. It was a wonderful few days of winding down and debriefing before having to say goodbye to our group who I had come to love.

It was overwhelming and wonderful to finally return to the U. S., but the separation from the other students was not. We had bonded during the three months we had been together, and it was an abrupt end to strong friendships. It was also a return to Lawton, and what was undoubtedly a completely unchanged situation at school and at home.

What had changed, however, was my perspective on the world and myself. I stopped saying things like, "I'm starving" if I was hungry. I finally knew what real starvation looked like. I learned to be grateful for all that I had in the U.S. I had experienced just how strong and resilient I was, both physically and mentally. I knew what I was capable of, and that I could effect change for other people as well as myself. I had learned what it was to thrive without being controlled and held down. I had learned that independence suited me and that I had huge reserves of inner strength.

After everything I had experienced – hiking and living in a third world country, the hurricane, an armed militia, living in tents, doing laundry and bathing in the river, being ogled by the locals, living in a completely different culture – I learned that I could be fearless. I had discovered a whole world out there waiting for me to explore and I could not wait to get underway to see it.

Less than a week after returning from Haiti, I started my senior year of high school. As I suspected, nothing had changed in my home. My family was great when I returned and threw me a party with cake and lots of visitors. There was a brief honeymoon period where I enjoyed all the comforts of a modern house: air conditioning, running water, a comfortable bed and electricity. But Jeannie continued her reign of terror, and Don continued to enable her and build those paddles. My social life remained crippled except for sports, and games, and the time I spent with Fiona and Nikki, mostly at school.

From the time I got my drivers' license on the day I turned 16, I loved to drive and was the family chauffeur at every available opportunity. I would cart my brother and stepsisters back and forth to school, and my mother to run errands, or whatever it was she wanted to do. A little more than two months after I got home from Haiti, I turned 18 and celebrated my birthday in a typically perverse fashion because, thanks to a cruel twist of fate, my mother and I have the same birthday.

At the time, 18 did not seem so special, but I would soon find out just how important and special it was. About a month after my 18th birthday, Christmas break was fast approaching, and I needed to go Christmas shopping. Off to the mall my mother, Frankie and I went.

I was driving and listening to a tape that Fiona gave me for my birthday. The song on the tape that she had given me for a dedication for our friendship was "Friends are Friends Forever". It meant so much to me that Fiona had given me that song. And because it was sung by a Christian singer, I was allowed to listen to it. I loved that tape and was having a great time listening to it while enjoying the freedom of driving (even though my mother was in the car with me).

Mother was talking over the music, which was not loud because I knew better, but apparently the music irritated her, so she turned it all the way down. I turned the music back up, only very, very slightly, so I could still hear it in the background while she rattled on. I was not trying to be rebellious; I just wanted a little background music. It was quite out of the ordinary for me to do something so bold.

My mother flipped out. I had defied her! She started screaming and yelling that she was not going to take this behavior from me. I kept driving, trying to stay calm so we could stay safe. My mother loved anything dramatic, so long as she was the one in charge of the performance. As I have said, she tended to make her point during her fits of rage in cars by either hitting me in the head while I was driving or trying to jump out while we were still moving.

So, four blocks away from our house, Jeannie opened the car door and threatened to leap out. That was it. That was the final straw for me. Something shifted in my head. I stopped the car, did not say a word, and just looked at her, locking eyes with her and saying nothing while she continued screaming at the top of her lungs.

She got out and slammed the door and stormed away. Whatever. So, I would get the shit beat out of me when I got home – that wasn't new. I drove on to the mall with my brother and did my shopping. I had been working since I was 10 years old and had my own money for gifts. I was tired of my mother's meltdowns always ruining everything and tired of her controlling my life. This was the day I was going to change all of that. Enough was enough.

The second I arrived home she called me into her bedroom. Laid out on the bed were a Bible, one of my stepfather's belts with a very large buckle, scissors, and one of my stepfather's wooden paddles. Many beatings were spur of the moment – a flash of anger and insanity that prompted my mother to just start laying into me wherever, whenever and, however. But sometimes they were premeditated, as was this one.

It began, as did the other premeditated ones, with readings from the Bible, this time illustrating how I had disobeyed my parents or had transgressed against God.

I recognized her kit for what it was, except for the scissors, and braced myself for the religion and horrible beating she was about to unleash on me. I was also bracing myself for the end of the ordeal, which was always the same. After beating the shit out of me, she would always demand that I hug her and tell her I love her – such a sick and perverse way to obtain love and maintain control.

Before she began, Jeannie demanded that I go to the car and get the tape that Fiona had given me. I knew right away as I walked to the car to get Fiona's tape that my mother planned to destroy it just as she had destroyed anything and everything she hated, or thought was evil or bad. I brought it back to my mother who immediately started pulling yards of tape out of the cassette and cutting it to shreds as I cried and cried.

My anguish mattered as little to her as it had when she, in the throes of one of her more notable religious manias, destroyed a little sculpture my brother Kent Jr. had made before he died. It was so precious to me, and I guarded it with my life, keeping it safe through every move we made into a new house. It was a piece of wood that he had glued stones to and painted to look like a frog sitting on a log. I loved it and kept it close to my bed in my room.

My mother and Don got it into their heads based on a scripture in the Old Testament of the Bible that frogs and owls were agents of the devil and any representations of frogs or owls had to be destroyed. It was the late 1970s, early 1980s, when owls and frogs were a standard part of the décor in many suburban homes, so they had a lot of clearing out to do. We were made to bring everything that had an owl or frog on it into a pile in the living room and they smashed it all to pieces with a hammer and their feet while casting the devil out of the décor by praying, dancing and singing in tongues.

My mother knew a critical piece was missing when she didn't see my brother's frog art in the pile. She demanded I go to my room and get it. I became hysterical, begging her to let me keep it so I would have my brother near me. She knew exactly what that sculpture meant to me and did not care. I brought it from my room crying, and she smashed it to pieces on the living room floor with all the other offending items in our house. I was devastated.

The same thing happened early on in the cult formation, when my mother demanded I bring all the albums and records I had to the living room for the same ritual. Much of my music collection had been given to me by my father who was a DJ for many years; and often when they pulled a record out of the playlist, he would give it to me. I cherished them because I loved music and singing and dancing around my room (prior to the cult), and because my father had given them to me, they meant something special.

Once those records were in a pile in the living room, she smashed them in exactly the same way she would later smash the owls and frogs. She destroyed the records with a hammer, broke them with her hands and stomped on them with her feet, all the while casting the devil out of them and me for having them. All I could do was cry, heartbroken every time she took something from me and destroyed it, something that I loved and that meant something to me.

She treated the tape Fiona had given me no differently. Destruction was at the forefront of my mother's mindset. Once the tape Fiona gave me had been reduced to pieces with the scissors, my mother picked up the board and began beating me on my back, head, legs and occasionally my butt, until it broke and then she went for the belt. She went at me with the strap and the buckle, hitting me with all her might, anger, and strength. It hurt so much, and as I fell down, she would pull me back up by the hair, ripping out clumps of it, beat me some more and then throw me on the floor, beating me until she was ready to pull me to my feet and start all over.

My mother kept at it, over and over; I was like a rag doll as she shoved me to the ground and then yanked me back up all the while hitting, punching, slapping and choking me. The last time she shoved me to the ground, I brushed the side of my face on her bed post. As I landed on my hands, I sprained my wrist and could not regain my balance to get back up. I was on all fours, and she just kept going at me with the buckle end of the belt, keeping my long hair in her fist and ripping more out every time she moved and brought the belt buckle down on me.

As she was beating the life out of me for turning the music up slightly, it occurred to me in a flash of clarity that I was 18 years old. What was I letting her do to me? I was on all fours like an animal and being beat within an inch of my life. I had dealt with this madness my entire life, 18 long years, and I had had enough. This was sick! No more!!

I managed to get up onto my knees and swung both my arms backwards, hitting her legs as hard as I could to push her away from me. I had little left in me after Jeannie worked me over, but I had enough to make her lose her footing and stumble backwards.

At that moment, I jumped up and ran out of her bedroom. I ran and ran as fast as I could, but she ran after me. I could feel her grasping at my long hair trying to catch me while screaming at the top of her lungs for me to stop and get back in her bedroom. She chased me all the way through the house as I ran for the front door.

The second we were both out of the house and in the front yard she changed her tone immediately. My brother and his friends were playing outside and some of the adult neighbors were out in their front yards as well. Under no circumstances would Jeannie allow herself to be seen for what she was, and the minute she hit the front yard she stopped screaming at me and started calling after me, "Please stop honey! Come back! I love you!" She sure knew how to put on a show.

I had no idea where I was going. The sun was starting to set, and it was a freezing cold December evening. I had no coat and was beside myself running and crying, missing handfuls of hair, bruised with welts, scratches and cuts all over me. I looked exactly like I felt. I kept running and she did not come after me; it was one of the few times I thanked God that she was lazy. Instead, she would just wait for me to eventually come home so she could beat the shit out of me some more.

Once I got a few blocks away and knew she was not coming after me, I slowed to a very fast walk. Around the curve of the road, I saw my stepfather's car driving directly towards me as he was coming home from work. I slowed my pace to appear as though I were taking a leisurely walk, and as he drove past me, I smiled and waved at him so he would think everything was fine – but behind my smile were tears, fear, and a lot of pain, both physical and emotional.

I had no idea where I was going but once my stepfather was out of sight, I knew I had to hurry because he would no doubt be coming for me soon, maybe with her in tow. I picked the pace back up to a fast jog. I decided to go to a convenience store about 1.5 miles away, where I could call my father to come pick me up.

Once out of my neighborhood and onto the busy road heading to the store, my stepfather caught up to me in his car. Who knows what story my mother told him as to why I ran out of the house, but I am sure she feigned total innocence and put all blame on me because I "disobeyed" her. I did not stop my fast pace as he pulled alongside me, focusing only on getting to that store while still crying uncontrollably. I was in a tremendous amount of physical pain from the beating. I hurt all over from my head, my back, face, legs and arms throbbed in pain and my wrist hurt terribly from the sprain. As I hustled, sobbing, and freezing with no coat, he rolled down his passenger side window and drove alongside me. "Sissy (as he sometimes called me), why don't you get in the car and come back with me – we can talk about it." Emphatically, I sobbed, "No!"

As he was trying to convince me to get in the car, a police car pulled up behind him flashing lights for him to pull over and stop. I am sure the cop was trying to figure out what this older man was trying to do with this young girl. The police officer got out of his car, came to Don's side of the car, and asked him what was going on. Don said that I had had a fight with my mother and that he was going to take me to go back home. The cop looked at me, crying and a total mess, obviously beaten up, mascara running down my face. He asked me how old I was. When I said that I was 18, the cop looked at Don and said, "Sorry, she is an adult, so she does not have to go with you. If she wants to leave, she can leave." Relief flooded over me.

I do not remember if the police officer gave me a ride to the convenience store or if I walked the remaining quarter of a mile, but I got there. I was still crying, and I looked even worse for having been out in the windy cold; but I managed to ask if I could use their phone. The people at the store were horrified at my sobbing, welted face and messy look and let me have whatever I needed – the phone, a cup of water, tissue, and a chair. My father was not at home, but my stepmother was. When she arrived at the store to pick me up, relief yet again swept over me, and I knew it was all over. I was never going back. My mother could never hurt me again. The next chapter of my life had begun.

CHAPTER FOUR

BEGINNING ANEW

People who have not lived in abusive households often ask, "Why did you stay?" The answer is simple. I stayed because it did not occur to me to leave. I was not stupid, uninformed or weak. I did not secretly get something out of that incredibly, horrifically messed up situation. I was systematically broken down until I lost any sense of self or autonomy. I became someone who could not imagine any other way of living.

That last bit is important. When you are not able to imagine any other way of living, the only alternative is death. So, there you are, stuck between the possibility of death at the hands of your abuser, or death at your own hands to get away from the abuser. That is a very depressing and terrifying paradox in which to exist, day in and day out. That is draining beyond belief and adds to the disorientation and bleak hope-lessness about what the future looks like.

Then add in the physical abuse that wears you down, and repeatedly reinforces the notion that you have no autonomy, or that you might actually deserve the abuse. And as I have said, I always felt that I deserved all that was happening to me as punishment for my brother's death. That feeling continued through my adulthood.

I believed all the bizarre and painful injuries and inexplicable events that happened to me, were because I deserved them. My friends would say, "Of course that happened to you because anything insane always happens to you." One can become stuck in a brainwashing loop of constant verbal, emotional and mental abuse that takes extraordinary external circumstances or an extraordinary inner revelation to stop. I know many people reading this book can relate to this. I could have left my mother's grip at 13 to live with my father, per Oklahoma law; but I was so brainwashed, manipulated and controlled that I was too afraid to leave. Also, I did not want to leave my brother with her. But after 18 years I had to go. I could not take it – not for one more second. So, I left.

For me, the strength to finally leave began building months before I finally did. Being in Haiti showed me that there was a way to escape from my mother, the cult, and all the pain of life in Oklahoma. It was a defining external circumstance for me because it took me out of that brainwashing loop. For three months, I was free from my mother's terrorizing violence, or the bizarre reasoning behind it. I was also free of the enablers and fellow victims around me reinforcing the message. What I did have was a new community of people who just lived their lives and experienced joy or irritation or whatever emotions came up in an appropriate way. The topsy-turvy world of my mother's logic, which kept me working overtime to figure out what was going to come at me next, was gone. My mind was free to explore ideas and thoughts other than fear and survival. I was free to live my life and enjoy it.

The bottom line is that living in Haiti was completely liberating, as was my time away from my mother and her religious cult. The time in Haiti helped me realize that I deserved better, and that I was strong enough to walk (or run) away. Not everyone in an abusive situation has that kind of opportunity to realize there is so much more for them. Instead, many people in abusive situations are caught in a downward and vicious spiral of abuse and find it impossible to get out.

I am grateful for that time in Haiti because it helped set the stage for my independence. As they say, once you have seen something, you cannot unsee it. My time as a missionary shifted my perspective. I had seen a free life – and that liberation was not something I could unsee or unfeel. For whatever reason, I managed to hold on to my innate resilience, and Haiti had helped it to flourish, and grow stronger. I had been exposed to fresh air and light just long enough for Jeannie's hold to begin to crumble away.

The night I left my mother's grip and home, I looked like hell. The beating had left me cut, bruised, scratched, welted and missing pieces of hair. I am not sure how my dad was unaware of the extent of what was happening to me, but he was. Unlike my mother, my dad was not psychotic or a liar, so I chose to believe him. I had not spent much time with him in my teens, which contributed to his lack of awareness. Every time I went to my dad's, Mother made it hell before I left and when I came back, so I stopped going to my fathers as much. Also, I was a teenage girl and dad was not the most emotionally available guy; and he was also busy with his wife and three young sons, my little brothers.

I loved my little brothers so much and always had a lot of fun playing with them. But vacations were tough with three boys and a teenage girl. Dad loved taking long road trips in the family van on the open road without any hotel reservations. In the days before the internet, no hotel reservations meant there was a decent possibility that you would not find a hotel or food until very late at night. With three young boys and a teenager this was not much fun.

I finally drew the line the summer I got a painful ear infection while we were on a family road trip. My dad was so focused on his quest to clock as many miles as possible without stopping that my pleas to see a doctor were ignored. By the time he relented, I was crying in pain, throwing up, feverish, and had to go on an extended course of antibiotics. After that, I opted out of road trip vacations – for all those reasons, my time with Kent Sr. was minimal.

Another possible reason my dad did not do anything about my mother's abuse is that because of his family history, abusive behavior had been normalized for him. My dad grew up with a brother who was both delusional and violent, especially toward my father. Although his brother was committed to a psychiatric institution at the age of 19, my father had to live with the unpredictability and fear for his entire childhood. I imagine my dad was conditioned to accept insane behavior. More than likely, it is also what conditioned him to deal with my mother as long as he did.

The skewed tolerance that comes from living with insanity during your formative years can have ongoing, cascading effects through generations of a family – and it definitely worked that way in mine. Dad's reaction on seeing how thoroughly my mother had beaten me was genuine; he was horrified and enraged – but only after he could no longer turn a blind eye.

My dad had become a father when he was just 19 years old, so he was likely not ready for a family. I do not blame him for not removing me from the hell of Don and Jeannie's house. I am just glad that his fierce anger and protectiveness surfaced when he finally saw the reality. His anger, surprise, and disgust also helped me feel loved and safer than I ever had before.

Today, we take for granted that the police and social services protect children and battered spouses; but in the 1970s and 1980s there were not many laws in place, and awareness was negligible. The warning signs of abuse or what to do was not part of our national consciousness back then. At that time, people had a strong sense that problems in a family were for that family to solve. Lawton, Oklahoma, was not a hotbed of groundbreaking social justice. It was all about, "We wish you well. Please close the door to your house, so we cannot hear you screaming in there."

That put me in a situation where, if I wanted to be saved, I would have to save myself. When I was 18, it didn't make me angry that no one helped me; it was just the way things were. I was so happy to finally live away from my mother, I didn't give her a conscious second thought after I left.

As an adult, I can look back and see that my brain was a mess of chaos, terror, and alarm. I had no voice, no way to represent myself or my interests, and zero respect at home, which taught me to be circumspect, quiet and fearful. Feeling like you have no voice, or actively silenced, is a horrible thing. As human beings, our deepest instinct is to communicate who and how we are – and use that information to connect with other human beings. It is in our DNA. Having no voice is a constant chipping away at your humanity; it's a slow death. That feeling was my daily baseline. Now when I look at the neglect, manipulation, collective blindness, stress, and ruined childhood, I am enraged – which is progress.

In spite of having been in the dark for so long, Dad freaked out when he saw my condition. He and my stepmom examined the cuts, welts and bruises on my body from that day's beating, as well as a few that had come from previous beatings. My stepmother took pictures, and in my dad's rage, he wanted to press charges against Jeannie, which at first, I thought was a perfect solution to get some vengeance.

However, I realized fairly quickly I just could not endure that. Once again, it was not because of weakness, stupidity, fear, or anything like that; it was because I had had enough. I was out. The idea of staying tied to my mother and her bullshit, or listening to her lie, scream and degrade me or anyone else for another second, was more than I could take. I did not want to go through that legal process or have to talk about what had happened to me. Once I was away from all that, why would I elect to stay enmeshed with it?

For me, the strongest choice was to walk away and start rebuilding immediately. It was behind me, and I wanted to keep it that way. I had spent so much of my life compartmentalizing and shoving things down for my survival, now I was going to shove all of that into one of the rooms in my psyche, kick the door closed, and lock it forever. I wanted it over, and dad relented.

The only thing that was hard about living with my dad was leaving Frankie behind. The feeling of guilt was heavy; my only solace was knowing that she was not abusive to him, and hopefully that would continue. Many years later Frankie told me that the mood in the house changed after I left, and not for the better. I had always been the clown and played games to make my siblings laugh when my parents were away. Taylor and Cary were very quiet, and no one was there to manufacture any more fun; Frankie was stuck in that house with our crazy mother, two older, silent stepsisters and Don, who was under our mother's heavy thumb.

Despite the trauma and regret over leaving Frankie, I settled into life with my dad, my stepmom, and the boys to finish out my senior year of high school and plan my escape from Oklahoma. In hindsight, I went through a period of shock from the drastic change in my life. It was a huge change to be able to watch TV, listen to the radio, talk on the phone with my friends, and do things a normal teenager does. And I loved playing with my baby brother Clinton and my little brother Ronnie. I have always loved babies, toddlers and children in general; they are so present and force you to be equally in the moment. Clinton was no exception – such a sweet and cuddly little guy who was all love and fun. He was the perfect antidote to the total lack of love I had experienced for so long – and Ronnie was fun and lovable too.

That kind of love was a huge departure for me, and television was too. In my mother's house, we only watched an hour or two of TV each week, and only carefully selected church-approved programming. The lack of exposure to TV, movies, music, magazines, people outside the church, restaurants, clubs or time with my friends had kept me completely uninformed about pop culture. It had totally suppressed my ability to function outside of the small world that Jeannie had created.

Under normal circumstances, staying glued to the TV is not something I would recommend; but for me, in that moment, it was perfect. I caught up on what everyone else was seeing, wearing and thinking about in 1985. I devoured MTV, Three's Company, Cheers, Growing Pains, Family Ties, and anything else I could find. I particularly liked The Facts of Life, possibly for the loving mother figure of Mrs. Garret, but mostly for the girls on the show. They were so pretty and fun and – pretty.

Less pretty were the horror movies I discovered, and, for a time, I was totally obsessed. Jeannie had banned all scary movies because they were the devil's work (and as we know, the devil can reach out and invade a soul right from the TV). Once I could watch them, I loved them for their weirdness, but also because they represented my new freedom. The first horror movie I ever saw was Children of The Corn; and, like most people of my generation, Malachi will always have a special place in my heart.

Nikki had introduced me to Prince; but now I got to listen to Madonna, Tina Turner, Gloria Estefan, Corey Hart, Duran Duran, and all the other gods and goddesses of MTV and radio. Nikki continued my pop-culture intervention and introduced me to General Hospital, about which she was obsessed; and, like millions of other people at the time, I was drawn into the on-again-off-again relationship between Luke and Laura. As silly as it may seem, it was a big deal to be connected to other people through knowing who those characters were and being invested in what would happen to them. It connected me to the larger world. It confirmed that I was not confined to the narrow, isolated life that Jeannie had created for me. Nikki also took me to see St. Elmo's Fire. If you were a child of the 1980's, you know that if you could identify the members of the Brat Pack, you were keyed into the zeitgeist.

After I moved into my dad's house, all of the things I did with Nikki were emblematic of my sudden and almost complete adolescent freedom. I still attended the Christian school – changing schools in the middle of my senior year would have been more trouble than it was worth – and Nikki and Fiona were there, as were my sports teams. There was no deep conversation with either of them about what had happened at home; but they both knew I had relocated to my father's house. Maybe they had been told to stay sensitive and not trouble me with questions. Maybe they knew but did not bring it up because they were lost in their own adolescent dramas. It did not matter to me at all; being with them and having that continuity made the seemingly endless number of life changes easier to process.

The thing that constantly amazed me was what it felt like to experience real freedom – not the freedom I tried to grasp when I lived with my mother, or the freedom that had an expiration date like when I was in Haiti. The new door that had opened onto making choices for myself was thrilling and overwhelming. I put my toe in the water when I went to the mall with friends. In the 1980s, going to the mall was the ultimate teenage escape. It was not about shopping: it was our town hall, our clubhouse, where we ate, dated and played. Malls were teen-towns that represented freedom, which was one of the reasons I loved going.

Everyone was trying on new and liberated versions of themselves at the mall - and I could blend in there.

Blending in also meant looking the part; and the prissy dresses and skirt-and-blouse combos that my mother and my Christian school demanded went out the window outside of school. When my friend Brian, who I had known for years, invited me to his prom at the local high school (because, of course, my school did not have a prom), I was happy to go. I knew many of the students from when I had attended public school, and I was excited to see all my old friends.

I dressed up in a full-on Madonna look with a white lacy dress and fingerless gloves, and sashayed out of the house and into the limo that Brian's mother had rented for us. He gave me a corsage and we had dinner out - things like that would not have been possible just a few months earlier. That prom was the first time I ever danced with other teens in public, and I discovered that I loved it. I found it very freeing and danced all night. Brian eventually dragged me off the dance floor to go home. To this day I love to dance and do it often.

I found out later that Brian's mother had arranged for all the little luxuries of that night, hoping that it would spark something between us. The spark did not happen, and her disappointment left her very unhappy with me. I had not been allowed to date; so, I was not equipped or eager to be someone's girlfriend. But I was interested in seeing all my old friends, meeting as many new people as possible, and learning everything I could about them and myself.

Nikki continued to be the best passport to a fun teenage life imaginable. After we graduated, we would go to a club called Sound Stage where we would dance like fools and meet guys. My dating experience was zilch, and going out with these boys kickstarted my connection with a wider world. If Jeannie had known that I was dating, she would have had a complete meltdown, which contributed to the pure joy of dating, even if I really had no interest in boys.

Sound Stage was only one of my happy hunting grounds for a social life. I was still working at Don's grocery store, and at a Christian bookstore in the mall, which gave me the opportunity to meet tons of people every day. Without the weight of Jeannie's expectations on me, I felt free to actually make eye contact and connect with some of the people, boys in particular, who shopped with us at either store.

Yes, working with Don after I left was awkward; but a job's a job, and I knew that money led to freedom. The hustling I did as a child had never let up, and my jobs were the key to my plans to eventually leave Lawton. This is a good place to note my view of my stepfather, Don, in all that happened to me as a child. While Don had been both a bystander and a participant in all the nightmares of my pre-teen and teenage years, he was mostly only a witness and abettor. He made those paddles at his store and did beat me a few times, but I knew that it was not really who he was in his soul. I am not sure how I knew that. Maybe there was some reticence in the way he went about the grim task of assisting Jeannie, or his kindness and generosity when he was not swept up in her dementia.

Whatever it was, my mother was the clear cause of the abuse; and her behavior eclipsed anyone else's. I also knew that Don's parents had not used belts or paddles, but instead favored switches they made him cut off of a tree in their yard. Once again, violence normalizes and begets violence. There might have even been a little Stockholm Syndrome going on there as well; I saw how Jeannie manipulated Don and took her rage out on him on rare occasions. I identified with Don too much to hate or blame him.

After I left my mother's house, I learned some things about my mom. Growing up I had not known much about my mother's family history, especially since they lived far away. Mother not only cultivated a cult of secrecy around anything that happened in our house, but she also did the same about her own background. What I learned about my mother's parents happened completely by accident.

After I left my mother's home for good, I attended a large church that I had never been to before, in my hometown of Lawton, with my friend Teresa. After the service, a woman who could not have been a day under ninety-years-old came up to me and asked if I was Jeannie's daughter. Good lord! How could she know that? It could only be that we all have a strong family resemblance.

She shared things about my mom's family with me that both shocked and upset me. She said that my grandfather had been the pastor of that very church many, many years ago. She went on to tell me, "We loved them so much but it's a shame what happened. We had to let your grandfather go because of your grandmother's breakdown." What a shock to learn that my grandparents had lived in the same town that I did many years before I was born, and that my grandfather had pastored a large church there and was fired because of my grandmother's breakdown (whatever that meant). As far as I knew, my grandparents had always lived in Texas.

In a short, five-minute conversation with a total stranger, I learned more about my mother's family history than I had in my entire 18 years. And it was very upsetting. I found out later from my father, that my grandfather, a very stern man, had taken my mother and her brother away from their mother leaving her with their youngest, a baby girl. He did not tell my grandmother where they were going and lived in another town in secrecy, far away, and for over a year. What could have been so terrible that a man would take his children and leave his wife and other child behind to fend for themselves in the early to mid-1950's? Something nasty must have happened.

My grandmother could not find them for a long time, but she eventually did find them, and they got back together although never a real couple again. She wound up on lithium for the rest of her life and her son, my mother's brother, who was unstable and violent, was institutionalized when he was in his twenties. He was diagnosed with paranoid schizophrenia and was institutionalized until his death in his 70's.

My father's family history was much more transparent. As I mentioned earlier, his older brother Wayne was institutionalized when he was 19 and lived the rest of his life there until he died in his seventies.

It helped me to understand that mental illness had been present for generations in my mom's family. Mother was an undiagnosed manic bipolar narcissist with sociopathic tendencies, and her mother and brother were mentally ill as well. I have often wondered why I was fortunate enough to not have inherited the mental illness. Although sharing a birthday with my mother was far too close for comfort. I never have a birthday without thinking about my abusive, violent mother.

While these insights were disturbing but helpful, I was so glad to be free and living a new life of freedom. My new social life, post Jeannie, was busy. Lawton had an army artillery base which, of course, also brought a lot of potential dates into the store and the Sound Stage. None of these guys were keepers. They were nice enough; but they were young, immature, and sometimes married, which I would find out after a few dates. They were learning how to blow things up with cannons and grenades and rocket launchers, and were performing maneuvers over thousands of acres of land. You could hear the explosions all over town and they would rattle the windows in my dad's house. Whatever their shortcomings were, those soldiers were instrumental in helping me to cut my teeth on the dating world. They were sweet and we would make out and fool around a little – I had a lot of fun. I cannot remember most of their names or faces anymore, probably because the thing that cements boyfriends in your mind did not happen for me. I never had a crush on a single one, nor did I give up my virginity to any of them. I kept dating them because I was hoping to feel something.

I did, however, have crushes on girls. I was unaware that what I was feeling for those girls was romantic, but I knew it was different. Another weird part of growing up in my mother's crazy religious cult was that sex and romance were never, ever, discussed. I was so innocent that I could not know what went on or how to identify what I was feeling. I had no idea that feeling nothing for those guys was actually telling me something.

When I was in high school and still living at my mother's house, I was even more shut down than what my ignorance dictated. My constant anxiety and fear eclipsed any feelings or recognition of feelings I might have had. A girl transferred into the Christian school from San Diego my senior year and she seemed jealous of my close friendship with Fiona. She was much more worldly than I was, and in her jealousy accused me of being in love with Fiona. I was shocked and deeply offended. What the hell was she talking about? Fiona was my good friend and I cared about her deeply; but falling in love with her was absolutely ridiculous. It was like accusing me of loving someone's cat, or a lamppost. Being in love with another woman was totally absurd.

I dated boys in order to shake off what I presumed was an indifference brought on by 18 years of religious doctrine saying that everything going on between the guys and me was bad. Although I would not sleep with them, and did not lose my virginity until my twenties, learning to date was a very important part of my coming of age. Dating was part of the process of joining the non-Jeannie world; as was attending college, which I did right after graduating from high school.

My grades were good enough to earn me a full ride four-year scholarship to the university in our city, which caused a few problems because I desperately wanted to leave Lawton and never look back. My dad had no intention of paying for an out-of-state school, even though my parents' divorce agreement dictated that he pay for my brother's and my college.

I buckled and agreed to give the local university a try. It helped that he celebrated not paying for my education by buying me a brand-new, red Chevy Cavalier with all the bells and whistles.

Even with the car, college was a disaster. Five years at the Christian school did not prepare me at all for college. It was essentially home-schooling without a teacher, or a bunch of autodidacts held hostage, depending on how you choose to look at it. When I got to college I had no experience with listening to lectures, learning as a collective, taking notes, waiting for other students to catch up or taking timed tests. The Christian school made me more of a visual person and it was difficult to "hear" professors and learn verbally. It just did not work.

To make it worse, I was still in Oklahoma and had my sights set on getting out of Oklahoma. So, the combination of living where I did not want to live, and attending a school that I hated was too much to bear. I stopped going to classes. My father went nuts and insisted I go back, so I went occasionally. But my heart just was not in it, even though it was already paid.

I made the decision to leave Oklahoma and go to whatever school would accept me as long as it was not anywhere near Oklahoma. I am not a huge risk-taker by nature; I was not just buying a plane ticket to New York or Los Angeles (the two cities I had settled on as my next home).

I bided my time to figure out a plan. I spent months considering my options. I combed the classifieds. I considered joining the Coast Guard or going back to missionary work with the Peace Corp. I even went to Dallas for a few weeks and stayed with an aunt to see if there was any work for me there. While I was in Dallas, my dad called to tell me that he had found me a job at a bank back home. Work was work, so I drove back only to find that there was no job. It was an interview; and since I did not have banking experience, no bank job for me. That was the last straw. I had to get out of Oklahoma. I had to leave – and I had to leap if I was going to leave.

The classifieds I had been looking at for months were more than just local – there were national ads in the paper too. I figured that my plan would work if I could get a job in one of my chosen cities. I did not have any real skills; but I did have experience with my little brothers, which I thought set me up pretty well to be a nanny. There was a nanny position available in Summit, New Jersey, near New York City. The family would pay for me to get there; would give me a bedroom in their house; would feed me; and pay me a small stipend every week so I would not be jumping into the abyss.

Summit, New Jersey, was less than an hour from Manhattan, so I knew this was a stepping stone for my new life in NYC. I could work for a year with this family, establish my residency for college, and then move into the city to go to school and work. I knew it would mean I would have to work multiple jobs to pay for school and living expenses in NYC, but I did not care. That was my dream. Even though no one in my family had graduated from college, and it was not a conversation my parents had with me, I knew I needed to go to college. I did not want to get married and have children; I wanted to focus on a career and big city living as far away from Oklahoma as I could get. I wanted a career that would provide well for me and make me independent.

I told my dad what I was planning, and although he did not agree with my plan, he knew I already had one foot out the door. He did not really have a leg to stand on because he had left his family's farm when he was young to pursue his own career dreams. While he did not like me moving so far away, I think he understood. He insisted that because I was leaving, he was not going to pay for my school – but he gave me his blessing to leave, probably thinking I would eventually be back. I told him I did not care if he helped me financially or not; I told him if I had to work three jobs to pay for school I would. I knew there was a far better life for me out there than living in Oklahoma, where I had experienced so much heartbreak.

While he did not pay for my college, he did sell the Cavalier and sent me $1,500 a semester until the money from the sale of the car ran out, which was about halfway through school. This hardly covered subway fare in NYC; but I was grateful for the help. That was the final negotiation I did with anyone in my family. I packed, promised to be in touch, and got the hell out of Oklahoma, forever.

After I had left Oklahoma, my mother up and moved to South Carolina, with Don, Frankie and the girls, to get my brother away from our dad. They lived in South Carolina, for several decades. My father insists to this day that it was to separate him from his son, and I believe him. My mother hated my dad for leaving her and was a vindictive person. When my brother was out of high school, he moved back to Oklahoma, to be with our dad.

Mental illness leads to all kinds of strange behavior, and my mother eventually facilitated the death of my stepfather. He developed Lewy body dementia in his early sixties and my mother was not a caregiver. She preferred to be cared for, not care for other people. So, when my stepfather could no longer care for her, they moved back to Lawton,

Oklahoma, to be close to my brother Frankie, so he could carry the burden of caring for them both. Which, like the amazing man he is, he did.

Upon arriving in Oklahoma, and perhaps even before, my mother starved my stepfather. There was never food in the house, not because they could not afford food. When I visited, I would bring groceries to their house. But mother would say they could not eat any of it and throw it out. When my brother would take Don out to eat, he would eat like he had not eaten in weeks.

Mother was also physically abusive to Don. She would call Frankie and tell him Don had "fallen" and she was not able to get him up. My brother would go to their house and pick Don up off of the floor. However, the cuts, scratches and bruises Don had were not indicative of a fall. I knew my mother all too well; an abuser continues to abuse when their victims get away – they just find someone else to abuse. My mother preyed on the weak, and Don had become weak because of his disease.

I believe these things facilitated Don's death. He was six feet tall and barely ninety pounds when he was put into a home to receive the proper care that my mother would not give him. He died not long after. It was a very sad day when we buried him, and mother did not attend his funeral – just like she did not attend her own mother's funeral. My mother was selfish to the core. Everything was always, always about her.

CHAPTER FIVE

NEW YORK CITY HERE I COME!

Getting a grip on reality is difficult when you have primarily dealt with a total lack of reality your whole life – but I was determined to do so. Oklahoma and the insane world in which my mother had trapped me for 18 years were loathsome to me; and I finally broke free from her hold when I left her home. And although I had moved to my father's house in the middle of my senior year of high school, that was not enough for me. I knew there was a much better life out there; and I was going to find it.

The idea of leaving Lawton and starting a new life on the East Coast was very exciting. My plan was to work for a year in New Jersey to establish residency there, and then move into New York City to go to school. I decided to say goodbye to Jeannie before I left for my new job as a nanny in New Jersey. I did not have any love for her, but I knew how to deal with her at that point – and she did not scare me. Did I go to say goodbye out of a sense of duty? Maybe. Did I want to confront her about the damage she had done? Absolutely.

After the break with her, I actually had gone back to the house a few times to visit my siblings and my stepfather, even though I had seen him at the store. Seeing Frankie was particularly great because I missed him terribly; but most of my visits were decent at best, mildly unpleasant at worst. During these visits, she did not attempt to hurt me or verbally abuse me; but my mother is the kind of toxic person who can fill a room with a smog of simmering resentment, rage, religious mania, and just plain insanity.

One upside to going back, aside from seeing Frankie, was that the food was far better at my mother's house than my dad's. My stepmother was a lovely person – a former high school beauty queen – but not very invested in mastering the domestic arts. My dad never cooked, and even if he had tried, I am sure the food would have had to go directly into the garbage can. So, they ate out a lot, including a lot of fast food – which sounded good at first, but was actually kind of gross.

Anyway, I was always working or in school, so I was not often available to go out to eat meals with my dad and stepmother. And because there was never food in their house, I usually ended up fending for myself.

The only good thing about living with my mother and Don was that there was always food to eat. All of us had our scheduled night to cook. My stepfather enjoyed cooking, so he would cook Sunday meals and sometimes another day during the week. Whatever food was made at my mother's house was heavenly compared to the fast food I was now eating every day at my dad's.

I decided to make my way over to my mother's place right before I left for New Jersey. We had dinner, and then I sat out in the backyard with my mother for a while. We made small talk before I launched into what I had to say.

I asked my mother what was behind the constant beatings and thrashings. I asked about the many, many instances of choking that continued until things went dark and I saw sparkles of light. I asked her about the incessant, daily, verbal, emotional and mental abuse and rage. I needed to know what she thought about everything that had happened, and if she had any feelings about my brother that connected to those events. I certainly would not have blamed her for thinking that my brother's death was my fault, or for directing her anger at me about it for a decade – I certainly blamed myself. I was angry at myself for causing the loss of the most important person and protector in my life and ruining my family.

When I finished speaking, she turned to me, looked me straight in the eyes, and said, "I don't remember any of that." Was I floored? Yes. Should I have been surprised? Probably not.

At that point, I hadn't even begun to truly process my childhood and my relationship with my seriously mentally ill mother. The depths of her madness – which could have been anything from a combination of narcissism and psychoticism to manic bipolar disorder to some unknown mental condition – were not for me to explore, nor did I want to. I was totally appalled, shocked and disappointed by her response. Then and there, I decided I had no desire to ever again get to the bottom of what motivated her. All I needed to know was that she was insane, that she always would be, and that I was leaving.

The family I worked for in New Jersey turned out to be lovely; their baby, Christopher, was sweet and adorable. He was a baby, and I made sure I was an extremely loving nanny. My work ethic and love of babies went into my work; but I knew that it was also vital that I keep the job so I could establish residency in the tri-state area. Resident status would mean that I could go to school in Manhattan and not pay out-of-state tuition.

To help fund a future move into Manhattan for school, I took a second job at a high-end department store at the Mall at Short Hills in Short Hills, New Jersey. The mall was super-posh, which was an environment to which I had never been exposed. It was a real eye-opener for me at 19, and really made me want to strive for "the better life," which would include making money and buying nice things for myself.

One of the managers at the store was a woman named Perry, who completely intrigued me. She was this type-A serious person who dressed in trousers and flats all the time. She had long dark hair and was very pretty. She was nice enough, but there was no friendship or connection between us. Even so, I would lie in bed at night and think about her. I was so perplexed – why was I thinking about this very pretty woman all the time, and what about her was so riveting?

Finally, during one night of again lying in bed thinking about her, and trying to understand why she was always in my thoughts, I had a revelation. I decided it must be a crush – therefore, I must be gay! And that was that. I was gay.

I had needed to get out into the world to understand that 'gay' was even a thing. That word was not in my vocabulary in Oklahoma. I only learned that word after leaving home and experiencing the "real world" of New York City and the tri-state area. But by using a word to describe it, I was now able to understand all the strange feelings and crushes I had on pretty girls while growing up. Not that I ever acted on those feelings, anyway – I had no idea at the time that they were actually crushes; and I would have been way too scared to do anything about them.

Even with the revelation that I was gay, I decided I needed to understand what it really meant before I started to try to date girls. I needed some time to come to terms with, and embrace, my new identity. Plus, I had no idea how to meet girls.

I was with the New Jersey family for 10 months, but I was eager to get into college. I started applying to schools the second I was eligible. I knew I could not afford NYU or Columbia; but I was determined to go to school in Manhattan. I investigated every other university there and soon found the Fashion Institute of Technology. It was perfect. FIT is a well-regarded school with programs centered around the fashion industry; moreover, it is part of the State University of New York system, so it was – comparatively – reasonably priced. And the likes of Calvin Klein and Michael Kors had gone to school there – so I knew it had to be fabulous. I would still need to work two or three jobs to keep myself fed, clothed, housed and in school, but it would be doable.

So, I made my decision – I wanted to live in New York City to go to FIT. I gave the couple in Summit my notice and prepared to rent a room in the city, enroll in school, and take care of anything else I needed to do in order to start college. I knew I would need to find at least a couple of jobs in NYC. But no matter how difficult it would be to work that much, it would be infinitely easier and more fun than returning to Lawton.

If you are not a New Yorker, you may not know that there is an intricate network composed of people who hire nannies, people who refer nannies, and the nannies themselves. You can whisper, "I need a nanny," to someone on the corner of 77th Street and Madison Avenue, and by the time you get to your office at 54th Street and Park, someone from the Unofficial Nanny Network will have left a message for you: "I know exactly the person for you! She doesn't mind walking around with peanut butter in her hair and is nice to the children even when they try to set her on fire!"

That is what happened to me. The lovely mom I worked for in New Jersey heard that a friend at her work needed a nanny. She referred me for the job, which I got. So, I went to work for Cheryl and her family almost immediately; they lived on Park Avenue near 94th Street.

Cheryl was a bigwig at an advertising agency and her husband was the head of the legal department for one of the major TV networks. They had three sweet children: Katrina was the eldest at 9 years old, and the twins, a boy named Kyle and girl named Stacey, were 7.

Thus began my stint of hobnobbing with the children of the rich and powerful. The girls went to a private school with Carolina Herrera's children, and the little boy was friends with Richard Nixon's grandson. Who knows what other luminaries I was introduced to, or had to hover near, at 3 p.m. pickup? It was all very posh, very luxurious – and consequently, a memorable gig.

Cheryl and her husband were very nice, and I really did enjoy living with them on Park Avenue for a year. I would go to school at the same time the children did, get out in time to pick them up from school, help them with homework and make them dinner. Then, I would retire to my room when the parents came home, and I would work on my own homework. Even though my bedroom was the size of a shoe box, it was an oasis of peace for a year on Park Avenue on the Upper East Side.

After I left the Park Avenue nannying job, I started a job at the legendary Rainbow Room at Rockefeller Center. I stayed there throughout my entire college career, primarily because I made a lot of money and had a flex schedule for my classes. Keep in mind that this was decades ago; I was happy to start at $9 per hour. I received a raise to $11 per hour pretty quickly; plus, I made a lot of tips. Back in the late 1980s and early 1990s, it was a lot of money.

The Rainbow Room was – and is – a place where tourists and locals alike go when they want to drop a lot of money and have a classic New York City experience. The locals who showed up were either seriously well-heeled or famous. Needless to say, the tips were terrific and made a major dent in my tuition bills. Depending on the day, I worked as a page, did coat check, walked around as a cigarette girl, or was a concierge. All that running around the Rainbow Room and working there for so long meant that I had ample opportunity to meet a lot of very famous people. These were people who I never could have dreamed of meeting when I was back in Lawton. Growing up in the cult in Oklahoma, I would not have known who a lot of the celebrities were; but after moving to NYC, I dove headfirst into pop culture, music, and movies. I wanted to learn about and understand the world that I had missed out on my whole life.

I met Ron and Nancy Reagan, Mike Tyson, Madonna, Robert DeNiro, Jessica Lange, and so many others. I hung out with the likes of Tony

Bennett, Rosemary Clooney, and Phyllis Diller while they rehearsed for their upcoming performances at the Rainbow Room Cabaret. I had many interesting and entertaining conversations with them. Phyllis would always have me cracking up; she was so funny to be around. And I just loved listening to Tony and Rosemary sing. It gave me such joy. I did a photo shoot for the cover of New York magazine with Frank and Kathie Lee Gifford, and was an extra in a movie that had scenes shot in the Rainbow Room with Dana Carvey and John Lovitz. Dana was very nice and friendly. John was a bit of a prima donna and cranky; but it was still so much fun to be a part of that. It was such an amazing time in my life. But then – I met Barbra!

During the day, the Rainbow Room was the Rockefeller Center Club, named for the Rockefeller family. It was a private business club where David Rockefeller often dined. It was on the 65th floor of the RCA building, later known as Top of the Rock. The views were absolutely incredible. During the day, we let people come in and check out the view for a minute – but if they were not dressed appropriately, we would ask them to leave – jeans and sneakers and very casual wear were definitely not acceptable. Men had to wear collared shirts and jackets. One day, I was standing near the entrance and a big group walked in. There was a woman at the front of the pack. I presumed they were there to see the view, so I gave them a couple of minutes to take it in before I would do my duty and inform them they would have to leave. They were all dressed in jeans.

I did not really look at anyone except the woman who seemed to be the leader. I figured I would have to be cordial but stern with her; but when I turned to face her to inform her of our dress code, my jaw dropped – it was Barbra Streisand! I **love** Barbra. I think I even said, *Holy shit, it's Barbra Streisand,* in my head.

It turned out that she was with part of her film crew, scouting the restaurant to film a scene there for *Prince of Tides.* She explained why they were there and that they were waiting to be shown the room. Fine. No problem. What am I going to do, kick out Barbra Streisand? I think I just said, "Have a good day," but I really wanted to whisper, "*I love you very, very much.*" Yes, it's creepy and I meant it, but I managed to keep my mouth shut. Wow – I almost tried to kick Barbra Streisand out of the Rainbow Room. That's one for my diary.

Once I moved into Manhattan and was introduced to more of what New York City had to offer, I went out every chance I could. I met people and learned about their lives, and made lots of friends. During the course of all that socializing, I finally learned what it really meant to be gay. Realizing I was gay the year before was not a bombshell event, strangely enough. I had been going through so much change and such a complete rebuild of my identity that figuring out that I was gay did not really floor me. It is possible that I was unfazed because I still had no idea how to meet girls; so, the realization that I was gay was much more theory than practice at that point.

I still dated a few guys here and there, experimenting and finding out exactly with what kind of personality I was most comfortable. I met this nice guy who was sort of a rocker type. He was super-good looking and was always in black, and had long dark hair, and he made it fun to just hang out.

One night, we were in a diner, and he was flipping through a copy of the *New Yorker* magazine (don't judge a book by its cover). He paused while looking through the classified ads at the back. He laughed at something and pointed it out. I read it and chuckled too. Then my eyes scrolled down the page; much to my surprise, there were ads for people seeking different people for romantic interludes and relationships. I scanned some of them and then my eyes landed on an ad that listed a woman seeking a woman! I looked at it, but tried not to look overly interested. I handed the magazine back.

But immediately after the date, I went to buy my own copy. I thought, *Holy cow! This is how you meet girls in New York!* As I scanned all the magazines and newspapers at the newspaper stand, hoping to find other publications that ran the same kind of ads, I ran across the *Village Voice,* another now-defunct New York institution. The *Voice,* as it was affectionately referred to, was a local paper that also had rows of classified ads for everything you could imagine in the back pages. It, too, had ads for women seeking women.

I was so excited; I was beside myself! Armed with the *New Yorker* and the *Village Voice,* I started responding to ads. Here is how it worked: if you found an ad you were interested in, you would call the magazine or paper, and you would punch in the account number that was associated with the ad. You would leave a little phone message saying something about yourself. If the other party was interested, she would call you back. It was not as easy as today's dating apps, but it worked. I started talking to girls and met a few. I went slowly and found my bearings – and that is how I met my first serious girlfriend, Anna.

Anna was pretty, very feminine, with long dark hair. She wore makeup, had a very nice figure, and pretty eyes. She worked on Wall Street for Goldman Sachs. We went on a few friendly, chaste dates, and I guess she decided I was cool enough to introduce to her friends. She arranged for a group of us to go out. I was still only 20 years old, under the drinking age, but somehow I made it into the lesbian club (my first one) and met all these women who were friends of Anna's – some were her exes.

It was not a scene I had ever encountered before, but I tried to roll with it. The music was great, and everyone was dancing. I was still in 'recovery' from years of being banned from dancing, so I was not leaving the dance floor. Then a slow song came on, and there was that awkward moment when everyone paired up. Anna came over, took my hand, and took me onto the dance floor.

Slow-dance with a girl? I had never even slow-danced with a guy before. I do not know why it had ever struck me as odd or uncomfortable, but we started dancing – and it was OK. I had no experience dancing like that, and didn't really know what to do – but while I was trying to figure it out, Anna kissed me. Woah! Fireworks! *OH WOW! This is what everyone's been talking about!*

I had never felt anything particularly noteworthy when making out with any of the guys I dated. They were nice, but there was never a "wow" moment. It was all just OK. Now I realized that once you experience a fireworks-kiss, "OK" is quite bad by comparison. And there you have it. My love affair with beautiful women began.

Anna was eight years older than I was, made good money on Wall Street, and was already set up with a life that worked for her. She lived in the north Bronx, where she was born and raised. She had moved out as a single, young girl, against her mother's wishes, and against her Italian upbringing ("women don't leave home until they marry"). She had moved anyway into her own apartment near the Bronx Zoo. She was near her family, but far enough away to have independence.

I was still nannying in Manhattan, but would take the subway up to her apartment, where I would occasionally stay with her for the weekend. I was settling into my first relationship with a woman. I eventually realized that I could not work on my relationship with Anna in any significant way if I was still living with Cheryl's family; so, I gave my notice that I would be leaving.

Anna asked me to move in with her. After much discussion and thought, I agreed. I packed up my stuff and moved in with her. I was still in school and working a couple of jobs to keep myself afloat. Anna said she understood that I could not handle 50 percent of the bills, rent and all other expenses. Although that awareness seemed to evaporate over time, in the beginning we had a great relationship. I was learning about relationships and how to be a good partner. We did things as a couple; and we settled in quite nicely with one another. We took a few trips together and spent time with family and friends.

But because of our age difference, Anna began wanting different things than me. She loved decorating the apartment and refinishing antique wood furniture. She was very homey and wanted to be involved with projects around the house. I was not the stay-at-home type; I was busy with school and working lots of jobs. She wanted to own a home, and that became her focus.

She started to complain that I was not making enough money, nor was I carrying my weight financially, although I was paying what we had originally agreed. We also started to butt heads and argue about other things. And when we did, she would then launch into a narrative about how she was older than me, and that my arguing with her was a sign of disrespect. She would say that her parents were off the boat from Italy, and they had instilled values in her that dictated that everyone should respect their elders. I had no problem with that concept, except that Anna decided that it applied to our relationship as well. She felt that her eight years on me required me to respect her like she was my *nonna*.

Uh, no. And anyway, mutual respect was not what I felt from some-one who had a habit of running off to make out with random people when she was drunk, which occurred on more than one occasion. I should have known that staying with Anna probably was not the best choice when she chose to get cozy with a straight couple that we met at a gay bar. They were looking for a girl to swing with – but setting boundaries wasn't my strong suit then, so I elected to roll with it. I do not think she ever did anything with the couple; but she admitted to having a crush on the girl and they spent hours talking on the phone. Even then I knew that was not right, but so it went.

"Rolling with it" included finally agreeing to buy a house with her, even though I was not sure if I could afford it. We had been together for almost three years when Anna started focusing on a house. I was still in school, and my financial situation had not changed. To me, buying a house did not sound like a good idea; but Anna said that if I did not do it, she would buy the house with her mother. And her mother did not like me; I represented all of her disappointment about her daughter being gay. I was the reason Anna was not married, was not straight, and did not have children – even though Anna had other girlfriends before me. Perhaps they had received the same welcome from her mother – I am not sure.

One thing was for certain: if I wanted to stay with Anna, there was no way she could co-own a house with her mother. Her mother would have access to the house and walk in whenever she felt like it – this would not work for me.

So, at 23, I started to figure out a way that I could buy the house with Anna; I needed $5,000 for my half of the down payment. I first asked my dad if I could borrow the money from him, but he said no. So, I scrimped and saved, and even took money out on credit cards – and I finally came up with $5,000 toward the down payment for a house in New Jersey that I neither wanted nor could afford.

It was a 100-year-old colonial with a wraparound porch. It had great "bones," and at one time it undoubtedly had been a beautiful house. However, 100 years had taken its toll. We spent every weekend fixing up that house. We spent every penny that we had on it too, and I hated it more and more every day. I hated the very long commute into New York City for work and school; I hated that it was freezing inside in the winter; and I was not into the whole fixer-upper-feathering-our-nest thing like Anna was.

Over the course of our five years together, I had agreed to things that I really did not want, because relationships are about compromise, right? But I was very young and still learning how to live within a partnership. Anna was sweet, and in many ways, living with her was a positive part of my coming-out experience. But as partners, we were a bust.

Anna had a need to be respected and call the shots; she claimed that she had more wisdom and insight than I did due to her age. Yet, she ignored our age disparity and earning capacities when it came to paying bills. It was all too much.

I was certainly no picnic either. I was coming into my own. After escaping my mother's domination, I was not going to let anyone boss me, ever again. I also was dealing with a lot of anger – fallout from the trauma of losing my brother, sexual abuse, my parents' divorce, my mother's constant abuse, and the strict dogma of the religious cult. I had never learned how to properly deal with that anger, and it showed.

Plus, I was working many jobs to pay for school – and now, a house. I was now commuting three to four hours a day for school and work. To top it off, I was putting time, energy and money into fixing that house while enduring the freezing winter. All of it broke me. I was exhausted, and started to dislike New York – as well as New Jersey, where we now lived.

Anna and I started to fight constantly, and I finally told her that we had to call it quits. So, we broke up on a "trial" basis – but still lived together. I moved into one of the other bedrooms and we both started dating other girls. Looking back on that now, I realize that it was weird; but both of us had money tied up in the house, and neither of us could afford to buy the other out. It was a terrible situation.

I started going out to clubs, meeting girls, and dating, which I had not done before. I had jumped into a life with Anna without having any prior dating experience – and it was time for me to figure out who I was, and do some growing.

I also knew that I had gifts that I needed to explore and develop. I knew I was smart, resourceful, creative, loving, generous, and very strong; but I had to figure out how to put all those qualities to their best uses. Coming from an oppressive childhood, I was not taught or mentored. No one had guided me on how to put my best foot forward – I was going to have to teach myself how to do that.

I also knew that having survived living with my mother and all the other traumatic events of my childhood, I had some serious emotional shit with which to deal. But my natural instinct was to shove it down, suppress it, ignore it – do anything other than face it. I had already lived through so much horror and trauma – why would I want to relive all that by analyzing it?

And my dad, who did provide a home for me when I moved out of Jeannie's, was not entirely innocent either. He was loving, but he could also be rather disparaging sometimes. I knew he loved me because of his actions toward me, but he said very little. And then what he did say was often hurtful for me as a teenager.

I was always a small, skinny, but muscular girl, and had never been told by either my mother or father that I was pretty, or sweet, or even remotely presentable. My mom focused exclusively on fixing whatever physical flaws she saw in me. Mostly, she commanded me to wear makeup every day, do my hair, and wear horrific dresses. When it came to my dad, he was not the sort of dad who saw his daughter as his little princess. He treated me like one of his boys, which was fine when I was a small child, but not after I entered my teens.

However, as I mentioned, there were things he did to show me that he cared. Right after my brother died, my dad disappeared into his workshop in the garage. I did not have the awareness then to consciously realize he was hiding to avoid all the pain and sadness, but that is probably what was going on. But he was doing something else, too. When Christmas rolled around that year, there was a red, sparkly helmet for me under the Christmas tree at my grandmother's house. I thought it was cool – but what would I need a helmet for? It turned out that Dad had spent all that time in the garage building me a go-kart, so I could race the other neighborhood children with go-karts. He had wanted me to have something of my own to love and to be proud. And I did love it – and was so proud of it! As a family, we never ever talked about how we felt; but I felt loved because of my dad's gift. He had worked so hard to build it so he could surprise me.

By the time I was a teenager and living in his house many years later, it seemed as though he still had not revised his view of me as a tomboy. He didn't understand that growing teenage girls need emotional reinforcement from their fathers. The only time that my dad commented on my appearance was to tell me in a backhanded way that I was far from good looking. Almost every night, he would tell me goodnight by saying, "Get your beauty rest! You need it!" And in the mornings, he would say, "I think you should go back to bed; you didn't get enough beauty rest." One comment would have been funny, but they were constant, and they chipped away at me.

I never became comfortable with my body or my face. They were, in so many ways, battlegrounds for me – battlegrounds primarily because that is where my mother waged some of her insane wars. My body and face became battlegrounds because I had to cover myself with makeup to be acceptable or appealing; and because my mother or Don refused to take me to the doctor or hospital if I was sick or injured. There was not a part of my physical being that was not affected or invaded by someone else's desires, opinions, or rage.

So, after my relationship with Anna ended, I found that what I needed to work on was establishing boundaries. Maybe it was too late to do it with my mother – and maybe it would be a long, slow haul with my dad – but I could practice putting boundaries in place with the new people in my life. I had become so used to my mother's outrageous abuse that smaller doses seemed almost like nothing. So, I had to learn how to draw strong boundaries; but I also had to learn to define what would be unacceptable. I had to learn what it meant to truly feel good – not just relieved that things weren't crazy and horrible. However, as I have discovered over many decades since then, learning to set boundaries is a lifelong learning process.

CHAPTER SIX

BOUND FOR TINSELTOWN

My entire frame of reference had been my mother, her insanity, and her intricate set of arbitrary, constantly changing, domineering and controlling rules. Her influence was compounded by other tragic events in my childhood. In her mind, her rules were all justified by her religion and what God wanted. But I could never come to terms with the idea that God wanted someone to be so violent and cruel; it never added up for me. Still, emotionally it kept me in a constant protective crouch. Usually, I could only make plans for how I would get through the next 24 hours.

The concept of autonomy was totally alien to me until the day I walked out of my mother's house forever. Then, my almost eight years in New York City was an amazing adventure and crash course on entering the world. I started to see how self-determined people function. I feel so fortunate that my first stop in life outside of Oklahoma was New York City, in all its revelry and glory. It was truly an incredible experience for me!

After Anna and I broke up, I started dating as many girls as humanly possible, regardless of our proximity in the house. It was a lot of fun; but none of those girls really stuck. Anna and I lived together, platonically, mostly for convenience. We did not want to deal with the sale of the house, and with the task of finding new places to live in the NYC area – which was a nightmare. Mercifully, after a few months, some of the awkwardness dissipated between us.

Eventually, I started casting around for a new girlfriend. I heard from a friend that a girl named Brooke, who had been two grades below me in high school, came out after graduation and was living in Kentucky. The idea that someone else had also been through the weirdness and semi-insanity of a Christian school, and growing up in Oklahoma, would have been enough to make me call her. The fact that I remembered her as a very pleasant and attractive girl only added to my decision to look her up. What did I have to lose?

Brooke was exactly as I remembered her: she was sweet, kind, very feminine and pretty. Perhaps more important after my power struggle with Anna, Brooke made it easy to get along. We began to date, long-distance, but I soon found out that a long-distance relationship can get tiring pretty fast. If you have ever had one, you know that you have to be an expert at scheduling, restraint, maximizing time, and managing money for travel.

When you are young, none of those skills are usually in your wheelhouse, and Brooke and I were not any exception. Moving to Kentucky was not an option for me. However, after some time and discussion, Brooke agreed to come to live with me in New Jersey.

Why she agreed to move in with me and my ex-girlfriend I will never know, because I would not have been able to do it if our roles had been reversed. Perhaps the fact that Anna was also already in a fairly serious, new relationship helped. Maybe Brooke was just that secure. Maybe I was a bigger draw than I thought I was. But whatever the reason, Brooke did indeed join us, and we three coexisted pretty happily for several months.

Brooke and I did not fight, which was so refreshing. We had fun together; and we shared some reference points from our childhood and teen years. Those common experiences were unique enough to create a meaningful bond. When you come from an unusual background, and when you **know** that your experience growing up is not comprehensible to most people, having a partner who is a touchstone is grounding. That is the best way to describe Brooke – she was grounding. Our fabulous sex life didn't hurt either. I can only imagine what our life would have been like had we known more about ourselves, and each other. But presuming that all things happen when the timing is right, all that matters is that we did find one another for a time.

Before I left Oklahoma, my dream had been to live in both New York City and Los Angeles. But after nearly eight years in New York, I was burned out with the weather, the people, my job, and the commuting. Do not ever underestimate the importance of weather when you are thinking about moving! New York seasons are brutal – and more importantly for me, the arctic gloom of the winters made me yearn for more reasonable climates.

So, after checking the NYC box, Los Angeles was the obvious next move. Brooke was interested in LA and had no problem with yet another move and starting a new adventure with me. Only about four months earlier, she had skipped from Kentucky to New York – and now we were headed to LA. That showed me, yet again, that she was up for anything and an easy partner.

Brooke and I loaded everything we had into a moving truck, and we set out for Ohio to visit her dad. We also wanted to drop off our furniture and any non-essentials, with the idea that he could send them to us later. After a nice visit with her dad and stepmom, our next stop was my dad's house in Oklahoma.

My dad decided to give me a car for the next leg of my adventures. After a few days with my dad and stepmother, he gave me an older red Mazda RX7 two-seater. It was exactly what I wanted – sporty, fun and fast. I saw it as the perfect reflection of how my life would be in LA. Brooke and I packed up again and set out for the 1,284-mile journey to our new home.

Work and earning enough income have always been top priority for me; so, I made sure I had a connection in LA before I left NYC. I did not want to go days or weeks trying to find a job. Prior to leaving NYC, I had been tending bar and waiting tables at night after my day job in the fashion industry. I had focused on making extra money to pay off my university debt, saving money for the upcoming move, and providing myself with a cushion.

I found out that a co-worker had a friend who worked as the restaurant manager at the Embassy Suites Hotel right near the Los Angeles

International Airport, or LAX. Once in LA, we found a room in an old motel near the airport (because it was cheap), and then I walked into the Embassy Suites and asked for Jeff. Everything fell into place – I applied for a job as a bartender and got it right away.

I then found another hospitality job down the street, at a Marriott, waiting tables; Brooke was hired to wait tables at the Renaissance Hotel. These were crappy jobs; but we were young, and they set us up financially, well enough to rent an apartment in LA. It was a really old apartment, but it was within walking distance of our jobs, and it worked well as a landing spot for a bit in Southern California. It did not take long for me to love the sunshine and mild weather there, and I was very happy about the move.

After having worked nonstop like a maniac in NYC to pay for college and the lifestyle there, I was grateful that I did not need to work seven days a week in LA. Brooke and I had enough downtime to drive around, get to know the city, go to Disneyland, and do all the other fun touristy stuff. It was amazing to run around for a while without a crushing sense of responsibility on my shoulders, which was the way I felt on the East Coast.

However, the reality is that I am a type-A personality – I wanted work that would lead to a career, and four months of playing in LA was all I could handle. I started getting antsy. I had earned my bachelor's degree in marketing and communications at FIT, and I had presumed at first that I would pursue a career in a fashion-related field. In fact, Bloomingdale's had wanted to recruit me as an assistant buyer in NYC, which sounded good to me, but there was a required typing test that I just could not pass.

You see, having attended a self-taught Christian school when I was younger, I did not have the aptitude for it. In that school, there were two subjects that no one wanted to teach themselves – typing was one of them, and the other was French. But I also found myself thinking, *Why would I want to type? I don't want the kind of job that needs me to be a fantastic typist!*

Although the Bloomingdale's recruiter said she would hire me if I took a typing class, I had turned the opportunity down. Eventually, I made my way to a window design and merchandising job at a national, high-end, men's custom-made suit and shirt chain. I did it for a year and did not like it at all. I had also managed several retail men's stores for a few years before that, and those experiences were no better. By the time I left NYC for LA, I knew that the fashion industry was not for me – too many catty people, terrible hours, and not enough pay.

So, there I was, working in hospitality instead of fashion in LA to pay the bills and strategize my next steps to build a career. I knew I needed to find proper employment before I became too bored and too poor. The most important thing for me was to get started in a career – after all, that is why I had struggled for years to earn a college degree.

Back in Lawton, there was a mentality for many, that "having a job" was enough. I had gotten out of Lawton, and I had shed that mentality. I knew that I wanted more – advancement, the potential to grow, the chance to become a leader, the opportunity to travel. The only thing that would make my dreams possible, I believed, would be a long-term career.

Even though I hated retail management and was not in love with merchandising, I applied for a few positions in those areas as backup jobs in case nothing else materialized. I even had a few offers in those fields when I was contacted by a headhunter who was recruiting for a parking company.

I had never considered parking as a career – actually, I had never heard of such a thing. The truth is, I had never even thought about parking in any way, beyond simply finding a parking spot for my own car. But this particular company really wanted me to interview with them. They had me in for not just one or two interviews, but for a whole series of interviews. I met managers at some of their LA locations, toured the offices, had lunch with them – the whole dog-and-pony show.

I was still a little on the fence about what to do; then, during one of my last interviews with the company, I saw a map on their office wall. It had little stars all over it, showing the cities in which they were located. They were **everywhere;** and they were poised to expand into other countries. I remember looking at that map, thinking, *This is the kind of company that I want to work for, because somebody has to manage all of that, and that means room for growth.* Bingo! Three of my career aspirations could be fulfilled at that job. That map had communicated my future to me, and I accepted the company's offer the minute it came in.

When I started work for the parking company – Center Parking – I was assigned to Murdoch Plaza in Westwood, which is right near UCLA and Beverly Hills. I was to manage the underground parking garage and the very high-end valet service in the building. Murdoch Plaza housed lots of different kinds of companies; but it was also the headquarters for Interscope Films, Interscope Records, and Death Row Records. Ted Field, the founder of Interscope, would use the valet services sometimes, so we met, and I got to know him and his staff a little.

During the first year that I worked for Center Parking, I started to think that I was out of my mind for taking a position in parking. I felt I had made a mistake. First of all, Brooke and I had moved to LA just in time for the Northridge earthquake of 1994, which was quite terrifying. And being in a sub-level office in a parking garage, with a 17-story building swaying and creaking on top of me at each aftershock was very unnerving. But as it turned out, that would be the least of my worries at Murdoch Plaza.

Murdoch Plaza was a crazy place. It was filled with all kinds of people, but particularly entertainment types; and I found myself once again in the presence of many celebrities. We would park the cars of Arnold Schwarzenegger, Jodie Foster, Tina Louise, and so many others, but my favorite celebrity customer was Ed McMahon. He would drop his wife off at work and then sometimes come and hang out with us in my office for 15 minutes or so. Or, if he was waiting to pick her up, he would come over and chat while he waited for her. He was so friendly, smart, and he always made us laugh. He and his wife also gave the valets a very big tip every year at Christmas – and I received a nice gift as well. He was not pretentious at all; people like him and his wife made my job fun. The regulars were in and out several times a week; but a few were unsavory or unpleasant characters.

Mary Hart, of the TV show Entertainment Tonight, came to an event at Murdoch Plaza, and her husband provided one such negative experience. They arrived one evening for a very fancy black-tie event at the Regency Club, the private club at the top of Murdoch Plaza. They pulled up in a beautiful new red Mercedes. When her husband got out of the car, somehow he set off its alarm. Because the valet area was underground, the sound of the alarm bounced off the concrete ceiling of the garage – it was deafening. He was trying to figure out how to shut it off, with the help of my valets, as everyone arriving for the function stared at him.

I had a good idea about how to shut it off, having helped out in valet operations with different luxury cars at several of Center Parking's Beverly Hills locations. So, I thought perhaps the same alarm shuttoff method that I had seen work with a different car might work with his car. Because the technology was relatively new, not many people were aware of how to do it.

I went over and introduced myself, explaining that I was the manager. I offered to help, but he was very frustrated and embarrassed at the noise at that point. He yelled at me, telling me that he could do it, that he did not need **my** help, and to leave him be. I could tell by the way he looked at me, and by the tone he took, that he thought that there was no way in the world that a girl would know how to fix a problem with a car.

I was shocked. I looked at Mary and she was clearly embarrassed. I backed away and stood off to the side, watching him and the valets try to figure it out. Finally, after watching the ridiculousness play out for what seemed like forever, I went back over to him. I politely asked if I could see the key to the car, which is what I had intended to do in the first place. He angrily handed over the key. I calmly walked to the back of his car, put the key in the keyhole for the trunk and turned it. As if by magic, the alarm turned off immediately. His face turned bright red; I assume it was from embarrassment at not letting me manage the situation to begin with. Even though he had been an ass to me, I felt some satisfaction that I had solved the problem. He thanked me and quickly whisked Mary off to their function.

That incident was a minor one in the spectrum of all my dealings with difficult people at Murdoch Plaza, however. Thanks to the presence of Interscope Records and Death Row Records in the building, I came into contact with a lot of rappers and other artists who – by 1994 standards – were not considered the crème de la crème of society. In contrast, the private, members-only club at the building, the Regency Club, was at the opposite end of the social spectrum from Death Row. The Regency Club was an outpost for LA's old money, with most of the patrons being crusty, uptight older people. They were predictably snooty, and not particularly fond of the Death Row people who they encountered in the lobby, valet area or the garage. I cannot say that I was particularly in love with the record company people either; they made my job **very** difficult – often, just for the sport of it. Those conflicts did not mix well with my ambition and desire to make the operation at Murdoch Plaza a huge success.

My office was underground – it was a big glass box at the end of the underground garage ramp for the valet services. It was directly in front of the valet drop-off spot; if anyone wanted to use valet service, they had to pull up right there. So, I could see all the action – I could see who was arriving – I could see if the valet drive was clogged up – and I could see if there was any funny business.

Invariably, there **was** funny business going on – and frequently, Snoop Dogg was a part of it. Actually, he was Snoop Doggy Dogg then. Time has passed, and Snoop is mellower now. He is friends with Martha Stewart and co-hosts a show with her, where he shows viewers how to make pot brownies. On the show, he chats with equally mellow and cuddly guests, like Seth Rogen. Now that Snoop has settled into such an avuncular role, it is hard to remember that he was not always so sweet.

But I will never forget. Do not get me wrong; I really love Snoop's music and admire the person he has become – but we all have had our personal growth processes, and he is no different. My problems with him began right after I started at Murdoch Plaza. His first studio album, *Doggystyle,* was released at the end of 1993, and he was obviously really feeling himself in mid-1994 when we first met. He pulled up to the valet drop-off, so I could see his car right in front of me through my office window. The windows of his car were barely cracked open, but music was blaring out of the car stereo and billows of pot smoke were pouring out the windows. You could smell the weed everywhere – which, back then, was not legal.

He settled into a pattern. After arriving at that conspicuous valet drop-off spot, he would start bouncing his car on its hydraulics, and would blast music that reverberated off the garage ceiling. He would pretty much cause a scene every time, and he would never move his car if we asked. If any of my staff tried to approach him, he would simply ignore them; and he would make everyone else who used the valet service go around him. That type of behavior – and worse – occurred multiple times per week.

Snoop did not restrict his behavior to loitering, hot-boxing weed, and blaring music. He also did not feel the need to find a restroom in Death Row's offices or at home; sometimes he would pee on the columns in the parking garage – yes, like a dog – or a Dogg. Bill, the director of security at Murdoch Plaza, would hear, see, and smell what was happening and he would call management. In turn, management would call me and tell me to fix the situation. What the hell was I supposed to do? At 108 pounds soaking wet, was I supposed to take on a carful – or as was often the case, several cars full – of pissed-off, stoned rappers?

Things would get worse when the little old ladies from the Regency Club came downstairs to get their cars. They would get off the elevator, turn the corner, see Snoop and his friends – or any of the other Death Row visitors or employees – and immediately go right back to the elevator. Then, they would complain to Bill or to building management. The vibe for me was like one fluid motion – a nonstop flow from all business to all fear.

I say fear, because I knew what happened to the last parking manager (I will get to that) and did not want the same thing to happen to me – and because I did not want to lose my job. But I cannot say that I hated seeing the rich old snobby ladies freak out like that. Many were so snotty and so entitled that they were unbearable; so, I did not think a little shake-up hurt them much.

One typical complaint from them was about where we parked their cars. Those women would show up in Rolls–Royces, which we would park around the corner from my office in the garage. But the women would get horribly bent out of shape because they wanted to park directly in front of my office. They wanted to take up spaces that were reserved for delivery people, couriers, and Ted Field's personal assistant, who had to run things back and forth between his office and various other labels and studios. That assistant drove a really beat-up car, and when she would pull up in front of my glass box office, the Regency Club ladies would freak out if they were around. They would complain to me: "How **dare** you park that Toyota right there, when my Rolls is all the way around the corner?" I do not know if it was just the sight of the beater car that upset them, or if they thought they deserved a better spot – but it drove them nuts.

They became progressively ruder about it. And I had no idea why they would want their cars so close to Snoop's favorite spot in the garage to smoke weed, urinate, or harass people. I guess it was just an opportunity for them to be condescending and snobby.

I later realized that the artists at Death Row Records were equal-opportunity harassers. None of what they did was just about me. The reason that Center Parking installed me at that particular location under Murdoch Plaza was directly because of Death Row. Many of the rappers on the label had, prior to their music careers, been in jail. Hence, the name: Death Row. They were not a refined group in those days of them just starting out in the business; however, since then many have grown into their roles as leaders in the music industry quite well. But back then the only well-mannered one among them was Tupac. He always behaved like a gentleman and was quiet – never rowdy, or disrespectful – but he was not around nearly as frequently as the other artists.

I found out that one of the rappers from Death Row had had a sexual relationship with a former employee in the parking operation; but for some (presumably unrelated) reason, the manager – my predecessor – had to fire her. When he did, she flipped out and threw a can of Coke at him, covering the office in splashes and sprays of soda. In fact, I continued to try to clean up that mess long after the big event.

Anyway, the rappers were not very happy with the girl being fired; they actually threatened to kill the former manager on more than one occasion. Wisely, he decided that dying as a result of that person's termination was a bad idea. He asked the company to transfer him to a different location; they did – and then they installed me in his place. The logic behind their move was that I had spent eight years in NYC and had even lived in the Bronx for a time, which carried its own reputation. Moreover, I had at one time flirted with the idea of being a police officer, a fact that emerged during the interview process. So, they figured I must be tough – and they were right. It was a flimsy rationale, but I suppose it helped them to sleep at night.

The building's management company, my company's client, would go insane about the behavior of Snoop and his associates. They would demand that I do something. Again, what was I supposed to do? The client was also upset that Dr. Dre would constantly park in the handicapped spots. I would ask again, "What am I supposed to do?" They never had a good answer, so it became an uneasy stalemate.

Snoop, however, was not entirely satisfied with the status quo. He upped his game by driving into the parking garage one day in a convertible, with the top down, and a Rottweiler in the passenger seat. It did not look to be a friendly dog. Everyone in the garage warily eyed the hellhound, and we all held our breath waiting for Snoop to leave.

My valets refused to park the car with the dog in it (the four-legged animal, not Snoop) so we allowed Snoop to back into a space next to my office, thinking he would take the dog up to the Death Row offices with him. He did not. He left it sitting in the passenger seat, with no leash, and with the car's top and windows down.

My valets were all afraid of the dog, and so was I. They refused to park cars at that point, and they all crammed into my office. Terrified of Cujo, we begged Bill the security guard to go upstairs to tell Dr. Dre and Snoop that the dog had to go. Snoop eventually came down, but was furious, and gave every one of us the stink eye. We knew that could not lead to anything good.

As we expected, Snoop's reign of terror continued, with more peeing on columns and antagonizing everyone who was in his way. It was relentless, and my client was on my case every day about not controlling Snoop and his group. Finally, one day, I had had enough. The next time that Snoop pulled into the garage and relieved himself, I asked him to come with me. I took him to one side and asked him, nicely, to please quit pissing on my columns, if for no other reason than my client was up my ass about it. He looked down at me and said, "F*#k you, white bitch. I will kill you."

Great. From that day on, that was my name as far as Snoop was concerned. I was "white bitch." It was absolutely miserable – and it only got worse. On July 5th, he and his friends thought it would be hilarious to throw an M80 down the ramp of the garage toward my office. Thank God that it became stuck under the bicycle ramp near the top of the ramp and did not go off. But Bill from security had seen them throw it, viewing the action through a camera at the top of the garage. Bill called me and told me not to go near that part of the garage ramp, and not to let anyone else do so.

Bill called Suge Knight and told him what Snoop and company had done, and said that if he did not send someone to get the explosive, he would call the LA bomb squad. He also said that he would turn the videotape over to the police. Suge sent someone to retrieve the M80, and everything returned to normal – well, normal for that place.

Explosives, piss, drugs, death threats and rottweilers. Working for Center Parking at Murdoch Plaza was a lesson in patience and perseverance; but the whole situation never sat well with me. I hated feeling trampled on and not having a voice to confront someone who was so wantonly ill-behaved.

There is a postscript to the story. Over a year later, while I was still at Murdoch Plaza, my company won the valet contract with a big, new casino in LA, called Hollywood Park Casino, and I was asked to participate in the grand opening night, along with 40 other managers. The night was in full swing – cars were pulling into the valet area six lanes wide, backed all the way down highway 405. The highway patrol was complaining to us about the backup the casino had created. We literally had 100 valets and 40 managers parking cars – the volume of cars was insane. There I was, running around in a skirt suit, pantyhose, and high heels (required attire for women in my company at that time). I was opening car doors, greeting VIPs, and hurrying to park and retrieve cars as quickly as possible. We wanted everything to be perfect that night, so we were hustling.

A two-door Mercedes drove up to the main entrance. As I leaped to open the car door and greet the new guest with, "Good evening! Welcome to our Hollywood Park Casino!" out steps Snoop Dogg. *Ugh!* I thought. He looked down, hovering over me by about a foot. Shaking his head, he said to me, "What the f*#k are you doing here?" I looked back up at him, paused for a moment to think about my response, and finally said, "What the f*#k are **you** doing here?"

He then paused again for a few seconds, staring at me. I waited for him to start kicking my ass. Then he smiled, nodding his head in approval, and said, "Alllllllllllright." And into the casino he went. The harassment stopped that night.

This might seem like a "shaggy dogg" tale, but it is the absolute truth. There is a point to it, and it is an important one. When you find your voice, and you use it, you find your power – and with power comes more respect. That respect can come when you stand up to people who used to push you around, for sure; but it should also come from within yourself. Sometimes it takes an improbable act or statement at just the right time to demonstrate to yourself what you are really made of. Snoop set me up to feel powerless and – later – to understand that I could command respect. I am grateful to him for that.

While all of this was going on, I heard that Ted Field of Interscope was looking for an office assistant. I recommended Brooke for the job; she interviewed and got it. Thank God she was not the recipient of any shit as a result of working in that building like I was. If that had happened to her, I would have had so much guilt.

Brooke ended up really liking her job, and received all kinds of Hollywood perks from her involvement with the company. For example, when Oscar season came around, Ted would receive videos of all the nominated films; Brooke would bring them home and we would watch them together. She was also privy to all the dailies (recently shot, unedited film footage) of whatever Ted was shooting at the moment, like *Jumanji* and the Bill and Ted movies.

We had fun together and our relationship was going well. By the time I was given a promotion that involved relocation, there was no question that she would go with me. I had been working for the parking company in LA for about two and a half years when a new regional manager, a tough lady named Sydney, came to town. She took me aside and said, "You're going to move up in this company because you have high potential – but if you want to move up, you're going to have to move cities."

That was her mantra, as was the company's – to move up, you had to move. Faced with another giant location shift, I was not excited about leaving Los Angeles. I loved it there. I liked the people with whom I worked. I liked the city, the weather, the energy, and vibe – and I had a great group of friends. We were really tight-knit and had a ton of fun together. We went to Las Vegas and Tijuana – we had parties and played night golf – and we hung out every Friday night at a minimum. I had the kind of community around me that I had always wanted – along with the lifestyle I wanted.

So, making the decision to relocate was not only difficult emotionally, but also a test of how serious I really was about my own advancement and growing a career. It was a hard decision; but I knew that the added income would result in strength and security. Finally, I decided to take the new position, a promotion and move to Dallas.

I hated leaving LA – and I hated Dallas, which was my new outpost. Dallas was too much like where I grew up for me to ever really be comfortable there. Everyone had trucks and cowboy boots and country accents; it was the antithesis of the hard-won metropolitan life I had enjoyed for more than a decade in both New York City and Los Angeles.

Dallas was also way too close to Lawton, OK, for my comfort. It was less than 200 miles from Lawton and that proximity depressed me. In a way, I felt like I had failed, even though Dallas meant that I was actually moving up my career ladder. But it was good that I had experienced NYC and LA first, before moving to Dallas. The worst thing that I could have done after high school would have been to strike out on my own and still end up getting drawn back into the regional culture and lifestyle that I hated so deeply. True, Dallas was not Lawton, but for me they seemed the same. Brooke moved with me to Dallas, and we did our best to settle in.

I am not terribly proud of how things eventually went down with Brooke, especially considering that in a few short years, she had moved from Kentucky, to New York, to LA, and then to Dallas for me. But as with all relationships, it was educational. I learned a lot about functioning in a relationship with an equal; I learned what it was like to be with a woman who was not overbearing or strident; and I learned how nice it was to live with someone who liked to make a home together. I also learned – the hard way – what my own worst traits were as a partner.

I do not know if my feelings about Dallas (which were mostly disgust and depression, having grown up nearby) were major contributors to the dissolution of our relationship; but Dallas is where Brooke and I started to unravel.

Eight months after moving there, I received a promotion to general manager of San Antonio operations, which was the only thing that kept me from quitting the company and moving back to LA. Actually, it was incredibly exciting because I was promoted again so quickly. It was a big promotion this time. Running an entire city operation for a company was a dream; it was something for which I had strived. And it was a big deal at Center Parking.

The promotion required a move to San Antonio, and it was a real turning point for my career. As a General Manager, I was finally becoming acknowledged as a leader. I knew I wanted to grow in leadership roles; to advance my career by moving up the ladder, and this new position was the first step towards accomplishing that.

But looking back, I was establishing a pattern in my relationships. Things would be good with a partner for roughly four years, and then I would hit a wall. I would suddenly start to lose interest in maintaining the life we had built; and, to be brutally honest, I would start to lose interest in the woman. It was unclear if it was my age, and not wanting to settle down for a lifetime – or if it was because I saw my parents go through so many relationships. It was probably a combination. It would always take me some time before I ended the relationship, and that seemed to happen a number of times right around the five-year point. Then, I would finally call it quits.

When it was time for me to move to San Antonio, I encouraged Brooke to stay in Dallas while I settled into a new home and job. She agreed and let me do my thing, which prolonged the inevitable. By the time Brooke joined me in San Antonio, I was over it – I was over the relationship – I was over the monogamy – and I was over playing house.

Brooke never did anything specific that brought me to a breaking point. But I had a built-in timer that went off when I was with Anna, and now it was happening with Brooke. The relationship was becoming profoundly suffocating. I can see now that I did not handle the breakup well; but at the time I felt justified in my actions. I rationalized that it was the move that made me keep Brooke at arm's length. I broke up with her by degrees – small steps – because ripping the Band-Aid off would have been just too much for me.

It would become my lifelong relationship pattern: serial monogamy punctuated by geographical moves, a loss of interest, and fault-finding with my partner, which I used to justify moving on. It would take the end of two subsequent relationships – relationships that ended in the same manner – before I would finally truly realize my pattern and dig deep to analyze it. Terrible, I know.

Knowing why you do the things you do does not excuse your actions. Awareness of your own issues is not the end goal. The goal is not only to be aware, but also to understand why you do it – and to change your behavior so that you stop hurting other people, and yourself.

It is impossible to ignore that the patterns of behavior I experienced in my childhood were partially mirrored in how I conducted my relationships. First, I would fall hard for someone – delighting in the way she loved me, and how she lavished attention and affection on me, and I would do the same. It was a stark contrast to the affection, love, and tenderness I was denied while growing up in my mother's house. Then, I would create a cozy domestic life with my partner, creating an ideal home, which I had longed for as a child, but never had. After a while, a timer bell would ring in my head and signal that it was time to go. That I felt restless is not surprising, considering that I had lived with constant chaos and drama in my formative years.

And then I would feel suffocated, which is the absolute worst for me. It is how I felt in my parents' home, it is how I felt living in Oklahoma, and it is how I would feel when reacting to the emotional needs of my partner. It was like a weight was pinning me down and keeping me from breathing freely. Again, it is not surprising that I felt that way because I grew up with my activities insanely proscribed, and was conditioned to believe that my feelings did not matter. Any sane person rebels against feeling suffocated, which is why I rebelled against the pressing emotional needs of my partners. I found their reasonable expectations for my emotional responses to be stifling. And I was still working through all my PTSD from childhood, which did not help me in my role as a partner.

So, after dragging my feet for months, I pulled the trigger. Brooke and I split. Do I regret how it all happened? Of course I do.

Was I evolved enough at the time to step outside myself and understand why I acted the way I did? Absolutely not. Is it my responsibility now to look at myself unflinchingly, to not let my past dictate my future, and to make conscious choices about what I do? Yes, it is. Did I know any of that when I started the next phase of my life in San Antonio? Not a chance. And unfortunately, that would not be the last time I left a relationship badly.

In addition to the relationship pattern, there were other signs that all was not well in my world. The residue of violence and fear from my past would, at times, spill over into my present. My night terrors that started after my brother's horrific death have continued to this day. And while I was living in San Antonio, amongst the many night-terrors I would have, one stood out to be a particularly disturbing experience.

While I was still asleep one night, I ran out of my second-floor bedroom onto my balcony, naked as a jaybird. As always, I was running from whoever was trying to kill me in my night terror. I jumped over the balcony wall of my townhouse onto my neighbor's balcony, which was much lower than my townhouse because they were built on a slope. I then crawled over his railing, still asleep. Suddenly, a car came around the corner and the headlights in my eyes woke me up.

There I was, stark naked in the middle of the night, straddling the balcony railing, trying to escape death. By that point in my life, waking up in strange places because of my night terrors had become a fairly regular occurrence, so I had trained myself to react quickly. I realized I was not where I was supposed to be and had no clothes on. I knew I had to get to a safe place, so I climbed back onto the neighbor's balcony and ducked into the shadows, in hopes that the people in the car would not see me.

Scared and mentally fuzzy, with my heart racing, I was sweating and shaking from the night terror, I tried to collect my thoughts. I went back over to the wall that separated the townhouses to climb back up to my own balcony. As athletic as I was, I realized there was no way that I could jump up and grab the top of the wall to climb up. It was just too high due to the slope.

Oh my God, I thought, *am I going to have to knock on the door and wake up my sleeping neighbor to have him help me?* But I had no clothes on – how would I explain how I became stuck on his balcony? What would he think? He would probably call the police! I decided to crawl onto the railing, and then try to stand on top of it while pulling myself up, holding onto the bottom of my townhouse's railing.

It was not easy – especially with no clothes on – but I did it. The next day, I went out to the balcony to survey the scene. I could not believe what had happened, and that I had managed to not wake my neighbor! I looked down onto his balcony and saw two dents in a rain drainage tube where my feet had landed the night before. *I have got to stop doing this,* I thought to myself. But, that would definitely not be the last time I ran naked from my home or hotel room. It occurred so frequently that I finally started sleeping with some clothes on for that very reason.

CHAPTER SEVEN

LATINA FEVER

Not long after Brooke and I broke up, I moved into a townhouse in a community in San Antonio called International Residence. I have no idea what the "international" part of the name meant. It would have been far more accurate to call it "Lesbian Villas" or something along those lines – because, unbeknownst to me when I chose to live there, International Residence had many gay, female residents.

It was a lesbian Melrose Place. I had an instant community that was really warm and welcoming. It was also filled with enough drama and madness to rival that of the actual Melrose Place television show. Arriving there was like showing up at my own debutante party; it was my first time ever being out, single, and immersed in an actual lesbian community. Most importantly, I had enough money to have fun, which I did.

I had a lot of fun – particularly after I realized that I had a type – and that San Antonio was teeming with gorgeous, very feminine Latinas, who were my Achilles heel. I made it a point to meet as many of them as humanly possible.

The two women who managed International Residence were named Isabella and Sophia, and both quickly became my friends. They took me under their wing and introduced me to the lesbian and gay party scene in San Antonio. And what a scene it was!

The energy in International Residence felt like an ongoing party – every weekend, someone was having a get-together. One Sunday, as on so many other Sunday afternoons in the complex, I dressed for a party thrown by my friend Lori, a fellow lesbian. Each weekend, we all made cocktails and roamed around the pool or various apartments that were having get-togethers, my place included. We would visit with each other in and out of the apartments. On that particular Sunday, I made a Bacardi and Diet Coke with lime, my drink of choice for many years, and walked over to Lori's apartment. As I opened the door to her apartment, I immediately saw a stunning young Latina sitting on the floor, looking over some paperwork. She was so pretty that it took me by surprise, and I spilled my drink.

Olivia was 20 years old, very bright, and very straight. Olivia looked up at me, with my glass in hand and some of my drink on the floor, and nodded her head. I was captivated. I had to get to know her.

So, during the evening, I asked all my different friends at the party if they knew her; I held out the hope that she liked women. When my friend Amelia – another member of International Residence's sorority – saw how taken I was with Olivia, she pointed out that Olivia was straight. I answered Amelia's warning with, "So what?" and did what I would do with anyone else I thought was intriguing and alluring: I spent as much time with her as I could.

During the next few weeks, I focused on finding out what party or gathering Olivia would attend, so I could make sure I was there. I also invited her to any activity that my friends and I planned. I chatted with her, and flirted as much as I could without drooling all over myself. One night after about a month and a half of hanging out, becoming friends, and learning what made one another tick – it happened. We kissed. Kissing led to . . . and we became a couple not long after. That was the start of what has since become my decades-long fixation on dating beautiful, sexy, straight Hispanic women. It has been a delightful habit that I do not care to break.

For those of you who wonder how and why a straight girl embarked on a lesbian relationship way back in the 1990s, before it was a popular thing to try, the answer is very simple. There are loads of people who are less concerned with gender than the quality of the person they are with; Olivia was one of them. The things that women tend to care about having in a partner – respect, someone who listens, sharing life stories and opinions, genuine interest in them and their minds, and great sex – are frequently not forthcoming from men in straight relationships. So say my straight female friends.

I cannot tell you why men behave the way they do, and I am sure there is not any nefarious reason. I am sure their approach to connecting with women isn't mean-spirited. However, the things that women look for in a relationship are often difficult for men to deliver – again, according to many straight women. My straight female friends tell me that it seems like even the most loving, attentive, well-meaning men are somewhat handicapped in communication. They seem to come from across an endlessly deep and wide chasm that swallows up whatever point they try to make or whatever emotion they would like to express. Their messages to women can get lost; and their points often never quite reach the level of clarity and emotional connection that women can achieve with their friends.

For Olivia, and the other straight women I have dated – and there have been many – the attention and connection I brought to the table was equally as important as the incredible connection in bed. I cannot say if my straight girlfriends were predisposed to be sexually fluid; all I can report is my own experience with them. When push came to shove, genitalia were beside the point.

Olivia was 11 years younger than I was and she was truly an amazing partner. She, like Brooke before her, sacrificed her life, family and friends to move with me as I progressed in my career. I climbed the ladder, and I moved a lot in order to advance within my company. Olivia moved to Atlanta, and then to Chicago with me.

Olivia was the kindest, sweetest, most together woman I had met – as well as smart and very beautiful – but she wanted something that I did not. She wanted to get married and have children. That just wasn't for me. I never saw myself getting married or being a mother, even though I love children and get so much joy from them. Raising children with someone in a long-term committed marriage was something that I did not want. After all, my own childhood had been chaotic, traumatic, and very painful. My parents' relationship did not last, and represented a hotbed of anger and distress; marriage just did not appeal to me.

Feeling that pressure of Olivia's desire to wed and have children helped end the relationship. I finally said, "You know what? I don't want to get married, and I don't want to have children; so, I'm going to let you go so you can find all of that with someone. I don't want to hold you back."

The not-so-lovely truth, however, is that I was also bumping up against my usual five-year-itch. Five years was my cap for a relationship for some reason; and this would be the third, five-year relationship that I ended. I guess I had gypsy blood and felt the need to move on. That same gypsy blood that kept me from settling into a relationship also helped me stay strong with every one of the 13 moves to different cities for my career. Change – for the success of my career – was the one constant in my life, and it became the norm for me.

Looking back on it, it was sad we wanted different things, because Olivia was – and is – one of the best people I know. To this day, I always say she was the last normal, sane, kind, unselfish, and honest woman I have been with. Miraculously, we are still friends somewhat, which is a testament to how loving and understanding she is.

The postscript to our story is that after our breakup, Olivia and I remained distant friends, and she found the person she would marry. Surprisingly enough, I also met the woman I would marry. While Olivia was sweet, beautiful, nurturing, very kind, studious, funny and smart, Camila, my future wife, was an exciting, captivating, addictive, whirlwind of a human being.

The first time I met Camila was when Olivia and I were visiting San Antonio. We were living in Chicago by that time (my company moved me there after a year and a half in Atlanta). We were in San Antonio to visit Olivia's family and to meet our friends for Fiesta, a fun-filled annual festival. I had bought a townhouse in San Antonio, because I hate cold winters and it was a good place to escape from Chicago on the weekends, during the cold months. Plus, it gave us a place to stay when we went back to see friends and Olivia's family.

We were wandering around the Oyster Bake, an event at Fiesta, and bumped into our friend Ramona, who introduced us to her new girl-friend, Camila. Nothing really registered with me other than she was a very pretty girl.

Camila and I would not cross paths again for more than a year. By then, Olivia and I were no longer together – I had moved to Cleveland for work – and Camila and Ramona were also no longer a couple. Now single, I was in San Antonio visiting and Camila approached me while we were hanging out with a group of friends. There was no way I was not going to talk to her, no matter what her past connection to Ramona had been. Camila was smoking hot – absolutely gorgeous.

We were at a bar with an outdoor area with picnic tables, and a place for a band to play. While I was enjoying the music and drinks, Camila sauntered over. She straddled the picnic table plank to sit down and face me, and started talking to me. She was very engaged, making a lot of eye contact, and rubbing my back. That is the way to get me every time. Touch is my love language, so I responded very positively to her.

I stayed in San Antonio that week for Fiesta (again), which is an amazingly wonderful celebration and several weeks of pandemonium. I saw Camila all that week, but could only stay away from work for that week. We stayed in touch after my return to Cleveland, and the next time I went back to San Antonio, we seamlessly transitioned into a long-distance relationship. We were inseparable when in the same city.

My breakup with Olivia had been very civilized; but later she was furious when she found out I had started dating Camila. That was because Camila had a young daughter, Harper, who became a big and important part of my life – particularly after Camila brought her to Cleveland so they could spend the summer with me. Olivia could not understand how I had ended a relationship with her because I did not want children, but was now dating and semi-living with a woman who had a child. I can only imagine how hurtful that was for Olivia; and frankly, I cannot explain it either.

I guess there is no way to know where life will lead you. Camila and I did the back-and-forth between Cleveland and San Antonio for a time, but that was not sustainable. So, I invited her and Harper to stay with me for the summer, and I figured that we would see where we were at summer's end.

I love boating and bought my first boat when I was living in Atlanta with Olivia. We took it on our move to Chicago, and then I took it with me to Cleveland. So, the thought of enjoying the boat during the summer with Camila, Harper, and my new friends in Cleveland excited me.

A month and a half after Camila and Harper arrived in Cleveland, I was promoted to my first Vice President position at Center Parking, which was extremely exciting. However, it meant yet another move – this time to San Francisco. I had no clue what to do with Camila and Harper. Do I send them back to San Antonio or take them to San Francisco? I was absolutely crazy about Camila, but I started to see some weird behavior from her – behavior that I would have taken more time to examine if the San Francisco thing had not come up. The new job forced my hand. I had to decide if I was going to stay with her or cut it off because of my next career move.

I was too into her and getting too attached to Harper to let go. But a few things about Camila felt "off."

I knew that Camila's childhood had been tough, and this was probably causing some of her behavior, but I did not have the best childhood either, so I was not eager to judge. I learned Camila's history slowly over a period of time from her, her cousins, and her grandmother. And I met her mother, who was a lifelong addict. It was not a good meeting.

Camila's mother was a heroin addict and had used drugs throughout her pregnancy. Camila was born addicted to crack, even though her mother had been restrained in a hospital bed during the month before Camila was born so she could not use drugs. Camila was an adult before she got to know her father; and even then, it was not 100 percent clear he was her actual birth father. She was in and out of 26 different foster homes while growing up.

Camila's mom, Vivian, used to hook at truck stops so she would have money to score drugs, and would take Camila with her while she hooked. The one man in Camila's childhood who did stick around for a while was a boyfriend of Vivian's, who became Vivian's husband for a short time. He was only about 12 years older than Camila, and from bits of information Camila shared with me, it seemed pretty clear that he had sexually abused her.

Having been raised in an extremely religious household, I did not have any knowledge about alcoholism, drugs, and addiction. There was never even one drop of alcohol in my home while I was growing up, much less any drugs. And, for much of my life after my parents' divorce, my mother did not believe in doctors unless the situation was catastrophic; so, there was no medication to be found at home, either. The one exception was the occasional bottle of aspirin.

Because I was so naive about addiction, it took a long time for me to really understand what was going on with Camila. It turned out that she had a number of addictions.

Camila had run away from home when she was 15 or 16, started supporting herself, and moved into an apartment with a male friend. She had a relationship with him that resulted in Harper's birth; Camila was 17 years old. She floated from job to job, and was a cocktail waitress at a strip club when I met her.

She was convinced that the guy who was part-owner of the strip club was her dad. She idolized him. Whoever he was, he was also allegedly a leader, and one of the founding members of a very well-known and very dangerous motorcycle gang in south Texas. He was definitely a scary character, as were those in his circle.

I knew that Camila's life had been rough, and her ways of living, partnering in a relationship, and parenting were all mostly unknown to me. But I was captivated by her – and decided to take her and Harper with me to San Francisco as I started my new job.

Having a child around was not something I was used to. I had been adamant about not having children, so I was as surprised as anyone when I fell in love with Camila and agreed to bring both her and her 7-year-old child into my life.

Early in our time together, Camila and I were asleep in my bed-room, and I woke up in the middle of the night to find Harper stand-ing over the bed – staring at me. She was less than a foot away from me. She probably had a nightmare and wanted her mother – but what-ever was going on, it scared the shit out of me. I was quite rattled, but Harper was OK. She had probably learned early on how to adapt to her mother's dramatic life choices.

Camila was gorgeous, sexy, exciting to be around, and could light up a room – which had its upsides and downsides. The upsides were the usual ones that came along with having a hot, vivacious girlfriend. Moreover, those positives did an excellent job of smoothing over some of her less-than-lovely qualities and behaviors. Yes, it is easy to ignore the stuff you should be nervous about when the rest of what that person offers is dazzling. That is hardly a groundbreaking obser-vation – but it is very, very accurate.

As time went on, I learned all about her history, and realized that a rough, abusive upbringing could result in an adult with serious bound-ary issues, potential drug use, hypersexual behavior, a loose commit-ment to telling the truth, and serious anger problems. So? Who doesn't have some problems?

Again, my own absolutely screwed-up childhood made me unenthu-siastic about judging Camila. Just because the parental abuse I experi-enced was not "hooker at a truck stop" and more "crazy religious cult with a seriously violent mother" did not mean that I was **better** than her. It did not mean that I should write her off. What if someone had known about my mother and the world of insanity and pain she created, and then judged me as damaged, untouchable goods? Not cool. On principle alone, I could not dismiss her. Considering everything else Camila brought to the table, she basically had a free pass from me – for a little while.

The first sign of trouble (that I ignored) popped up at the beginning of our living together. We were living in Cleveland in the loft district where converted warehouses had been made into loft condos and apartments. The area had clubs, restaurants, and bars. There was even a club directly across the alley from my loft, and I could hear that music banging into the night. People always asked me if it bothered me – of course not. I just tried to be part of it. If a party's happening, what a waste if you do not join in!

Just across the river from the loft district was the Flats, with restaurants, bars, outdoor concerts and boating. It was not as upscale as our side of the river, but it was considered a cool party scene. It would also be the scene of a confusing and scary event in our lives.

I also liked the area because it was in downtown Cleveland, which gave me the easiest commute ever. I had to drive only five minutes to my office; it was almost like rolling out of bed directly into my desk chair. Another great thing about Cleveland was that everyone there was so uniquely **nice**. I was only there for nine months, but I made a lot of friends, in no small part because those Buckeyes really were salt-of-the-earth people – although I could do without their conservatism. One of those kind people was my secretary Barbara, who was a witness to the first evidence of what made Camila so problematic.

Camila and I were coming home from dinner at one of the local restaurants. Barbara was babysitting Harper for extra money, which she did fairly often. Camila and I got out of the car, and right away she started freaking out and causing a scene in the parking garage. I do not recall what it was about, but she had been drinking. I assumed that she was just drunk and acting up, and that it would die down into nothing.

When we entered the building, she ran down the hall toward our loft – screaming about what she was going to do in the apartment, in front of my secretary. My head started spinning. Why was she acting so crazy and why was she so loud and angry? The last thing Harper needed was to be awakened by her mother in that state. I was very confused trying to understand why she was so upset and irrational. Moreover, I felt that Barbara definitely did not need to witness that kind of madness – so I grabbed Camila and held on, refusing to let her go inside.

She broke out of my grip, and ran barefoot down the building stairs. She had taken her heels off in the car and then threw them down the hallway before she made a break for it. She ran out, disappeared into the middle of the night, and I was left standing there completely bewildered and wondering what the hell just happened. I had not seen that kind of inexplicable meltdown since my mother.

I followed Camila down the stairs and tried looking for her, which was ridiculous, because she was way ahead of me. But while standing outside, I started to worry that maybe she had gone back upstairs and into the loft and was making a scene in front of Harper and Barbara, like she had originally intended.

I ran back inside and asked Barbara if she had seen Camila – and thankfully, she had not. Eventually, Camila came back, and Barbara left. But I had a giant red flag waving in front of my face that I chose to ignore, which does not surprise me when I think about it now. I had been well trained in my childhood to push a whole lot of craziness to the back of my mind and just keep going.

Poor Barbara. I had been conditioned to handle the craziness, but she was not acclimated to it. Which was too bad, because Barbara would have to deal with a "Camila scenario" again soon, and it was a pretty dramatic one.

Right after I agreed to move to San Francisco for my job, I flew there to explore the city, check out the office, look at houses, and find a place to live. Immediately after I landed in San Francisco and walked into the airport terminal, I was paged to pick up a white phone to receive a message.

It was a message from Barbara. I called her right away, wondering what could have happened in the seven or so hours since I had left. Barbara was very upset, and her voice was shaking. She said that Camila had come back to the loft after working at her part-time job (as a cocktail waitress at a bar), and had come home a bloody, incoherent mess. Barbara said that Camila really needed to go to the hospital, but was refusing to do so. Instead, Camila was passed out on the couch. I freaked out, not knowing what had happened, and I asked Barbara to put Camila on the phone. She did, and I told Camila to please go to the hospital and to stop giving Barbara a hard time.

They finally headed to the ER, and Camila was patched up as best as the medical staff could manage. She had been battered and bruised, and she had puncture wounds all over her body – including her feet, legs and hands. Her skin had been ripped off her body in many places, and one of her nipples was hanging by a thread. Camila was not only completely physically incapacitated, but also a psychological wreck.

I had to complete my four-day trip to San Francisco, so I could not fly back to take care of her and Harper. I was panicky, wondering what on earth had happened. I tried to figure out how to arrange for around-the-clock care for Camila – who was unable to walk or use her hands because they were so torn up and bandaged – and care for Harper. Thank God for my friends, who all took turns nursing Camila's wounds, feeding her and Harper, and keeping them company.

Before I left for San Francisco, Camila had asked if I would leave the keys to my new Porsche at home. I had asked her why, considering we had two other cars she could drive, and she had never driven the Porsche. My Porsche was brand new, and I never let anyone drive it. She made up some silly reason; she suggested that she might need to move it in the garage or something. I was gullible; I did not want to argue – and I did not yet realize how diabolical she actually was. I left the Porsche's keys at home but made her promise not to drive it.

Well, that promise lasted all of two hours. As soon as I left for the airport, she left for her part-time job in my beautiful new Porsche. Now, it was missing. Camila said she could not exactly remember where it was, but thought that it was in a parking lot someplace downtown – which, by the way, was very, very far from where she worked.

I called my friend Alan and begged him to drive around to all the downtown parking lots until he found my Porsche. It took him a while, but he finally did find it. It was in a public parking lot, with the keys still in it! And Camila's purse, along with her money and ID and her cell phone, was in the trunk. *What the hell?* I thought. It made no sense to me. But Alan was able to return my car to the garage at my loft; and while Camila was a mess, she was safe at home.

A few days later, while still in San Francisco, I was able to get Camila's recollection of the events out of her. But I never really got a straight story of exactly what happened. I could only get bits and pieces from her at the time because she was such a mess. She had become hysterical, and then was quickly doped up on pain medication. Camila said she was injured as a result of jumping out of a moving car near the Flats on a bridge with metal grates.

She said that the chain of events started with a carjacking in the parking lot at her work. A guy got in the Porsche and made her follow another car, at gunpoint, downtown to a lot that she could not identify. Her purse, wallet, ID, and everything else of value was in the trunk of the car, which apparently did not matter to the carjackers. They had demanded that she get out of my car and get into the backseat of their car with a guy who was holding a gun on her. Camila said that as they drove toward the Flats, the men talked about raping and killing her.

Camila said she had started freaking out at that point, realizing that it was possible she would not survive the night. She said that the guys began arguing about what they were going to do with her, and were distracted by their bickering. The one with the gun who was sitting next to Camila had turned his attention to the driver and had taken his eyes off Camila, who quickly opened the door and threw herself out of the moving car onto the bridge. She said that because they were in the middle of moving traffic on the bridge, the guys were not able to stop and grab her again. She was severely injured in the fall, but she ran across the bridge barefoot until she found a cab driver who would agree to take her back to the loft. That was the story she told me.

I wanted to believe her, but it all seemed extremely bizarre and unfathomable. Still, I wanted to try to verify the pieces of her story. I called a guy that I worked with in Cleveland and said, "Listen, can you please go down to this particular bridge at the Flats and see what you can find? See if there's blood, or torn clothing, jewelry, shoes, or **any-thing** that would confirm Camila's story?" He agreed, went to inspect the bridge, and called me back a few hours later. He found nothing at all. His response was, "Dude, like, what the hell? Your girl is crazy and she's lying."

I returned to Cleveland after four days, with a lease for a new home in San Francisco in hand. I was planning for the move to San Francisco and my first Vice President position. It was a big promotion, and I was extremely excited. I had worked so hard in my career; I had made many moves and big sacrifices to arrive at that level in my firm.

This horrible incident involving Camila certainly put a kink into my moving plans. After weeks of mulling everything over, and asking as many questions as I could, it still did not add up to me. Camila would not go outside, for fear of those men finding her. She would not open the curtains at the loft. She would not return to her job – not that she could have anyway, because she couldn't walk. She also would not allow me to call the police, which to me was the biggest red flag.

I eventually came to the conclusion that Camila was lying. I figured that she had probably partied with some people that she met at the bar where she waitressed, and drank a lot, and maybe did drugs with them. Maybe they had wanted to have sex with her, or maybe she was supposed to pay them for drugs and couldn't pay, so they shoved her out of a moving car. Or maybe she really did jump because she couldn't pay them and did not want to have sex with them.

Although I could not confirm her drug use at that time, I was unable to reconcile any of the events that had happened with any logical explanation – so, it was either drug-related or perhaps she really was carjacked. To this day, the truth eludes me; but I suspect that it lies somewhere in the middle.

Either way, Camila buried the truth deep inside her, for me to never find out. While nothing in her story added up, I did not pursue it any further. I was not ready to let her go, and I suppose I knew in some stunted part of my brain that if I dug into her weird tale, I would find a lot of stuff I never wanted to know about her. Besides, I needed to get us ready to move to San Francisco and re-focus on my career. After all, I was now a Vice President, and that title came with a lot of responsibility. I had to be present and at the top of my game at work.

I also had this wonderful child, Harper, who was new in my life. I needed to help care for her, along with her now-invalid mother. There was so much happening, and it was a lot to juggle. Building my career was always my focus and the most important thing to me; but now I was saddled with so many other responsibilities. It was stressful – physically, mentally, and financially.

The moving company came and picked up everything in the Cleveland loft. The vehicle mover loaded up two of my cars, and the boat mover loaded up my boat. I packed up a car for the three of us, and we hit the road to San Francisco. We decided to give Harper a fun summer road trip with lots of stops before she had to deal with yet another big change.

We arrived in San Francisco about five days later and unfortunately the drama continued. The day that the movers delivered everything to our new flat in Nob Hill, Camila started in again with bizarre arguments that came out of nowhere. She would rush out of the house, dragging Harper behind her, and disappear for a while.

In hindsight, it is pretty clear that she was repeating her mother's pattern of looking for drugs – and most likely doing anything to get them. Unfortunately, it would take me several more years to finally come to that conclusion and wrap my head around it.

At the time I had no idea what she was doing – I was focussed on telling the movers how to set up the house. But I was struggling with the dilemma about what to do about Camila. Her behavior was disrupting my life. *What the hell have I gotten myself into? Should I cut Camila off and send her back to San Antonio?*

I could not do it. I had already moved Camila and Harper twice in four months, and Camila had been in a bizarre and horrific accident (that may or may not have been her own doing). I loved her. I was in love with her. When she was at her best, our relationship was more exciting and satisfying than anything I had ever known. The way Camila loved me was intoxicating. All that drama and passion was real – I know that – but now I also know that the high emotion and drama was consistent with how addicts tend to operate. When she wasn't high on whatever she was taking, Camila was addicted to me – and in my ignorance, it felt amazing and wonderful to be loved so intensely and deeply.

Camila had convinced me to bring her mother Vivian to San Francisco for a few weeks to help us get unpacked in our new home. She could also take care of Harper while I was at work, and while Camila was out looking for a job. The prospect of having Vivian with us made me a little nervous because I had heard stories about her – but we needed the help, and we had yet to meet anyone in San Francisco. So, I agreed.

We picked up Vivian from the airport – and she was clearly higher than a kite. After we got back to our home, she went straight to bed in Harper's room. She slept for two and a half days. I kept opening the door to the bedroom to make sure she was still breathing; and I kept asking Camila when she was going to get up and start helping us. Harper would take her some food and she would nibble a bit and then go back to sleep. Finally, she came out of the bedroom, looking like a mess. She finally helped unpacked a little – but not much.

Vivian did watch Harper for us at times; but without getting into too much detail, her overall behavior was just bizarre. There were several disturbing incidents that happened while she stayed with us. I shared my concerns about Vivian with Camila and said that we probably needed to send her home soon.

The day after I spoke to Camila about her mother, my assistant walked into my office at work and handed me a fax. It was from Vivian's boyfriend in San Antonio. It was a crude, handwritten message that chastised me for being a lesbian, and told me I was a bad influence on Camila and Harper. It also said that God would strike me down for my lesbianism and sins, and that I would be going to hell. It went on to tell me that if I did not give them $700, they would out me to my office.

Well, that was pretty much known now, since they had sent that disgusting fax to my office in order to bribe me. It was likely that several people had already seen the fax, including my assistant. I had been in the San Francisco office for less than three weeks, so I was certain that no one knew I was gay. It would have been a very long time before I told anyone, if I even had decided to share that at work.

I was shocked and so angry. I was proud of my career and took it very seriously. I could not have something like this interfering with my career aspirations and goals. I left the office immediately with fax in hand; I went home and gave it to Camila. She read it and was horrified. I told her to tell her mother to pack her things.

I tried to find a plane ticket for Vivian that had her leaving that day, because I did not want her in my home for another second. There were no flights available. I checked the Greyhound bus schedule and there was a bus leaving within a few hours. I showed Vivian the fax and said a few choice words about how disgusting she and her boyfriend were. I told her that they needed help and that she would be leaving immediately. I loaded Vivian's things in the car, and we drove her to the bus station, where I bought her a one-way ticket back to San Antonio. I then gave her $100 for the trip, and told her to never contact me or Camila again. That was the last time I ever saw Vivian, although I do know she made it safely back to San Antonio. From what I heard, she went right back into the drug-filled life with her boyfriend – the way that she had been living pretty much all along.

That first year in San Francisco's Nob Hill had its ups and downs, but things seemed to level out to semi-normal after Vivian left. Camila and I were getting more and more entangled in each other, and she calmed down briefly to a low-to-medium rumble. We were living what looked and felt like a somewhat normal life with Harper, and we made some new friends.

When we had first moved to San Francisco, we entered Harper into the city's school lottery; the lottery dictated which school the child would attend. Nob Hill is a really nice neighborhood, so we assumed that was where Harper would be placed. However, she wound up in a school in a really rough neighborhood because it was so late in the summer, and most children had already been placed for the upcoming year.

Camila was really upset when she met Harper's second-grade teacher. The teacher greeted the parents and children at the school wearing lots of tattoos, a nose ring, and other piercings. She was wearing a skimpy top that exposed her midriff, along with a belly button piercing. Camila was equally put off by the chant that the principal had the students recite before starting for the day – instead of the Pledge of Allegiance, these little children would pledge not to do drugs or go to prison.

Harper did not know anything about that kind of stuff, and Camila did not want her learning any more about the rough life to which she had already been exposed at such a young age. Many of the other students had at least one parent incarcerated, and the oath was probably meaningful for them; but for Harper it was just another cause for alarm. The final straw was when we found out that the other children were hurting Harper – giving her burns on her arms, pushing her until she fell to the ground, and bullying her verbally. I had not ever planned on being a parent; but when I heard about what was going on at school, it broke my heart. It also made me angry; and I became more involved in Harper's care and well-being. It was that overwhelming protective instinct for Harper that made me realize how much my relationship with Camila and her child was changing me foundationally.

Camila petitioned the school board to switch Harper out to another district, but was told there was nothing that could be done. So, after dropping Harper off at school every day, she would go and sit in the school board office, asking to be heard. That went on for several weeks, until they finally offered Camila an alternative: if she could get the principal of the other school to sign off on a transfer, then Harper could change schools.

There was a science magnet school about a mile from our house that was full and did not have any room for another student; but we found out that the principal could make an exception if she wanted to. The school board put the responsibility in Camila's hands to meet with the principal and convince her to make room for Harper.

Since Camila was very charming and could talk her way into or out of almost anything, she was successful. The principal of the science magnet school agreed to admit Harper. We finally moved Harper into her new school – where she thrived.

A side note: the last time that Camila picked up Harper from the school in which she was originally placed, Camila saw a little boy – a first-grader – sitting on the steps of the school. She leaned down to say good morning, and he replied by giving her the finger and saying, "F*#k you." We were so happy that Harper made her way to another school.

At that time, San Francisco was electrified because it started to look like gay marriage could be legalized there very soon. Everyone was buzzing about it, and there was always something in the paper about gay marriage and the surrounding political discussion. Camila wanted to get married and pushed for it from the moment that it seemed like it could actually happen. I was, of course, less enthusiastic. My parents' marriage as well as their other marriages were not a glowing recommendation for the institution. But I loved Camila and did not want to be without her. I had no intention of leaving Camila over the marriage issue and knew it would be useless to fight about it.

So, I thought if I proposed to her, it would create positive feelings in our relationship, and it still would give me a few years' respite before she started pushing to get married. I really was not thinking that gay marriage would actually become legal anytime soon. But I had not paid enough attention to the newspapers; I did not realize that the reality of legal same-sex marriage in San Francisco was literally just weeks away.

Camila's birthday was at the end of January, so I proposed at that time. I knew that it would make her really happy; but, looking at it less romantically, I also hoped it would put an end to her constant questions about marriage. It was not that I didn't want to marry Camila – I didn't want to marry anyone. It just was not anything I had ever wanted for my life.

But the fact that she wanted to be married to me made an impact on me emotionally – to think that she loved me that much. And since I thought I would have a long lead time before we would even be eligible to marry, I felt more or less OK about moving forward with a proposal. It sounds horrible – but it was the happiest, secretly-uncomfortable compromise I could make. She loved the ring and was ecstatic, and everything was settled and calm between us.

Two weeks later, Camila came to me, waving the newspaper around in a tizzy of excitement. San Francisco had legalized gay marriage. She was beside herself, and all I could think was, *What the hell is this nightmare?* I soon found out what the nightmare was: city officials were going to start performing marriage ceremonies that Thursday, February 12th. Camila wanted so badly to go down to City Hall and get married right away.

Fortunately for me, I had too many meetings and too much work, and I could not break away on that Thursday or Friday. I figured that then we would be busy celebrating over Valentine's Day weekend, and after that I would just keep making excuses about why I would not be able to go during the week. Maybe I would have to go away on a business trip? I was trying to come up with anything to keep me from having to say those two frightening words: "I do."

Camila woke me up on Saturday morning, Valentine's Day, with breakfast in bed, flowers, and a card. She handed me the newspaper, jumping up and down clapping her hands and screaming for joy. They were marrying people that day at City Hall! I could not believe it! I read the paper over and over with dismay, trying to find a loophole, while she ran down the hall to get Harper. They both came back excited and began jumping up and down on the bed. They were giddily screaming, over and over, "We can get married. We are going to get married. Woohoo!"

I was in shock. How did my plan of giving myself a two-year reprieve turn into only a two-week reprieve? After the shock started to ebb, I realized I could not get out of it. I was getting married. I no longer had any viable excuses; and Camila was a freight train of enthusiasm. So, we got dressed and went to City Hall.

When we arrived, there were hundreds of people in line. The line wrapped all the way around the building. We stood in line as part of an enormous throng, waiting our turn and watching all the couples coming out of City Hall with their marriage licenses. They were triumphant and happy. The media was everywhere, and the entire City Hall area was abuzz with excitement.

Camila was so excited that she seemed lightheaded, laughing one minute and weeping with joy the next. For my part, I was so freaked out that I was numb and felt like I was in a semi-coma. She kept asking, "Who should we call and tell?" And my response was always, "No one." We did not know for sure that we would be able to get married that day." The real truth was that I was not ready to get married – so I was sure not ready to tell anyone about it.

As we moved closer and closer to the steps of City Hall, I started to silently panic. *What am I doing?* I thought. We crept forward with the movement of the line until we were 20 to 25 couples away from getting inside. At that point, I was seriously on the verge of crapping my pants. Although I was cool as a cucumber outside, I was a total wreck inside.

A few minutes later, a clerk came out of the building to say that they were really sorry, but they had to close for the day. Because so many city employees had donated their time to help marry couples, they needed to go home and spend the Saturday evening with their families and their Valentines.

Groans of disappointment went through the crowd, but I quietly let out a long sigh of relief. Then, the person making the announcement continued, "But we will open bright and early tomorrow, Sunday, February 15th, so that you can get married! We are giving you numbers, so you don't have to re-wait in a long line!" The crowd erupted in joy; my heart sank. *Just stop fighting it, Kendra,* I said to myself. *This is happening, and you can't stop it.*

That night after dinner, I decided to get up early the next day to be at the head of the line. I did not want to wait behind the 25 other couples who would be there. I was not going to spend another entire weekend day in line.

We arrived about an hour before the doors opened, and we were the second couple in line. I had bought Camila a beautiful bouquet of flowers for the occasion, and all three of us wore matching dressy attire. I had finally decided: if I was going to do it, I was going to do it right. We were whisked in very quickly. Harper stood with us, the clerk officiated, and Camila and I were married. Just like that.

The day was extraordinary. No matter what my feelings about marriage were or are, it was a landmark event that still must be recognized and celebrated for all those who finally had the opportunity to marry their love. San Francisco's City Hall is gorgeous – very beautiful – and huge inside. Officiants were set up all over the main hall on different levels and plazas, and the press was all over the place because it was a major historic event. It barely registered with me at the time, but we were photographed and videoed all that morning because we were among the first to get married on that particular Sunday. I think you can still find footage of us online if you look hard enough. We celebrated with a fancy lunch on the water, and in true Camila fashion, she started a ridiculous argument at our after-wedding lunch. I thought, *Seriously – this is my life?*

In the typical bizarre fashion of my life, something extraordinary and embarrassing happened after our marriage. My phone started blowing up. I was getting calls from all over the nation – from friends, clients and co-workers – congratulating me on my marriage. How in the world could they know when I had not told anyone, you might ask?

They all had seen Camila and me on TV getting married. It turned out that we had been on MTV, VH1, the national news, and local news all over the nation. Who knows, perhaps we were even on international newscasts. Harper's second-grade teacher even called us one night and said, "Turn on VH1, you are on TV!"

Why we, as a couple, became so emblematic of those initial gay marriages was a bit baffling to me. The only thing I could figure was that Camila was a stunning woman, and that made for some eye-catching television journalism. To this day, that video clip of Camila and me at City Hall is sometimes still used when a news outlet talks about those marriages.

At times, friends will text me a picture of Camila and me getting married that they saw on the TV news. For some time after our marriage, we would go into restaurants and stores in San Francisco and people would recognize us and congratulate us. For a time, people bought us lunch or drinks to celebrate when we were out in San Francisco. It embarrassed me; but Camila absolutely loved every second of the attention. She soaked up her 15 minutes of fame, while I cringed.

CHAPTER EIGHT

IS THIS LOVE, OR IS THIS INSANITY?

Camila exhibited a lot of very strange behavior that first year in San Francisco. She would start fights randomly – over nothing – often imagining things that she claimed had happened. Or, she would start an argument over things that I had supposedly said. Then she would run away. It did not matter where we were – a house, a restaurant, a store, anywhere. She would just leave.

The first time she was physically violent with me was after we were married and still living in Nob Hill. Camila's crazy behavior reminded me of my mother's behavior. I now know that it was her way of leaving to buy or do drugs. Or, the behavior was a result of the drugs she had just done.

One night, she had been drinking and she started another unreasonable fight with me out of the blue. Then, she asked, "See this glass?" Before I could answer, she proceeded to smash it against the side of my head, shattering many tiny pieces of glass into my scalp. It was one of those really thick ornate glasses from Mexico; and although it hurt badly, it did not knock me out. But it stunned me for sure. I did not understand why she did that, but it set the stage for so much more violence to come.

Looking back, I see how everything added up to drugs and alcohol with Camila. Substance abuse was a major cause of her behavior, along with mental instability, no doubt. Like most addicts, she was always looking for money so she could buy drugs – and any way she could get that money was OK. Things were always mysteriously disappearing from our home.

With the benefit of hindsight, I realize now that she was taking those things and selling them. But at that time, I could not see that phenomenon as an obvious sign of addiction or drug abuse, because I had not been exposed to drinking or drugs while growing up. I was raised so sheltered; I was very naïve. I did not start drinking until I was 27, because I really never cared for it.

I know that Camila's violence and the instability between us had nothing to do with where we lived; the problems she had would have followed us wherever we went. Nevertheless, the chaos of that whole experience with Camila did not add to my love of Nob Hill. Frankly, I hated it there – for several reasons. The fog would roll in and give me terrible migraines. And it seemed like every drunk tourist in the city found their way to our street, their revelry waking us up in the middle of the night. Our bedroom faced the street, and we were constantly awakened by singing, laughing, screaming, shouting, or fighting, depending on the drunks' behavioral preferences.

It also seemed like every homeless person found their way to our street to camp out on our steps. We lived in a Victorian building made up of three levels – with a different apartment on each level. We lived in the middle flat and by San Francisco standards it was quite large at 2,000 square feet. The building was set up so that you walked up the front steps to a landing covered with a portico. From there, you entered the door for your flat. That portico overhang made our building very popular with a lot of homeless and unsavory people as a place to sleep almost every night.

One time, Camila and I came home from a night out around 11 p.m. We tried to walk up the steps, but a man and woman had camped out on our stoop, blocking our way. That is when we saw them shooting up. I asked them nicely several times to clear a path so we could get to our house; they ignored me.

It was late, I was tired, and I would have to get up to go to work the next day – and this type of incident had happened way too often. I got mad and finally said, "Get the hell off my stoop." The guy started getting confrontational while holding a bunch of needles in his hand, which was scary; but I was so angry I just kept yelling at him. Miraculously, they both finally started to walk away. On his way down the stairs, the guy screamed at me, "F*#k you and your f*#king $500 pants!" I turned to Camila and said, "Damn! Do these really look like $500 pants?" You never know where your next compliment will come from.

My deep disgust for our street and neighborhood, which brought about our decision to move, came to a head not long after that incident with the junkies. We had picked up Harper from school and parked in our garage, which was about a block away from the house. We walked to the top of our street, getting ready to walk down the hill toward our place, and we saw that our stoop was occupied by a homeless man. His pants were down around his ankles, and he was defecating on our steps.

Harper looked at the scene, gasped, and I lost my mind. I was carrying a glass vase that I was bringing home from my office, and marched over to him, waving the vase. I yelled at him, "Stop taking a shit on my steps!" He was so high that he had no idea what was going on. He just shuffled out of the way, leaving a pile of excrement. We watched him stagger off; and I went straight to my landlord and let her have it. She lived next door, and we were constantly telling her that there was urine and human waste on the property, druggies and homeless people sleeping on the stoop, and trash everywhere around the building.

Nob Hill was and is a fancy neighborhood, and we paid a lot of money for that apartment. I asked the landlord to improve the situation, but she had no interest in that. So, I gave notice that we would be moving, and we found a beautiful, brand new huge three-level loft in Potrero Hill, another San Francisco neighborhood. However, just as we got away from the shit of Nob Hill and into a much more gracious home situation, we entered a private world of shit at home.

The incident where Camila had smashed the glass on my head was outrageous and unacceptable; but you have to remember that because my mom was extremely physically abusive to me while I was growing up, I just thought that was how everybody grew up – with that kind of violence and conflict.

Now, whenever I occasionally tell people about the kind of abuse I experienced growing up, they always ask why I never called the police, or went to any other city agency for help. Back then, there were no levels of protection. If you were a child, always getting the crap beat out of you, the likelihood that you could bring about real change for yourself was very slim.

And it would not have occurred to me to look for help, because I just thought that kind of crazy, violent behavior was normal. It was also normal for me as a child not to tell anyone what was happening at home. So, it seemed completely reasonable to me as an adult to not tell my friends that Camila hit me. But eventually, something finally happened that was so terrible that I had to call friends for help.

Camila, Harper and I had just moved into the new loft in Potrero Hill, and life was rolling along. For a few months before we moved from Nob Hill, Camila had been working for a company that made copy machines. She worked in sales and did other representation work for the company. I met some of the people she worked with; they seemed happy with her, and she was happy with them. And I was happy because she finally had some forward momentum, she was making a little bit of money, and was actually productive. It gave me hope that things were on track for us.

Before this job, Camila had not worked, other than her three-week stint at the bar in Cleveland that ended with that violent night. I had not protested too strongly about her unemployment most of the time because we had been on the move. Besides, I was the one who had uprooted her and Harper, due to my promotion. But my work ethic and my drive for success was very strong. I feel that no matter what you do, you have to find ways to be a contributing member of the community. I do not care how much money you make; I do not care if you work at Starbucks, McDonald's, or Google. You just have to do something. You must get up every day, go out, and function as a productive member of society in some fashion.

With Camila working, that period in our lives had the potential to bring some peace and normalcy; no one was shitting or shooting up on our steps anymore, and the adults in our household were gainfully employed. What could go wrong?

Our idyllic life at that time included joining a boating community in Napa, one of my favorite areas in the US. I had fallen in love with boating in college when I worked as a waitress on City Island, a boating-oriented island in the northeastern part of the Bronx. Watching all the boats arrive for Sunday brunch was mesmerizing. It was new to me, and it seemed so fanciful. It was then and there, while I was waiting tables and bartending to pay my way through college, that I decided that one day I would own a boat. That may not sound so glamorous to many; but for me, growing up in Oklahoma, owning a boat was a symbol of success. Besides, it looked like a wonderful, fun way to spend Sundays.

I bought my first boat back when I was living in Atlanta, and I took it with me on each of my work moves: to Chicago, Cleveland, and then San Francisco. For the first year in San Francisco, I kept my boat dry-docked at the San Francisco Bay. At first, it was fun to boat in those waters – taking friends out, circling Alcatraz, going over to Sausalito, watching the sea lions and even venturing under the Golden

Gate bridge. The fun was short-lived, however, because it was foggy by the bay and the water was too rough, cold, and salty for my taste. I discovered then that I preferred boating on freshwater lakes over ocean boating. I liked being on the boat in calm waters where it was sunny, peaceful and relaxing.

So, after the first year of boating on the bay, I decided to move my boat to a freshwater lake in the mountains, in beautiful Napa – the heart of California wine country. It was a two-and-a-half-hour drive from the city. I rented a house on the lake for us to use on weekends. We made some good friends at the lake, and Harper found friends, too. It was a lot of fun.

We loved it so much that I bought a second home for us to use on weekends at the lake. We invited friends from the city to the new place in Napa – Camila would cook, and we would entertain. We spent summer weekends boating, and winter weekends wine-tasting. Camila and I had a lot of fun – a great love life – the whole nine yards. When she was not melting down or disappearing, it was wonderful.

Camila also helped me manage a few rental properties that I had purchased while I worked in different cities around the country. Camila knew the details that needed fixing at the rentals or in our own homes, and she took care of any issues because I worked so much. All seemed right in the world – for a short time.

But before long another red flag popped up. Even though Camila was on top of things at home, she could not hang onto a job. That job with the copier company ended with her being fired within the first year; I never got a straight story on what happened. She then cycled through several other jobs, making excuse after excuse, as she was let go from each one. I knew something was wrong, but was unaware of what it was. I know now that most addicts who are actively using drugs or alcohol cannot keep jobs; so, in hindsight, it was not that surprising. But at the time, it just seemed strange.

At that time Camila started displaying behavior that was even more frightening than it was bizarre. She developed a habit of waking me up in the middle of the night to start a fight. It was clear that she had not been to sleep yet. She would start fights over things that, once again, made no sense. I would talk her down from the rage and try to restore calm and order before I went to work the next day. Harper would be sleeping soundly in another part of the house, and I did not want her to be awakened. But sometimes, I was not able to calm Camila down – I would have to go upstairs to the guest bedroom so I could sleep.

One night, Camila started the fight a little earlier than usual. I had not been to bed yet, but I was winding down. Out of nowhere, she hauled off and punched me in the face. I went down hard. We had a thick, dense berber carpet that provided zero cushioning when I hit the floor. My nose exploded, spraying blood everywhere. I stumbled as I tried to get up, instinctively turning at the same time to run away. As I ran, Camila ran after me and tackled me from behind, pinning my arms to my sides so I had no way to break my fall. She landed on top of me, punching my head, neck and back.

I managed to escape and get up and run again. She ended up tackling me three times – and each time she took me down, I slid across the hard carpet, taking off a lot of skin from my hands, knees, and the tops of my feet. I was bleeding from my nose, mouth, hands, feet and knees. My head was ringing from having been punched so many times.

She finally let me go, and I ran upstairs to the top level of our loft, which is where the front door was. I grabbed my briefcase at the top of the stairs that had my house and car keys in it and ran outside. I had no idea where I was going – I was a bloody mess – but I knew I needed to get out of that house, and fast. I got in my car and drove away. I parked only a few blocks away from the house, but far enough away that she could not hurt me anymore. I was totally destroyed.

I locked the car doors and stayed inside the car for several hours, trying to figure out what to do. *Should I call the police?* I had never been in a situation like that as an adult where I had to figure out options to protect myself. I was so upset that I called my friends Candy and Carla, a lesbian couple I had been friends with for many years. I told them that Camila had beat me up, badly, and that I was bleeding everywhere and didn't know what to do. Calling the cops was not an option because I did not want Harper to be exposed to that kind of thing. And, I did not want Camila to go to jail. I cannot really recall what advice my friends gave me; but just having someone else know what happened helped me feel a little safer somehow. I am not a crier, but I sat in the car and I cried that night.

I was in terrible pain – so after two or three hours I decided to go back to the house. By that time, Camila was passed out in the bed, face up, snoring. She had been drinking – and probably doing drugs – and was completely knocked out.

I went to the guest bedroom, locked the door, and shoved a bunch of furniture up against it to make sure she could not get in. She would not be able to attack me again overnight. But sleep eluded me that night, because I was in pain, and very scared.

The next day, I was a wreck with abrasions, missing skin, and dried blood. As it turned out, my nose was broken. It would be the first of several times that Camila broke my nose.

I was afraid to go to the bathroom to clean up. I was traumatized, and when Camila finally found me that next day she was horrified. When I told her what she had done, she said that she could not remember any of it. She was remorseful and ashamed; she cleaned and doctored me up, and looked after me for the next few days. I had to stay home from work; I could not wear shoes because of the raw abrasions on the top of my feet. Besides, I did not want to show up in my office looking like I had been beaten.

Like a textbook abuser, Camila took care of me very sweetly and tenderly to try to make it up to me. She said, "I'm so sorry, I'm so sorry, I love you, I love you, it will never happen again." We wrapped my feet and hands with bandages. It was my turn to not be able to walk or use my hands, reminiscent of how Camila had been incapacitated at the beginning of our relationship in Cleveland. But she had been responsible for both incidents.

I did not know it then, but the type of unexpected physical attack I had just experienced would become Camila's modus operandi. I quickly developed a system of escape for when Camila had these violent outbursts, but never escaping before she would do considerable damage to me, my face and body. Looking back, I can see it was completely crazy to have an escape plan – but necessary – because Camila would become so enraged.

After those bizarre, random fights became a pattern, I began to put everything of value – such as money, jewelry, my laptop, keys, ID and credit cards – into my briefcase. I would grab the briefcase and run to my car or to a room where I could lock the door. It became necessary during those incidents to safeguard my things; I did not want them to be damaged or to disappear.

At the beginning of Camila's recurring abuse toward me, I did not see myself as a victim, or even as someone weaker than my partner. I was unaware that I could be overpowered the way I was. I was strong and athletic, and Camila was not bigger than I was. But when drugs take hold of someone, especially the kind of drugs that I later found out Camila was using, that person can become crazed. They can become much stronger than normal when high on those types of drugs. And the adrenaline rush they get from the drug makes them not just stronger, but also faster.

When her drug-induced adrenaline rushes kicked in, it was like a hurricane appearing out of thin air. It was always a shock to me, and a real advantage for her. I never knew when a punch was going to land on my nose, mouth, eye or ear. Her forceful blows rattled my brain and vision so that I could not see the next punches coming. I would end up completely overpowered and laying on the ground bleeding; she would either stand over me while kicking me or sit on top of me while punching me.

Sometimes when Camila woke me up in the middle of the night and started a fight, she would also wake up Harper. She would pull Harper out of her bed and drag her out into the streets, running away from her hallucinations. Some of those nights were cold and rainy. I never knew what was going through Camila's head at those times – now I realize that she did not know either.

When she ran and took Harper, I would drive around trying to find them. Sometimes I would find them; sometimes I could not. When I did find them, I would beg Camila to get back in the car for Harper's sake; but Camila would just refuse and yell at me. Harper, holding her mother's hand, would ask her to please get in the car so they could go home. I would try to reason with Camila.

I guess it did not matter to Camila whether she came home and got some sleep, because she kept getting fired from her jobs, and was unemployed. However, Harper would need to be at school the next morning and I would have to go to work. We had responsibilities; we had commitments. I tried to get Camila to understand that in the middle of her meltdown. I presume that the nights I could not find her wandering our neighborhood streets were probably the nights that her friends or drug dealer would take her to get high. I always worried for Harper's safety. That was partially why I felt that I could not just move them back to Texas; I was fearful of what might happen to Harper.

There were a number of times when I was on a business trip out of town, and I had to fly back early from my trip. Camila would not answer her cell phone when I called, and she and Harper would be missing. And then, sometimes she would answer her cell phone, but I would hear partying in the background. I would ask her where Harper was, and she would hang up on me and not answer when I called back. Or, someone else would answer her phone and not make any sense. When I could not talk to Harper on the phone to know that she was OK, I would cut my business trip short. I would get on the next plane to San Francisco late at night or early in the morning, to make sure that Harper was OK. That happened far too many times.

On one such occasion, I came home to what I thought was an empty house. Harper was in school, but Camila was who knows where. There were beer cans and alcohol bottles all over the place. Cigarette butts and empty cups were strewn everywhere. It was clear that Camila had had quite a party while I was away.

While I was trying to call her on the phone, someone walked out of the back guest bedroom in the loft, scaring the shit out of me. It was Camila's friend Zoe from work, who had been sleeping in my house with no one else home. *What the hell is going on?* I thought to myself. I asked Zoe where Camila was, and she said she didn't know. Then I asked her what she was doing in my house, and she nonchalantly said, "Camila had a party last night and I was too drunk to go home, so I stayed the night!" *Jesus, what in the world?* Things were literally getting worse each day with Camila.

One Camila meltdown that particularly stands out in my mind started at home when I was sleeping in the guest bedroom. I was sleeping there because I did not want to be in the line of fire if she had another violent middle-of-the-night episode.

Camila had managed to get my work laptop out of the room while I was sleeping and searched through all of my email correspondence. She was looking for something that would prove that I was cheating on her. Well, I absolutely was not cheating on her – but maybe she was cheating on me, and her guilty conscience led her to project such behavior onto me. Camila was naturally a very jealous person; but she also had a fiery, volatile persona. She was possessive and tried to limit who I had as friends, and who I spoke to.

I know now that her behavior was typical for an addict and an abuser; but at the time, it was just profoundly irritating and a source of conflict. My ex-girlfriend, Olivia, had remained a close friend after our breakup, and my continuing friendship with her drove Camila insane. For a time, I had to stop communicating with Olivia – as well as with several other friends who made Camila jealous – to try to keep the peace.

Camila would not allow me to be friends with any pretty girls whatsoever, and as a lesbian I had a lot of female friends – many of them feminine and pretty. I had to stop my friendships with all of them while I was with Camila. I mentioned that on the night of the laptop theft, she stayed up all night scouring my computer for signs of cheating and flirting. In the process of looking through my computer, she infected my laptop with enough viruses to render it useless. She essentially blew it up, and I had to get a new one. And there was no way I could possibly have been cheating on her – my hands were full dealing with her madness, caring for Harper, and trying to further my career. I did not have time for anyone else in my life – much less cheating or any other kind of clandestine behavior. The mere thought of such a thing was ridiculous.

Despite all of her issues, part of Camila's allure was her gregarious nature. She did not know a stranger. She could walk into a room and own it, talking to anyone she wished. She would always garner plenty of attention due to her exquisite beauty and sparkling personality. She made friends quickly, and somehow, easily made connections throughout the city.

One example of this was when we were at a fundraiser at Harper's school, and Mayor Gavin Newsom was giving a speech. There was a small group in attendance, and we all stood around in a circle listening to the mayor. Camila was standing next to me, holding my hand. As he made his speech, the mayor was scanning the group, and he saw Camila. He stopped mid-speech and with a big smile said, "Why hello, Camila." She replied, "Hello, Gavin." After his speech, she introduced me to him. It was an awkward and very strange moment. How did my wife know the mayor of San Francisco and how did he know her by name? WTF? When I questioned her about it, she was somewhat vague – something connected to the school – I cannot recall exactly but it seemed like a BS explanation at the time. However, I was not about to make her upset by continuing to question her.

During our marriage, Camila lost both her father and her grandfather. She was close to her grandfather, and it was a very sad passing. We went back to Texas for the funeral, and I tried to be as supportive as possible. But then when her father – or alleged father – Chuco passed away, it was a whole different experience. As I mentioned before, Chuco was a founding member and leader of a motorcycle gang. Camila learned as a young adult that he was supposedly her father. Her last name was the name of a different man; someone she never knew. As a child, Camila was told that man was her father. Then, in Camila's late teens, her mother told her that Chuco was actually her real father. What would you expect from a heroin addict that took her daughter along with her to truck stops when she was soliciting men?

Camila developed a father-daughter relationship with Chuco. She admired him and thought he was badass. And when he passed away, Camila was devastated; we went back to San Antonio for the funeral. While driving to the funeral home for the viewing the night before the funeral, we passed many unmarked police or law enforcement cars parked along the road nearby. When we arrived, there were hundreds of motorcycles and gang members in the parking lot. It was surreal.

I had never been around those kinds of people. Honestly, I was a little scared – and quite uncomfortable in my pressed slacks and a French cuff shirt with cufflinks. I was totally out of place. Camila knew many of the gang members, and they hugged her and cried with her over the loss of Chuco. As we stood in the parking lot talking to many of them, helicopters flew overhead. Red, one of the leaders and a friend of Chuco's, started flipping them off and cursing, saying "F*#k the police and FBI!"

I was shocked, but then I put the pieces together in my head. Law enforcement had come out for Chuco's funeral service in the hope of catching some of the members who had outstanding warrants. Internally, I started freaking out. I thought to myself, *Why am I here? This is dangerous and crazy; I do not belong here!* But I said nothing and stayed calm so I could support my wife.

The next day was the funeral service and burial. When it was time to drive to the cemetery for Chuco's burial, hundreds of various motorcycle club members mounted their motorcycles, turned on their headlights and rode in what seemed like a mile-long parade of bikes. There were at least 300 motorcycles. I have to say, it was quite a sight to see, and a beautiful way to honor Chuco. But I was happy when it was time to head back to San Francisco, and relieved that no trouble resulted from the visit.

Love and attraction are very unpredictable, and very strong. Those are the same adjectives I can easily use to describe my relationship with Camila and the feelings I had for her. So, considering the strong feelings I had, it was not surprising that I put a ton of energy into throwing her a 30th birthday party. I hoped to cheer her up from having experienced the deaths in her family, and to show her – despite all the insanity in our lives due to her issues – that I still loved her very much.

I invited a bunch of our friends from the city, our Napa friends, and even some of my co-workers to a surprise party I planned for her. It was to be held at a beautiful restaurant on the water. I rented a Hummer limo that took us to the restaurant, where all our friends were waiting to surprise her when she walked in. After a wonderful dinner and dessert featuring a beautiful custom cake, the limo then took many of us bar-hopping to all of Camila's favorite bars and clubs.

It was a magnificent evening. But as the night wore on, we ended up at a bar across the street from my friend Spencer's house; it was his favorite bar, and he was part of the party. Spencer had been one of my closest friends for years; we worked at the same company together, but we never lived in the same city until we ended up in San Francisco at the same time.

Before we both lived in San Francisco, the most time that Spencer and I had spent together was when we had to attend two weeklong executive meetings for work each year. We, along with all other attendees to these meetings, would bring along our own booze. The meetings were always at a resort in a dry county in Kentucky, so we would use our own liquor to make cocktails, relax, and catch up on each other's lives during our free time in the evenings. Sometimes, we would rent a boat on our afternoon off and tool around the lake while enjoying the sunshine and talking. We built up a lot of trust during those trips and Spencer became a really close friend. By the time Camila was in my life and we were all in San Francisco, Camila and Harper knew him very well. Harper had even begun to call him Uncle Spencer.

So, having him join us for Camila's birthday celebration was not just normal, it was expected. Unfortunately, less than a year later, Spencer became too comfortable partying and drinking with my wife when I wasn't around so that friendship ended. But true to form, Camila flipped out later that night at her birthday party in front of everyone. It happened later in the evening, so some guests had gone home by the time we arrived at the bar. I do not know if Camila found drugs there, kicking her into deranged, angry behavior – but all signs pointed to that probability. Part of Camila's flip-out that night included her dragging me into the bathroom for a round of verbal and emotional abuse. She was so devastatingly vicious when she was drunk or high, and would say the most horrible and demeaning things to me. It would crush my soul and heart because I could not believe that someone who insisted that they loved me could be so cruel.

I remember being doubled over in the bathroom, like she had hit me, and drowning in tears. I was stunned because of the terrible things she said to me, especially after I had thrown her such an amazing party. As I was crying, I just kept thinking, *What the shit? This is supposed to be a fun time!*

She flew out of the bathroom and out of the bar, leaving her own party – and once again, disappeared. I had to clean myself up and tell everyone that Camila had left the party – and that I was so sorry that we had to finish the night on such a low note. I then took to the streets to find her, but could not. She came home around 4 in the morning.

I now know that some addicts will cause chaos and fights to have an excuse to leave wherever they are, so they can find and do drugs. Looking back, I suspect that was what she was doing that night for four hours – getting high with someone, somewhere. More drugs, more partying, more mayhem, somewhere in the city – but I would never know where.

More craziness ensued on Thanksgiving of the same year while at the lake house in Napa. I had to go through yet another nightmare of sprinting upstairs to my bedroom and barricading myself inside. It was supposed to have been a relaxing and fun Thanksgiving at our lovely home in the mountains of the wine country. But that did not happen. I didn't open the bedroom door for hours, and only spoke to her through the door. I told her to just stop; her daughter could hear her. Miraculously, she **did** stop, and went to bed in another bedroom.

Camila's pattern of picking fights and raging became such a frequent part of our daily life that I finally told Camila that she was either mentally ill or doing drugs. Either way, I advised her, she had to get help. Camila screamed back at me that she had no such issues, and that all of the discord and violence in our house came from me. I was making her behave like that, she said. She repeated those kinds of statements over and over and over until I started to question myself. Eventually, though, I would pull back and say to myself, *Kendra, you're a highly intelligent, successful executive; you get up every day and you have functioned at a very high level with the same firm for over 13 years. You have consistency in your life and are stable and successful, and you don't have any problems whatsoever with substance abuse, any other kind of abuse, or mental issues! Come on!*

I had never done drugs. Well, I tried marijuana twice in my 20s, and did not enjoy it. My body and mind did not like it. I hated drugs – still do – and never wanted to be around people who did them. I also did not overindulge with alcohol. I realized that any drug- or alcohol-related drama in my life had all happened since I had been with Camila.

Camila's manipulative tactics were so much like my mom's that she would get into my head. My mother had trained me to believe that everything bad that happened around me was my fault – or that God was punishing me for my transgressions (whatever those were for a timid, scared girl). Some people with mental illnesses and addicts are similar in that way – the mental, physical, emotional, and verbal abuse that they throw at you pulls you into their way of thinking. They are often skilled manipulators and will successfully gaslight their victims for years before the person on the receiving end reaches their own breaking point.

Because Camila had convinced me that I was the problem, I even saw a counselor for several sessions and took antidepressants for a hot minute. I was willing to do anything to save our relationship and make things better. I made an effort to normalize her behavior, but I finally had to draw the line at taking medication. I knew it was not needed. Even the counseling was not helpful in the way that Camila made me think I needed it, so I stopped both pretty quickly and came to accept that I was absolutely not the problem.

And then I thought, *Why isn't she in counseling or taking something to help her? She is the one, after all, who has been beating me and leaving me mentally broken on a regular basis, not the other way around.*

The only thing that the counseling accomplished was to remind me that I was dealing with an ongoing crisis that was not of my own making. Meanwhile, Camila was ramping up her drug use. She also escalated the intensity and violence of the insane scenes she would create. Later, after I had moved her out of my home, Camila admitted that she was addicted to crystal meth, among other substances.

Near the end of our time of living together, Camila actually started inventing jobs for herself. She would actually get up, get dressed for work, "go to a job," and then come home at the end of the day and tell stories about what she did at work. Because things were so bad by that point, I was very suspicious; so, I started calling the places where she insisted she was employed. When I would ask for her over the phone, no one at any of the places had heard of her. One time, I went to an Ann Taylor store where she said she was working. I asked for her and was told that no such person worked there. I called several times after that, thinking that perhaps the person with whom I spoke just had not met her yet. But it was confirmed each time – Camila did not work there.

This happened a number of times. When I would confront Camila, she would say, "Oh, those are new people," or "My manager doesn't want me to be disturbed at work." I knew it was all lies after the first time it happened, but it took a few more times for me to truly realize the severity of her deception. I dealt with one Camila issue after another. It was a traumatic time for me – I loved her so much – but I knew I needed to get out. I would say to myself, *I'm a smart, professional, successful person. How did I end up here?* And then my next question to myself would be, *How do I get out?*

I turned it over in my mind for a long time, trying to let her go. But when you are manipulated by an addict, it is hard to unwind yourself from the sick dynamic that has been created. Before Camila, I used to be very critical of people who would stay in abusive situations, or of those who would be involved with addicts or alcoholics. It is similar to dealing with extreme mental illness or any other situation that lies outside the bounds of normalcy that we expect in our lives. The reality is that you really cannot understand such behavior unless you live through it.

That was my situation with Camila. Plus, I had a lot of guilt because I had moved them twice so they could be with me. Because we had gotten married, that formalized bond played a huge part in my constant efforts to try to make the relationship work. For me, marriage was an entirely different kind of commitment than any other I had ever made. It meant for better or for worse; I had to try to help her.

I have now learned this about myself: I am a rescuer and a fixer. Maybe in some way, I have tried to make up for the death of my brother and soothe that enormous guilt I felt by finding women in need and trying to help them.

Over and over, my friends would tell me, "You can't save her, you have to get out." And I knew that she had manipulated me into that abusive relationship. Time and again, she would beat the shit out of me when she was high, and then would say, "I love you. I love you. It won't happen again," when she was sober. I agreed to put up with it, even if it was not a conscious decision.

When Camila was sober, she was gregarious, irresistible – just amazing. She would walk into a room and heads would turn; she was the hottest, most sparkling woman in the room. I was madly in love with her. She just was a magnet – my magnet – that I could not leave.

There were just so many incidents with Camila. Toward the end of our relationship, I stopped by the house at lunchtime during a workday to check in on her. I wanted to see if she was at home, or at one of her made-up jobs (which would actually mean that she was off somewhere getting high). I was really just looking for further confirmation about how f*#ked up she was to give me more reason to leave her. She happened to be at home, and so I started to question her as to why she was not at work. The questioning angered her, and we started to argue. But I was tired of the lies and the insanity. I packed some clothes and said I was leaving; I told her that I couldn't live like that anymore.

I started putting suitcases full of my clothes into the car. I planned to head back to work and then to a hotel to be alone; I needed to try to work out a plan to separate. But Camila became so angry that I was packing to leave. As I started to walk back in the house for one last thing, she ran toward me like a linebacker and tackled me – my arms pinned to my sides so I couldn't brace myself for the fall. With this latest tackle, my skin was scraped and bloody all over from contact with the pavement on the driveway. I was in pain and my suit was ruined.

I quickly changed my suit, but would take time to clean my abrasions later. I rushed back to my office, closed the door, and sat at my desk – shaking and traumatized. A fellow that I worked with – also a good friend – came in and could see I was visibly shaking. He sat down, looking worried, and asked me if I was OK. I said, "Yes," but I really was not OK. Then he looked at my bloody hands. His eyes got big, and he asked if I needed anything. Still shaking, I said, "No thank you, I will be OK." He knew, without me going into detail, that it was Camila's work again. Because he had become such a good friend inside and outside of work, I had somewhat confided in him as things had gotten worse with Camila. He was not aware of the full extent of what had happened, but he knew enough to know that Camila was dangerous and could not be trusted.

I finally decided that I needed to end it with Camila once and for all, because – despite her promises – she could not lift herself out of the dark mental and emotional hole where she existed. The violence and chaos just kept rolling – onto me – and I could not see any way for me to live a calm, productive life if she was in it. And frankly, I had become afraid that one day she would kill me.

I made a pact with myself that I would grab the first good opportunity to leave her. I left reminders for myself around the house (usually blood from a beating) of how bad things had become so I would not lull myself into a false sense of security. On one occasion, I was sleeping in the guest bedroom so I could avoid any middle-of-the-night craziness; but Camila still came for me in a high and drunken stupor. She was banging on the door, yelling at me to come out. All I wanted was for her to shut up, and for all of us to be able to get some sleep.

Finally, I opened the door to speak to her. She sucker-punched me – and busted my nose, yet again. Blood went everywhere. I left that blood there on the guest bedroom floor and door as a reminder for me. I am sure the cleaning lady was horrified, but I needed that blood residue in front of me. I needed it there to remind me to stay strong and resolute in my decision to find a way to leave.

Soon after that incident, we were at the house in Napa, and Camila put crystal meth in my drink – for the second time. Yes, for the second time. The first time she did it was at our home in San Francisco, and I had no idea what was happening to me. I did not sleep for days, and I kept talking, shaking, and grinding my jaw. I realized that somehow she must have given me something. She probably did not want to stay awake for days alone, since she too had taken the drug. That first time, the crystal meth shut my digestive and intestinal system down and I had to go to doctors to get help.

I had never had any such problems. My entire life, I went to the restroom every day at 10 a.m. like clockwork. But after crystal meth entered my system for the first time, it completely shut my system down, and to this day I am still not able to use the restroom without the help of medication, which I have to take daily.

The second time she put meth in my drink, in Napa, Camila did it to both our neighbor and me. Our friend and neighbor had come over to visit and have some wine. Yet again, I did not sleep, and I experienced the same physical effects as the first time she gave me meth. It felt horrible. I knew right away what she had done and was very upset.

The next morning, our friend called the house and said, "What the hell did you girls put in my drink?" She went on to say that back when she was young, she had done every kind of drug, so she knew she was high on something. I was mortified! I acted as though I had no idea what she was talking about, but I knew that Camila undoubtedly had put drugs in her drink as well.

When I confronted Camila, she denied it and we started fighting. She started screaming and yelling that I was hitting her, even though I wasn't anywhere near her, and had not hit her. I was dumbfounded and confused. Harper got out of bed and ran out of her room to see what was happening; she was understandably distraught, so I tried to calm her down. In the meantime, I asked Camila to stop. At that point, Camila picked up the phone and said she was calling the police on me.

That was it. She was literally insane, and I was done. It was yet another breakdown that made no sense. Crystal meth – and who knows what else – at its finest. I told Camila to be my guest and I left the house. I got in the car and started driving back to San Francisco. On the drive back to the city, she kept calling me and begging, "Come back, come back. I'm so sorry. I'm so sorry." I told her I was not coming back.

Toward the end, when Camila would get physical with me, I started fighting back instead of just trying to escape. For a long time, she would knock my lights out and then I would get up and run. She would run after me, tackle me, punch me, kick me and slap me. She would not let up. But finally, I stopped running and started fighting back. I did not want to hurt her – and I didn't – but I would put my hand around her neck and push her against a wall. My goal was not to choke her, but just to hold her there with my elbow locked so she could not get at me.

Even so, doing that made me sick to my stomach, because my mother was a choker. I never wanted to put my hands on anyone like that – even if it was just to hold them back. So, by fighting back against Camila, I had become someone who I never wanted to be. That is when I knew that I absolutely had to leave the relationship.

One evening back in San Francisco, I saw Camila put something in her pocket. I suspected it was drugs and because I wanted physical proof of it, I asked her what it was. She said it was nothing. I did not believe her and continued to ask her to show me what was in her pocket. When she would not show me, I went over to her and tried to put my hand in her pocket to pull out whatever it was. A huge struggle ensued. We began to wrestle on the ground, me trying to get in her pocket and she trying to not let me find whatever it was. The more she pushed me away, the more I knew I needed to see what it was. Camila had really long, manicured nails. She dug them into my hand, drawing blood. Then, just as I was almost all the way in her pocket, she bit right through the skin on my arm. I held on as long as I could, but she came up with a mouth full of my bloody skin. She was trying to rip the skin right off my arm!

I let out a blood-curdling scream, which surprised Camila enough to let go of me. Our next-door neighbors heard my screaming, and immediately raced over to our house. They were pounding and pounding on the door, worried about what was going on. I could not blame them for trying to get in or to at least get an answer. But I didn't answer the door; I didn't want them to see the bleeding bite marks on my arm. I was horrified.

To this day, I have scars on my feet, knees, face, hands and in other places on my body from Camila. Some of the bite marks on my arm have faded, but I still can see several leftover teeth marks. The scars and marks are constant reminders of that night when Camila's teeth tore through my skin – and the many, many other times she was so physical.

I will never allow myself to be in that kind of relationship again. Camila had provided an endless number of episodes over the years that should have prompted me to end our relationship and our marriage. However, it was her unabashed claim during that fight that she was a victim that made me fully realize that it was crazy. No way – I was the victim, not her!

I hated seeing myself as a victim, because I had always associated that word with weakness; but it was the truth, and the harsh reality that I needed to face. I had worked tirelessly for years to try to make Camila happy. I had tried to keep the peace, get her help, and save our marriage. But no more.

I did not want to be the victim anymore – not to her or anyone else. My mother may have trained me how to live through a continuous round of beatings, but it was a skill I no longer wished to use – I deserved better. I saw with searing clarity that the way to handle abuse was not to cope with it, but to leave it. I told her, "Camila, we're done. You're moving back to Texas."

CHAPTER NINE

I LEFT MY HEART IN SAN FRANCISCO

If my break with Camila had been clean and easy, who knows what my next career and relationship moves would have been? Of course, what happened was anything but simple; and, as with all things related to Camila, the fallout left me so bruised. I found myself struggling to rise above yet another whirlpool of chaos and destruction. Opportunities for good life choices don't usually flow from traumatic situations like that, and my situation was no exception.

Once I told Camila that we were finished, I realized that I would have to invest a fair amount of energy into untangling the threads of our lives. Even though Camila had not contributed financially to our household, she had helped me manage other parts of our lives, including the household errands. Of course, she had handled those activities only when she was well enough – or should I say, sober enough.

Still, she had access to my cars, my houses, my boat, and everything else that she shared with me in our relationship. And asking an addict like Camila to simply hand over the keys to everything would end up requiring more than just a polite request. There was also the fear that she might take or sell some of my belongings, which would have been typical of her (and most addicts).

One thing that worked in my favor – as twisted as it may seem – is that the legality of gay marriage had been reversed by that time. Separating from Camila did not legally require anything more than saying we were finished. Anything that I would give her as support or a settlement would be at my discretion. Even though I would have been entirely within my rights to leave her with nothing, particularly in light of her abuse, I chose not to do that. It just was not – and is not – part of my emotional or moral makeup to leave someone I love, or had loved, in financial or physical peril. And in this case, the emotional package included Harper, as well as her mother.

I told Camila that her behavior and abuse was damaging my mental health, my body and my work, and that I could no longer find a way to justify putting up with it. I told her that I would move her and Harper back to San Antonio, and that I would give her a one-time cash payment. I also told her that I would set her and Harper up in an apartment and would even provide her a car. Was I disappointed that she flat-out refused the offer? Yes, of course. Was I surprised? Absolutely not. Camila did not want to leave San Francisco, and still believed that she could get herself together and we could continue to be a couple.

My love for Camila was so consuming that, even with our breakup looming, I agreed that we could still work on our relationship as long as we did not live together. I had been asking Camila for several months to look for an apartment; I would cover the cost. She refused and continued to live as she had for the past four years. So, I started to look for an apartment for her, although she did not like any that I showed her. Little did I know that everything would come to a head very soon.

One afternoon, Camila was furious with me because I did not meet her at the salon where she was getting her hair done. It was a Friday; I was always beat at the end of a very busy work week that often also included some travel. So, I decided to go home to relax instead of joining her at the salon. The fact of the matter was, I needed some peace and quiet before I started a weekend with her. It was always impossible to predict because who knows what would happen on the weekend. How many different ways would she torture and antagonize me?

Camila was in a fury by the time she arrived home; she had taken my rejection of her request very personally. She was also higher than a kite, which meant she would rage on for hours. She immediately launched into yelling and screaming at me, telling me what a horrible wife I was for not meeting her at the salon. I tried to ignore her and watch TV, but that only stoked her anger.

Harper had not had dinner yet, so Camila took a few minutes out of her tirade to go into the kitchen and stick a chicken pot pie in the microwave. She then proceeded to carry it up to Harper's room, along with a bottle of Smirnoff she had opened for herself. We had a loft on the second level of our house that looked down into the ground-level living room, where I was still trying to watch TV. As Camila climbed the stairs to take Harper her dinner, she kept screaming like a banshee at me. I did not see that Camila had paused at the top of the stairs, where she decided to use that vantage point to launch the pot pie and plate at my head.

It all whizzed past me, just brushing my ear and smashing into the wall. The impact sent shards of crockery and bits of scalding hot pot pie everywhere – and I mean everywhere. Then, before the attack could even register with me, Camila sent the Smirnoff bottle sailing in my direction. It hit me directly on my left elbow, which immediately exploded into unbelievable pain. I knew my elbow was badly injured or broken – the swelling was immediate. It all completely shocked me.

I turned around in time to see Camila flying down the stairs toward me, and I ran as fast as I could. Sharp pain was shooting throughout my elbow and arm. She was acting so insane – no question that she was high beyond reason. I was scared for my life, and I admit I truly thought I was going to die that night.

I barricaded myself in the downstairs bathroom and called the police. Unbelievably, during all the years of abuse and beatings and fearing for my life, I had never before called law enforcement. Yes, I had threatened to do it, to try to get her to calm down during other crazy episodes. But I had never followed through. I was always too embarrassed to do it – and I never wanted her arrested. I especially did not want Harper to see that. But this time, I felt I had no choice.

The police came almost immediately and arrested Camila for assault with a deadly weapon. She insisted on taking Harper with her to the police station – which was irrational and wrong – but she refused to let Harper stay with me.

The police officers thought that either my arm, or my elbow was broken, so they called the paramedics. Upon arrival, the paramedics confirmed that my elbow was at the very least severely fractured, and they advised me to go to the hospital. But I refused to go. My trauma was so severe that going to a disorienting place like a hospital would have been just too much.

After the police hauled Camila away, I cleaned up the mess she had made, although I was still in shock. Because my left elbow was disabled, I could only use my right hand and arm. There were pieces of the broken plate and splatters of pot pie all over, not to mention remnants of the broken Smirnoff bottle and splashes of its contents all over the wall.

It took me quite a while to clean up everything, and by that time, the pain in my arm was excruciating. I have never been one to take pain killers or any strong medicine, so I took an ibuprofen and laid down to try and sleep. Just as I started to fall asleep, the phone started ringing. And it kept on ringing – for hours. The caller ID revealed that it was Camila calling from jail.

The first few times she called, I answered. But each time I did, I was subjected to an insane level of screaming, threats, and curse words. I had always heard that a prisoner was only allowed one phone call, but that clearly was not happening in this case. Finally, I unplugged my phone and fell into a fitful, painful sleep.

When I woke up a few hours later, I immediately thought about Harper. I knew I had to get Camila out of jail, so I pulled myself together and drove down to the police station; it was about 4 a.m. I was told that Camila was already out on bail! Some unnamed person had taken her and Harper somewhere. Then, it was my turn to call incessantly, and Camila only picked up after several hours of me trying to get through.

Of course, she would not tell me where she and Harper were, and she would not give me any logical explanation of how she had posted bail. She insisted that she had called a bail bondsman, but she had no money or assets. I could not imagine how she had made such arrangements. I wanted to gain an understanding about what was going to happen in her case, and I had a strong feeling that she was with someone who was providing her drugs. So, I paid the bail bondsman the $5,000 that Camila owed him, and started making arrangements to get her out of the house.

I would not allow Camila back into the loft after that. I paid for a hotel room for weeks for her and Harper while I figured things out. Then in order to put my plan in motion, I suggested to Camila that she take Harper up to the Napa house for a week, as it was Harper's spring break. Camila liked the idea, and off to Napa they went. I was supposed to go out of town for some meetings that week; but I canceled my trip and stayed home in San Francisco. I packed up all of their belongings, called a moving company and sent all of their stuff to storage. I changed the locks in the loft, and made sure there was no sign left of her there.

After I had been threatening for months to end our relationship, taking such measures was the only way I could make a clean break. But Camila must have asked someone to keep an eye on me and the loft; because she called me while she was still at the Napa house. "I hear there were moving trucks in front of our house. Is that for you or for me?" she asked. *Like I would move out of my own house!* I thought. "It's for you," I said. "You need to come back to the city and find a place to live. I will continue to pay for a hotel for you and Harper; but you have to find a place."

The most astonishing thing for me was that Camila was shocked that I had finally drawn a line in the sand. She seemed not to have any comprehension that her actions had resulted in consequences. Was it because I had capitulated so many times before? Was it because I had ignored or excused her behavior for so many years? Sure, it was. But she not only continued to refuse to take responsibility for her actions; she couldn't seem to connect the dots. She could not understand the extreme harm she had done to me, or that the chaos she brought to our lives was not sustainable. It had become a situation that no human being should have to endure, even for someone who loved her with the intensity that I did. Even getting arrested had not penetrated Camila's resolute obtuseness – which was brought on by drugs, denial, and her sheer force of will.

A glimmer of survival instinct had kicked in within me, although I still harbored a fantasy that Camila and I could work things out. I got her and Harper an apartment in San Francisco and I financially supported them for the next two years. We all spent time together on occasion; and I tried to get Camila help in the hope that she would get better. My goal was for us to find a safe common ground.

Instead, Camila spent all the money I gave her on drugs. When she ran out of money, she would call me and demand more. And of course, she could not work because she was screwed up and high much of the time. She was still incapable of holding a job. So, for two years, we would try to work on our relationship from time to time; but she would inevitably become the abusive person she always was. I would separate from her for several months; then, somehow, we would reconnect, and we would go through the cycle all over again.

At one point she came to my door at the loft, beating on it. I opened it and told her to go away or I would call the police. She sucker-punched me so hard – yet again – that I went flying. I landed on my back, and she came in and started kicking me. I rolled over into a ball to protect myself, but she continued to kick me – in the stomach, in the back, in the head, anywhere she could. I finally gave up and rolled over on my back, exhausted from being beaten.

She saw the blood all over my face, stopped kicking me and panicked; she grabbed towels and tried to help clean me. I told her to get the hell out or I would call the police and have her arrested again. That was enough to make her leave. But I left that blood on the floor for a while as a reminder of her destruction. I am sure that Nancy, the cleaning lady, thought, "What the hell goes on in this house?"

During the separation from Camila, I was distraught over losing my family – my wife and daughter. Even though the situations had been so tumultuous, I still loved them both very much. And – typical of the dynamic in an abusive relationship – it was difficult for me to get out and let go. Camila had convinced me – and I had convinced myself – that I could not leave.

So, I decided to go to counseling to try to make sense of it all. I had never been to counseling for any of the trauma earlier in my life; but I felt like I needed some assistance for what I was going through at that moment. I still had PTSD from all my childhood trauma; but I had added a new level of PTSD due to the abuse from Camila, and losing my family.

Jody, the therapist, listened to the stories of my marriage and Camila's abuse. She gave me some textbook feedback, but was never very insightful or helpful. At one session, about five weeks into the counseling, I told Jody that I was completely overwhelmed with trying to manage my life, because Camila used to help run our household and now it was all on me. I explained that I was having a hard time figuring out how to juggle tasks. I had to look after the houses and rentals, get the cars and boat serviced, make meals for myself, and run errands, among other activities. And I still had to work and travel while trying to make sure Camila and Harper were OK, even though they were not living with me. After Jody listened to me vent, she tilted her head far to one side, looked me directly in the eyes, and said, "And you only pay me $50 an hour!"

I could not believe it. Was I putting her out or taking advantage of her in some way? Never mind that the $50 was just my copayment, and that my insurance covered the majority of her fee. I cannot recall how that session ended, but it definitely upset me.

Soon after that, Jody convinced me to attend a group that she had put together of former addicts and spouses of former addicts. I was not sure if I wanted to talk about my life with a group of people I did not know, as I had never shared my feelings much. In fact, I felt that I had already branched out quite a bit just by seeing Jody. Finally, though, I decided to give it a try.

It was a small group, and I did not share much during the first meeting. I managed to open up a little more in each session I attended. At my third session with the group, I started sharing more about Camila, and at one point I referred to her as "crazy." That was actually a fact, and not intended as an insult. But the moment that I said "crazy," I saw Jody's head tilt far to one side again. I thought, *Oh great, I made her mad.*

After I was finished, Jody said to the group, "I want to address something Kendra said." She went on to ask the group how they felt about me calling Camila crazy. The entire group of former addicts immediately started hammering away at me; Jody allowed them to verbally beat me up. They went on and on about what a bad person I was for calling Camila crazy, and how inappropriate it was, and that I had no idea how Camila felt. I was in shock.

The spouses of addicts in attendance did speak up a little for me, which helped soften the blow – slightly. But the fact that Jody allowed people who knew nothing about me to attack me in a therapy session – just because they were offended by the word I used about my crackhead spouse – was mind-blowing.

I was so hurt and angry. When they were done beating me down and had established what a bad person I was, I said to the group and to Jody, "Camila beat the shit out of me for years, she broke my nose multiple times and broke my elbow, I had to have her arrested, she spent tens of thousands of dollars of my money on drugs, she lied constantly to me, and she cheated on me and stole from me." I added, "I have spent hundreds of thousands of dollars to support her and her daughter over the years. I tried to give them an amazing life and tried to get her help; in fact, I am still doing so. She was physically, verbally, emotionally and mentally abusive to me, and I have scars all over my body from her beating me so many times – so, if I want to call her crazy, I will f-ing call her crazy!"

After I was done defending myself, I really wanted to just get up and leave. But I did not want to be dramatic, so I waited until the session was over, and then I left. And I never, ever went back. I thought, *So much for counseling. I will clearly need to get through this on my own, just like I have with all of the other traumatic events in my life.* And I did.

What had become the "volleyball" nature of my relationship with Camila – of separating and not speaking for months, and then reuniting to try again because she swore she was clean – went on and on. After a separation, we reconnected again for one final concerted effort to make it work. In a desperate attempt to make her happy, I agreed to get us a different apartment "together" when I started my new job in Chicago. I would be living in a corporate apartment in LA and in Chicago, dividing my time between two cities by that point.

So, I moved out of my loft, put most of my things in storage or in the Napa house, and got a bigger apartment for Camila and Harper. I moved a few of my things there too, so that I would have them when I would visit with her and Harper. We would either stay there in San Francisco or we would go to the Napa house for the weekends.

But as usual, a few months into that new arrangement, she fell off the wagon again. One night in Napa, she kicked the shit out of me. That was the last time. I was really done – for good. I told her she had to move back to San Antonio; I would not continue to pay for her to live in San Francisco. I left for Chicago for work the following day, and did not go back to San Francisco for a month.

I had a vacation coming up, and I planned to go to Aruba. Since Camila and I were now officially broken up, I took my ex-girlfriend Olivia, who was still a close friend. When I returned from Aruba, I went back to

Chicago for work, where I also met my dad and his wife to celebrate my birthday. It was during that trip that my father told me that he and his wife, Rosie, had been discussing the Camila situation. Knowing how devastated I was, they offered to allow Camila and Harper to come and live with them in Oklahoma. He said that they would make sure Harper went to school every day and that her needs would be met. He added that they would get Camila into a rehab program near where they lived so they could keep an eye on her.

I thought about it, and thought it might just work – one last effort to save her and our marriage and our family. So, I flew back to San Francisco to tell Camila the news. I was excited.

But from the moment I stepped into the apartment we "shared," I knew I had been too optimistic. I could see men's clothing everywhere and drugs strewn around. There was a pile of unpaid traffic and parking tickets issued to people who had been driving my Hummer, as well as another car I had bought for Camila. Some of those tickets had been written out to a guy by the name of David Stallone. I saw his name and address on the tickets.

Something snapped in my brain. This guy had been driving the cars that I was paying for; using the money I gave to Camila, and staying in the apartment that I was paying for so that Camila and Harper could have a home. Clearly, he was someone who had been providing Camila with drugs and doing them with her.

I immediately got in my car and drove to the address on the tickets, which was not far away. My black Hummer was sitting in the driveway in the front of the house. I immediately called the cops to report my Hummer stolen. While I was waiting for the police, Camila came out of the house and saw my car blocking the driveway so the Hummer could not leave. Then a man – who was obviously David Stallone – got out of the driver's side of the Hummer. I had no idea that he had been sitting in the car the whole time.

Camila started screaming at me to move my car. I told her I wanted my Hummer back. She was screaming that it was her Hummer too; well, I had paid for it, but she had convinced me to also put her name on it. Big mistake. When David got out of the vehicle, I saw him stick something in his pocket. *Jesus, what was that? Drugs? A gun?*

When the police pulled up, I told them that the car in the driveway was mine and I wanted it back. "And by the way," I continued, "the guy standing in front of my Hummer just put something in his pocket when he got out of the car." The police frisked him and pulled whatever it was out of his pocket. When they told him to put his hands against the car, he took the stance as if he knew it well.

The police were not any real help. Because the car was sitting on private property, and because Camila's name was on the registration with mine, I couldn't take it. Even though my name was listed first on the registration and I paid for it, I couldn't take it. The police pointed out that if it was in a public parking lot or on a street, I could have access to it – but because it was in a private driveway, there was not anything they could do.

I was still incensed; and I tried to tell the police exactly how f*#ked up Camila and David were and how bad the situation was. They stunned me; they said that they knew. They informed me that both Camila and David were well known to the Burlingame police (Burlingame was where the apartment was located, and conveniently enough, where

David also lived). They advised me to just look after myself, and that possession of a car was not worth a tangle with these two.

Even though I knew that Camila was a hard-core addict and a source of never-ending trouble, I had always avoided thinking about how she got her drugs and who she was with when she got high – it was too hurtful. I never wanted to believe it was as bad as it was; but the confirmation by the police officer forced me to think, and think hard. Once you know something, you cannot unknow it.

Now I knew – really knew – and I could not come up with excuses for Camila anymore – or excuses for me to take her back. I drove directly to a storage place and rented a storage unit. Then, I got a U-Haul truck, drove to Home Depot, and hired several workers from the parking lot there. We drove to the apartment that I had provided for Camila for two years, and moved nearly everything (except for personal effects and some furniture and kitchenware) out to storage.

I emailed the apartment management and canceled the lease. I did not care how much money it would cost me to break the lease; I was not going to pay for Camila and her drug dealer boyfriend to live there anymore. After that, I loaded up the men's clothes and drugs and threw them in the trunk of the car I had bought for Camila and then I took off in the car for the Napa house. I needed to sleep.

Not long after I got on the road to Napa, Camila called and started screaming at me for taking the things from the apartment (which actually had been my apartment and my things). The only thing I had taken that was not mine was the men's clothing and drugs. I am not sure exactly why I took them – and had no idea what I was going to do with them – but I suppose it was some sort of revenge on David for being with my wife, living in my home, spending my money, driving my cars, and giving Camila drugs.

David took the phone from her – he was high and furious – and started threatening my life if I didn't bring his "things" back. I said, "Your things? You mean, your drugs that my money paid for, that you left in my house?" He then said that if I didn't bring his things back, he would kill me and kill my family. He said he knew exactly where my family lived in Oklahoma, because Camila had told him all about it. And then I could hear Camila screaming in the background, also saying that they were going to kill me.

I hung up, shaking, scared for my life. I called my dad to ask him what he thought I should do; he advised me to call the police. I then called my good friend and neighbor in Napa, who Camila had previously drugged. Her husband had been with the local sheriff's department for several decades, so I asked to speak to him.

He advised me to take all of their stuff back and leave it somewhere convenient for them to pick up. He added that I should then call them after dropping everything off, and that I should tell them where I left it. He said, "You don't want to mess with people that are high like that and who definitely have arrest records."

So, that is exactly what I did. After it was all done, I was exhausted. It was late, so I decided not to go to Napa; I checked into a nearby hotel. I thought it would be a safer place to stay than the apartment that I had leased for Camila, where I had just broken the lease. I thought that Camila and David might be there, or might return – and that could be dangerous. I knew that they must have driven back there earlier that day, because they knew the drugs were gone. Who knew if they were still there? I was afraid they would follow through on their promise to kill me. After all, Camila had a long history of violence with me; and after David threatened to kill me and my family, I had no doubt that he was the same type of violent person, if not worse.

After checking into the hotel, I lay down – completely wiped out. I breathed a sigh of relief that I was safe, and that the drama was done. But the relief did not last long. A police officer called me to tell me that Camila and David had filed a temporary five-day restraining order on me. I was floored. I am the most nonviolent person on earth! "Why would anyone need a restraining order against me?" I asked the cop, who explained that they alleged that I had gone back to David's mother's house to harass them about the Hummer. "That is an absolute lie; why would I do that?" I asked. He told me there was nothing that could be done; he also told me to steer clear of Camila and David because they were trouble.

I am not in the habit of breaking the law. I also believe in following police officers' instructions, so there was no way I would have gone back to the house. I told the cop that I could prove that I had been at the apartment packing and moving things out. He said he knew that the restraining order was a false filing. Nevertheless, he said, he would have to serve it to me, and he could not do anything about it. It was clear that Camila and David filed the false restraining order to keep me from trying to take the Hummer. Evidently, they were worried about that.

Still shocked, I told the police officer which hotel I was staying at so he could come and give the order to me. When he arrived, he had some very sound advice for me. He had once been in a similar situation himself with an ex-girlfriend who filed a false restraining order; she had also lied to get it. So, the police officer kindly led me through the steps of what I would need to do over the course of the next 24 hours. I will never forget that guy. He did not have to take the time to give me all that information – essentially giving me a roadmap to safety and freedom – but he did. He spent about 45 minutes talking to me.

I had never had to deal with such legal issues or with the police in that way, so I would have been at a complete loss without that officer's valuable guidance. One vital piece of information he provided was that I needed to file restraining orders against both Camila and her boy-friend – the very next day. He told me exactly how to go about filing the orders, and I immediately started that process the following day.

I also quickly hired an attorney to help me through the steps of get-ting a long-term restraining order on them both. It meant that I would need to go to court to testify to a judge about what had happened and explain why I needed such an order. I was successful; the judge gave me a five-year restraining order on Camila, and a three-year restraining order on David. The restraining order on David was shorter than Cami-la's because I did not have a history with him.

I felt that it was necessary for Camila to move back to San Antonio; but it took me time to negotiate. I started off by telling Camila that the apartment had been canceled and she would have to find somewhere else to live. But I also told her that I would move her and Harper back to San Antonio; I said I could help get them set up there and I would give her some money.

I was willing to help her get a new start even though I felt so much pain and anger – even a tinge of hate – over what had happened. I could not help but wonder, *Where is her loyalty to me?* I had taken care of her and her daughter for six years; I had given them an amazing life. I married her and let her take my last name. I gave her whatever she asked for, and I treated her like a queen. She had professed her undying love for me, yet she had made my life miserable. Even though she beat me, and verbally and emotionally abused me like my mother had, I still loved her.

How could she have cheated on me with that loser, and most likely with many other losers, over the years? For drugs? I was devastated. After discovering the sickening truth about Camila's drug dealer boyfriend, I had no love for her anymore. I just wanted her out of my life for good.

Still, because I had moved her and Harper to San Francisco to be with me, I felt obligated to set her up in a new life. I felt strongly that she should be in San Antonio, where she was from, and where her family still lived. She said no. She continued to live in the apartment until the 30-day notice was up. I assume that during that time, she was negotiating with David to live with him and his mother. But apparently, David dumped her when he realized that the gravy train was over.

Camila called me several times during the last week of the apartment lease, screaming at me for ruining her life and leaving her stranded. Mind you, this was an adult woman, who – if not for being a severe drug addict and alcoholic – should have been perfectly capable of working and supporting herself. Finally, when Camila realized she had no other options but to take my offer to move her back to San Antonio, she finally agreed to go.

There would be more drama first. She almost totaled my Hummer while high and in a fit of anger. She also had hidden some of my mail for months. I had not realized that, and because I never saw my car insurance bill, my insurance was canceled. With no car insurance to cover the damage she had done to the Hummer, I ended up paying over $16,000 out of my own pocket to fix it.

Camila's trail of terror seemed to have no end. But I endured it, dealt with it, and moved her and Harper back to San Antonio. I was so relieved and glad that that part of my life was over. And to make the whole situation land a little softer, my marriage to Camila was no longer legal. Six months after we got married, the California Supreme Court voided all the gay marriages from earlier that year. So, I did not have to actually divorce Camila. What a big relief. I thought I was finally free.

But, as my dad says, "That's what you get for thinking." A few months after I moved the girls back to San Antonio and tried to start moving on with my life, I had to go to Minneapolis for work. On my way home, while sitting in the airport, I saw a news report on TV in the airport that should have been something to celebrate. Instead, it terrified me. The newscaster announced that all gay marriages in San Francisco that had been voided were now legalized again; all former gay marriages were grandfathered in as legal. I almost threw up. *How could that be? It is four years later.*

I did not want to be married to Camila! How could they just decide that my marriage was legal again? There had been no legal action that I needed to take when we split. But now, I was tied to her again, and the idea of having to engage with her as a partner was horrifying. I got on my flight in a state of panic. I thought that if Camila happened to hear about the reinstatement of our marriage, she would want to divorce me and get "half," per California law.

Strangely, by the time I landed back in LA, the marriages were not legal again. However, all the agonizing I had done over the four-hour flight was enough for me to decide: *Screw this, I'll hire a divorce attorney anyway and I'll figure out what I should do.*

I thought that it would probably only be a matter of time before the marriages were considered legal again, so I would need to be proactive. The divorce attorney I hired told me that we needed to file for a dissolution of marriage. So, he filed for me, and he had to track Camila down to get her to sign it. Predictably, I ended up having to pay a settlement to her so that she would sign the papers. But I figured that it was a small price to pay to really be done with her forever. The marriage was dissolved, and Camila – her addiction, her violence, and her chaos – was gone. So was her fierce love, but that love was too dangerous and it could not compensate for the immense damage she created.

CHAPTER TEN

A NEW BEGINNING, IN HELL...

I should have known it was too good to be true. But I saw no signs of criminal activity or danger when I first met Dick, the CEO of a small, virtually unknown Chicago-based company called ZVL Parking. Dick had heard about me through the industry grapevine and approached me a few times during 2007 to try to hire me away from Center Parking. I had been with Center Parking since I had arrived in Los Angeles, 14 years earlier. During that time, I moved around a lot with the company, because every promotion brought a geographical move along with it.

My strategy to build my career was to move up the ladder as quickly as I could. It helped that I was willing to move to wherever a promotion took me. After Los Angeles came promotions to Dallas, San Antonio, Atlanta, Chicago, Cleveland, and lastly San Francisco – all with Center Parking. I have managed thousands of properties in over 180 cities in North America, as well as thousands of team members, involving hundreds of millions of dollars in revenue during my tenure. It has added up to a lot of airline miles. Those promotions and moves sometimes occurred every other year, but I did not mind, because I was swiftly moving up the corporate ladder. I worked hard, very hard, harder than anyone else I knew – and still do to this day.

That has been my MO – to be faster, smarter, and more persistent than anyone – and to work incessantly to win. I was and still am extremely competitive, which has also contributed to my success. Growing up with lots of brothers and a competitive father created an edge in me. And because I do not like to lose, I worked at lightning speed to accomplish my goals. I always juggled more work than I should have – more than most people are capable of doing – while "keeping my eye on the prize."

I knew how to win potential clients over and close deals with them. I showed them the considerable value we could bring to their properties. I showed them how we could increase their profit margin – sometimes significantly, depending on how poorly their property had been managed up to that time. I dug deep – exceptionally deep – into every property's operation to retool them. I found ways to increase existing forms of revenue, create new revenue streams, and reduce expenses.

I negotiated contract after contract to bring more profit to my company. I also negotiated union contracts all over the country; doing that was never a favorite activity of mine, but it was necessary to our business. I was exceptionally detail-oriented and very good with numbers, which helped me find all kinds of nuggets of hidden profit.

I built trust with my clients. One of the keys to my success was to always deliver on my promises – never over-commit, always under-commit, but over-deliver. I was no-nonsense at work – I expected my team to work hard – but I was also a compassionate, kind boss. In every new territory that I took over, I usually became friends with some of my clients, as well as with my team members. It is inevitable that you will form bonds when you work closely with people and spend so much time together. Those bonds served us all well, because people want to work with people they trust. Those friendships are still intact for me today, in many cities across the US.

Both my industry and my company were male-dominated, which was and still is a huge challenge. It was a miracle that, as a woman, I was successful at Center Parking. Being a woman, as well as a lesbian, made my rise in the industry very difficult. It was a good ol' boys club through and through. Center Parking was based out of Nashville, Tennessee, and the founder was about as old-school and Southern as they came. Therefore, he did not look highly upon women, and that attitude trickled down through the company. Women were to be secretaries – or at best, on the human resources staff. Maybe, just maybe, if she was lucky, a woman could be part of the marketing team in business development. But run a piece of the company? No way! But it wasn't just my company's owner who thought that way – it was an industry standard that has changed little over the years.

There was one other woman who worked as hard as I did, and also created a tremendous amount of success for the business. The only reason I received attention and opportunity is because I created it for myself, just as she had. I was always looking for, and closing, new deals – always finding ways to make the company more money.

The company's focus was profit, so that became my laser focus as well. It is hard for management to deny someone an opportunity when they are consistently making the company lots of money. And so it went, year after year, move after move. I kept my focus on moving up the corporate ladder. Yes, I was fortunate and lucky; but I also created my own path.

However, I started to feel like the glass ceiling was pressing down on me at Center Parking – and since I was not ready to stop growing in my career, I felt it was time for a change. I had been a vice president at Center Parking for about six years. It was at that time that the company was sold and taken private. It was evident that there would not be any upward mobility for some time to come – for anyone. It was right around that time that Dick, the CEO of ZVL Parking, called me about the number two position in his firm – directly under him, in Chicago.

I had not cared for living in San Francisco – never did. It was not my kind of culture or weather – and after five years of living in hell with Camila in that city, the thought of getting away was extremely enticing. Everywhere I went in San Francisco, I was reminded of Camila, and it was heart-rending. I knew we were not going to last much longer. Leaving San Francisco would help me make a clean break.

As the glass ceiling at my job and the need to sever my relationship with Camila came together in my mind, ZVL and Dick came up on my radar. Or, more accurately, the opportunity came calling and would not stop calling until I finally answered the call – and the voice on the other end was Dick's.

Unbeknownst to me, several people in the industry had told Dick that I was talented, very good at running and growing a business, and making lots of money for my company. His excitement about hiring me did not seem sketchy at all. I had been in our industry for 14 years, and my reputation for kicking ass and getting excellent results – as well as being willing to travel or move wherever I was needed – preceded me.

No matter what else was going on in my life, I always made sure that my career was the constant, my biggest focus. Everything else in my life had to accommodate my career, if for no other reason than I had had enough of scrimping and saving when I was younger. I had started working at my stepfather's grocery store beginning at the age of 12 and continued humping it through college with multiple jobs – which included the many hours at the Rainbow Room, nannying, bartending, and waiting tables. I truly had learned the value of a dollar.

The focus on my career meant sacrificing a personal life in many respects, as well as the comforts of long-term romantic relationships and friendships. I also was never able to put down roots. But the sacrifice paid off when I started making more than six figures by the time I was in my very early 30s. "Six figures" does not have the same meaning today as it did in the late 1990s; but back then it was a lot of money for a 32-year-old living in Atlanta.

My income and lifestyle had quickly escalated when I moved to Chicago as a regional manager, when I was making over $250,000 in 2001. But it was not until I got to San Francisco in 2003 that I really hit my financial stride. I started making about $500,000 a year, plus company stock and full benefits. I was only 36 years old and very proud of my success, even though it came with so much personal sacrifice. I felt as though I had finally made it. I had definitely found success in a man's industry. But I had given up a great deal personally for my work – definitely more so than most men.

I bought my first boat at 33 years old, and my first weekend (second) home by the time I was 34. When Camila and I lived in San Francisco, I bought a second home for us in Napa. I also bought other places as investments, such as a condo on Miami's South Beach, another home in San Antonio, and land in Utah. And even though life was difficult because of the drama with Camila, we lived a very comfortable life.

While money and material things cannot buy you happiness, for me it was a measure of success. Even when I was 10 years old, I was hustling in my neighborhood for various jobs – lawn-mowing, cleaning houses and dog kennels, helping teachers grade papers, shoveling snow, holding garage sales or babysitting. The focus for me was to get out there and earn money.

Money equaled freedom, and that was and is the most important thing to me – freedom. When I was a child, that freedom meant I could buy the forbidden candy I wanted, or a toy I had been eyeing. As a teenager, it meant the freedom to buy a sweater or shoes that I had fallen in love with at the mall. Making money back then also meant that I could have the resources to get out of Oklahoma as soon as humanly possible.

As an adult, earning has also meant freedom; but I have moved on from buying candy to real independence – lots of world travel, nice homes, cars, and the ability to take care of myself without relying on the whims of a parent, a partner, or anyone else.

The bottom line is that I learned early that money is power, and I liked existing in the power position. Taking care of one's self and planning for one's future cannot be overrated. While I was growing up, no one else had done that particularly well on my behalf, so I had no illusions about whom the job would fall to as an adult.

Now, many years later, I have learned that the true measurement of success and happiness is not based on material things, but on one's inner soul, happiness, peace of mind, safety, and both physical and mental health. Still, because the idea of a dependent old age fills me with dread, I am saving money and planning for my eventual retirement.

While my career at Center Parking had afforded me financial and lifestyle freedom, growth usually comes with change. So, after Dick reached out to me several times, I finally agreed to meet with him. He was excited about the future of the company that he was running as a new CEO. He told me that he was considering buying several more companies, and then he wanted to take ZVL public. He said he wanted me beside him on Wall Street ringing that bell on the day when that would happen. He also set my bar (the bottom line) – I would earn 20 percent more to start than my then-salary. He also indicated a clear path to more than doubling that already large salary.

Dick had done his homework, and he knew that I was ambitious and always interested in a new challenge. He was also new to the parking industry in terms of operating and running companies, and he needed support and expertise to back him if he was going to shine in his new job as CEO. Dick came up with a high-level executive title for me as number two; I would oversee three of the companies and draw a salary commensurate with the title.

He dangled it in front of me. How could I resist that bait? That is how you move forward in the corporate world – you climb the ladder by changing teams. And joining a company at an executive level when it goes public is how you build your personal net worth. All of that was music to my ears. Who could say no?

In hindsight, I should have said no – but I did not.

At that point, everything about Dick and the company seemed completely normal – there were no warning signs in sight. So, I left Center Parking, accompanied by all the upheaval that naturally came from leaving the only job I had ever had in my chosen field. I then began to settle in as my new company's number two; I was determined to increase ZVL's market share and profitability. I knew I would be very good at accomplishing both goals.

ZVL was a privately-owned company started by six men in the mid-1950s whose children eventually inherited it when their fathers died. The company had been a big deal in its heyday because it had been the largest landowner in downtown Chicago. The money flowing through the company was no joke.

What was a joke, however, was how the company's heirs behaved and how they ran the company. I was not privy to the fact that the company was a shit show because of the chaotic, inept ownership and leadership – until I joined them. Nor was I privy to the fact that there was considerable illegal activity within the company, which had been going on since it was founded. And when I say illegal, I mean activities that could bring someone multiple life sentences in the federal penitentiary – that kind of illegal. The company participated in the types of activities that get people killed – and did.

The owners hated each other and fought constantly. If they were not trying to get each other fired from the board, or the company, they were suing each other, spying on one another, and taking part in all kinds of shenanigans that made it a very uncomfortable work environment.

Dick had not told me anything about the stress and tension these people created at the company, because he was part of it; and I did not do enough snooping around to find out about ZVL's ugly little secrets before I joined them.

It would be the most toxic and dangerous place I ever worked. Friends in the industry that knew of the company were horrified to find out about my new employment. One of them actually said, "Why would you work for that company? They're really, really bad people, they're criminals!" But gossip is gossip, until you live it. And man – did I live it!

When I received the job offer, I flew out to Chicago to see ZVL's new offices. They were incredible, particularly for a parking company. They were on the 41st floor of a very swanky Class-A office building downtown. They had half of the floor, which was a lot of space. When I walked in, the first thing I saw was a beautiful entryway and waiting room with a receptionist, and gorgeous conference rooms – all glass, with amazing views, big screen TVs, and beautiful custom-made conference room tables with chairs. Each conference room could seat 20 people. The ZVL offices had bells and whistles that parking companies never have.

Then I saw what would become my office. It was Dick's old office, and it was enormous – again, with beautiful views. I could not believe it. Normally, when you walk into the offices of any company in my industry, you would immediately think, *Ah, that's right, margins aren't huge in parking*. Parking company offices are often less than inspiring – even dreary.

Dick was no dummy. Once I saw the glitziness of ZVL, I was fully seduced, and I threw my lot in with Dick and his team. I did not notice how sketchy everything was about Dick and the company until things started really going sideways later. There may have been some red flags; but I was ready to leave Center Parking for a better opportunity, and ZVL had all the right stuff to lure me.

For the first 10 months or so with ZVL, I was on the road all the time. We were in the early stages of due diligence research in buying two parking companies. One was based out of Los Angeles and the other was based out of New York, but both had operations in many cities throughout the country. A big part of my job was to help work through acquisitions; and after the purchases, I would help merge those companies into our overall parent company. I always enjoyed working on mergers and acquisitions – M&As – in my previous company as part of a large team.

Those new company acquisitions were the front and center of my focus during and after the purchases. And everything was fairly positive in the early days with ZVL, except for all of the fighting among the owners, which was stressful and unprofessional.

Dick made a big effort to make me a part of things in the beginning. He even invited me to his house for Thanksgiving that first year I joined the company. By the time Thanksgiving came around, I had already been with ZVL for 11 months. I was happy to be included and to get a chance to know my colleagues better. Dick lived in the suburbs and drove a long way to get to work; he enjoyed having a huge house, and the only way to afford that in the Chicago area was to live far away from downtown.

His house was indeed spacious; you walked in through a big entryway with lots of dark wood. It had a very pretty sitting room, and formal living and dining rooms downstairs. At the back of the house was a pretty kitchen in the French provincial style. It too had nice dark wood but was fussy. In fact, the whole house was very stuffy to me – my taste in home decor is very modern, bright, and minimalistic.

Dick had two little girls that were dressed up in pretty dresses, tights and Mary Janes. I brought them gifts and played with them for a little while. Mrs. Dick was all dressed up too, with an apron over her holiday attire. She was plain and petite, with mousy brownish hair. She seemed to be a conservative housewife, wearing a preppy headband to hold back her straight shoulder-length hair while she cooked. Dick was in his usual gray slacks, white oxford shirt and black sweater, a combination that his wife bought in multitudes so he would never have to think about what he would wear to work.

But isn't that a sign of a psychopath – when dressing is so unimportant that blandness becomes a sign of personal expression? Is wearing the same outfit day after day a signal that there isn't any person inside there to express anything?

I have a difficult time relating to women who lose themselves and their identities in their husbands – giving up their career and goals and dreams for a man. It is not that I have a lack of respect for women who choose to do that – but I made a concerted effort not to follow that path, because that was what was promoted in my family and religion while I was growing up. My mom and dad wanted me to be that way; but it was not ever going to happen. I could not imagine how such a circumscribed life could make someone happy.

That is what I thought when I met Dick's wife – that she had put her own life on hold to accommodate Dick's career and priorities. She seemed like a Stepford wife.

When I was introduced to her, she immediately made a catty comment. She made an exaggerated show of being welcoming, and said, "Ohhhh, you're **THE** Kendra that Dick can't stop talking about." She decided to make her point even clearer after we sat down at the dining table. I was seated next to her when she responded to something Dick said about me; she rolled her eyes and muttered, "Kendra, Kendra, Kendra."

I am not easily offended, and did not care whether or not this woman and I would be friends – but it was a clear sign to me that something was not quite right in Dick's world. I had no idea if the weird vibe at the dinner was entirely created by Mrs. Dick, or if he had given her reason to act like a sullen teenager. Either way, there was an unmistakable black cloud of tension hovering over those two. Maybe it was because she knew she was married to a liar and a lunatic, facts that would take me just a little longer to figure out.

Dick had only a few years of practical experience in our industry; he did not know how to do many things necessary to run a financially healthy company. He had been in-house counsel for a parking company that had been sold and broken apart. When he found himself out of a job after the sale, one of his former company's owners advised him to talk with one of the owners of ZVL, Jack Bloom. Bloom offered him a position as in-house counsel, but Dick did not want to be limited to that role – especially for a smaller firm. He wanted to do more – he wanted to work in operations and help run the company – even though he knew nothing about operations and the field work of the industry. Smelling an opportunity, Dick made his hiring at ZVL conditional – he would join, but he needed to be more than an attorney. So, Bloom agreed to make him an executive vice president, or EVP, as well as counsel.

When Dick accepted the job, ZVL was a small company that had been doing business with some very large government clients in Washington, DC, for over 20 years – and they were very big, complex operations and deals. You do not just walk into getting those kinds of contracts – particularly in DC – without experience or connections. ZVL did not have substantial experience or the references to land those deals – so they figured out how to make the right connections. To be more blunt: a small business does not get those kinds of contracts and keep them for many decades unless there are questionable practices going on for a long time. Think about it – there were bigger, top-notch companies that already had the local infrastructure and support in place, and they could easily handle big operations. Those bigger parking companies were equipped to do a much better job.

So – why would a client go with a small, family-run company that was based far away in Chicago, and had no other operations in the DC area? There was only one answer: big payoffs of the less-than-legal kind. It took me some time to discover that information – but that only scratched the surface of ZVL's illegal activities.

I learned just how shady ZVL could be, and here is an example. Part of ZVL's business was with government agencies, which require that their contractors provide work for minority-owned companies. ZVL had a contract like that in New York City with a very large, very lucrative, city-owned property. The property was a cash cow, generating millions and millions of dollars every year. It was a sweet gig for ZVL, because New York City had parking rates that were so high that any parking garage would produce a **lot** of profit. That one definitely did. ZVL had held the contract on that city-owned garage for a number of years when the city finally audited the operation.

The audit revealed that $8 million was missing over the term of the contract. To put it more accurately, $8 million had been stolen. As in-house counsel and EVP, Dick had to negotiate a settlement between the city and his company for that huge breach and theft. The minority business partner had fled the country and therefore became a convenient scapegoat. So, Dick blamed the partner. Who knows how much of that $8 million the partner had pocketed, and how much went to ZVL – but the disappearance of the partner helped Dick divert some of the blame.

Of course, the city wanted the full $8 million back; and there was no way that ZVL was going to pay that. When he started figuring out how to settle with the city, Dick quickly saw that he had even more leverage than he anticipated. Moreover, he saw how he could personally benefit from the negotiation.

I learned during the more than three years that I worked at the firm that Dick is a narcissistic psychopath who lies so much that he cannot keep his lies straight. He charms his way into situations, and then lies his way out of them. Lying for him is as normal as breathing. It is in his nature; sometimes I am not even sure that he knows he is doing it.

Anyway, remember how Dick was not satisfied to be just in-house counsel? Well, he also was not satisfied to be in-house counsel and EVP. The deal that Dick cut with New York City stipulated that ZVL would return $4 million to the city (half of what was stolen); and Jack Bloom, the longtime CEO at ZVL, would have to agree to step down. It was actually the most bizarre negotiation and settlement I had ever heard of in our industry. Obviously, someone within ZVL – other than Dick – had it in for Jack Bloom, and blamed him for the enormous loss.

Naturally, as number two, Dick then stepped into the role of CEO. This is the same Dick who had no real understanding of parking industry operations; he had only started dipping his toe in it a few years before. I knew the lead auditor for the city in the case, and he later confirmed the amount of money that was missing. He also confirmed the agreement was that Bloom had to step down for five years. Bloom did step down, but he remained an owner and worked behind the scenes. Meanwhile, Dick was promoted to CEO, but he was left without someone to actually run the operations and grow the company. That is why he needed a number two and made me an offer I could not refuse.

Interestingly enough, right around that five-year mark when Jack Bloom was scheduled to return to ZVL, Dick stepped down as CEO and left the company, claiming it was for personal reasons. Bloom came back as CEO, but unfortunately, his return to the top was short-lived. Less than six months after his return, Bloom would be knocked off – literally, killed – seemingly by some of his partners.

Evidently, his associates were upset that he had put the company in peril and had hired someone like Dick, who further cratered the company and created more legal risk. But I suppose when you are involved in a plethora of illegal activities, it could be any one of many things that would get you killed. Dick may not have known much about parking operations; but he clearly knew how to get what he wanted – regardless of the fallout.

Once I started working at the corporate headquarters, I noticed that there were cameras all over the office. You would expect to see that kind of surveillance at New York City's diamond exchange, but not at the offices of a parking company. What did we have on site that needed that kind of security? An unsuspicious mind would say *nothing*, which is what mine did at first, even though I thought it was weird.

An even weirder detail about those cameras is that there were more of them on the executive side of the floor than on the other side, where the majority of the staff worked. Until you have been in a situation where a fact like that matters, it might vaguely register with you; but you certainly do not think about the meaning behind it. There were four of us on the floor's executive side: the new in-house counsel, Dick the CEO, me, and the vice president of Human Resources. The chief financial officer was on the other side, with all the accounting people.

The cameras and other surveillance equipment soon became the bane of my existence. The significance of those cameras was not entirely mysterious; I presumed they were linked in some way to the fact that ZVL operated – unofficially – as a cash business. The arrangement was very old-school. They would bring cash in from their 90-plus downtown parking locations that they owned, and people tallied the cash in a very secure money-counting room. It was then bagged up and sent to the bank.

With all the technology available to a business like ZVL, that should not have been happening at all – and certainly not happening on the 41st floor of a Class-A office building. Nonetheless, Dick and the owners had a secret cash-counting room in our amazing suite of offices that housed the executive team, and also served as the corporate headquarters. You might ask: Why would the cash flow in and out of the corporate offices, when ZVL had operational offices elsewhere throughout the city, which were more accessible for counting money? Good question.

Equally bizarre was how secretive Dick and his cohorts were about such potentially not-kosher behavior. No one was allowed in the counting room or was to know anything about how it was run – including me, the number two person, right under Dick. I could only come up with three reasons why that would be.

The first reason was to keep anyone from helping themselves to whatever cash they could get their hands on. However, I could not see how that could be possible, considering the company's Fort Knox approach to the safety of the money. The second reason – and I now know that this was the case – was that the counting room was also used to house all the closed-circuit TVs to view footage captured by all the office cameras. And the third and most important reason was that – like many mafioso groups – they were laundering money, and did not want anyone to be able to trace it back to them or that counting room.

Keep in mind that just one parking garage can generate millions of dollars in revenue per year. Multiply that by over 80 properties in downtown Chicago alone, and that adds up to an insane amount of cash flowing through the counting room in our headquarters. Now, extrapolate that kind of money over the hundreds of properties that ZVL ran across the United States. It was a **lot** of money.

I discovered another suspicious thing: ZVL would not take credit cards at our parking garages and lots – only cash. I would regularly propose my business case to ownership regarding the advantages of accepting credit cards over cash; I even presented a cost-benefit analysis. I insisted that we needed to get with the times – after all, it was the new millennium. I explained that credit-card payments would create streamlined revenue control, because cashiers were stealing money. That was proven through many audits. I tried to convince them that not only was it necessary for the growth of our business, but also that our customers were asking for it. It was an idea that fell on deaf ears every time I brought it up. Dick told me it was a fight I would never win.

The resistance to accepting credit card payment was an obvious red flag for me. Why would they be OK with the employees in the lots and garages stealing so much money? Well, the answer was: even though the employees would take their relatively small cut of the money, there still would be hundreds of millions of dollars of cash per year to launder. Taking cash meant there would be no way to trace how much money they needed to report in order to pay taxes.

The employees who were skimming money off the top were also the same employees that tried to attack our general manager, Doug. I had hired Doug from a competitor to oversee our Chicago operations. As a new manager, he knew right away that things were not right in the operations, and he was determined to bust the employees that were stealing. So, he started performing more spot audits in the lots – counting cars and money, and comparing them to the tickets issued and collected to try to prove that theft was occurring.

One day, he arrived at a lot where the attendant was visibly bothered by his presence. The employee got on the phone and called someone while Doug proceeded with his audit. A little while later, two men showed up on the lot and aggressively asked Doug what he was doing. He replied that he worked for the company and was auditing the lot. They came closer to him; one of them pulled out a taser and lunged at him. Doug dropped to the ground, out of fear of being attacked. The man began hitting him in the head with the taser while trying to tase him, but the taser was not working. When Doug realized they could not tase him, he jumped up and ran. Doug escaped with just a few bumps on his head; but if the taser had worked, the story certainly would have gone a different way.

At one point I shared some of these stories about ZVL with a friend of mine in Chicago, who had been in the industry for decades. He looked at me like I was crazy, and said, "Kendra, everyone knows those families do all sorts of illegal, sordid activities; and everyone in Chicago who has been in this industry for a while knows that they have always kept two sets of books."

Right before the financial crash of 2008, the company that Dick used to work for was about to file for bankruptcy. Dick wanted to swoop in, buy the company, and save the day. He would get to be the hero and his friends at the company would not have to cancel their country club memberships, turn in their Lexus company cars, or give up all the other niceties that they had amassed with their ridiculous spending.

A normal CEO works closely with his mergers and acquisitions team to do considerable due diligence on any potential acquisition to make sure the deal is in the best interest of his company. Dick and his initial team did some cursory due diligence, but either did not know how or did not care to dig deeper. So that task fell to our CFO and me, along with our teams.

Dick's associates had contributed to the aforementioned company's instability by undertaking many very bad deals. I quickly unearthed facts about those catastrophic deals during my research. The company had executed agreements on properties that were under construction, so they had not started operations yet. I found that because of the bad deals that the company had finalized, they would ultimately need to file bankruptcy or sell.

My analysis determined that a lot of the missteps could be fixed, but there were a couple of deals – deals that had not started up yet – that had serious problems. Those particular deals were so bad that ZVL's purchase of the company should have been called off when they were revealed.

Those deals would wind up costing ZVL Parking millions of dollars to fix. Still, Dick was so romanced by his own role as his buddies' savior, and by the power he felt in putting the deal together, that he brushed everything I said under the rug. He moved ahead and purchased the company. I was shocked.

The more that Dick worked with his old crew members and people like them, the more I could see that my downfall at the company would not just occur because Dick would run ZVL into the ground. I could see that it would also happen because I was a woman. And trust me – I do not say that lightly. Working for decades in a male-dominated industry, I never played the woman card. But in that particular situation, the gender issue was real. All of the work I did was criticized. I received constant pushback from most of the old white men in the companies that ZVL was buying. They thought of themselves as hotshots and desperately needed to be right. It follows that they certainly were not going to be told what to do by a woman – and especially a much younger person. Yet, these same men had put their companies in peril and almost bankrupted them.

The parking industry was and is a completely male-dominated field that embraced the good ol' boy network – and I was definitely not one of the good ol' boys. If the person doing my job had been a man, he might have been able to openly go to war with the old guard, and then reconcile on the golf course or over some scotches and cigars. Such a scenario would have still adhered to the outdated social codes they followed.

But a woman advising or contradicting them was insupportable and unconscionable in their minds. They did not have any socially acceptable mechanisms to deal with me. Their only choice was to blindly flail against whatever I did – to try to wear me down to a state of submissiveness, sabotage me, disrespect and disregard me – and try to make me into a soldier in Dick's army of yes-men. It was an insane battle of wills, and it made my job impossible. I had absolutely no chance of success.

When Dick bought his first company in an attempt to save it from bankruptcy, the number two person at that company was Harvey, who had the title of president. Harvey was incompetent – not only at running the business, but also at hiding his feelings in meetings. He was very old-school, meaning that he still wanted to run everything out of a cigar box. He refused any technology initiatives that were presented to him or any operational improvements that could turn a losing property into a financially prosperous one.

He soon made it clear what he thought about me. *How could this much younger woman be my boss? How could she know more about this industry than I, and how can she come in here and try to change everything?* As I remember how Harvey and other older executives in similar positions treated me, I am sure that those thoughts were in all of their minds when we interacted.

The "all" that I speak of were men who were mentally and emotionally stuck in a time when contracts were sealed on the backs of cocktail napkins. Their assessments of potential deals were made as they eyeballed properties from the comfort of their company Lexus or Caddy – not by using solid, historical, predictive data analyses and detailed financial proformas. And that is how they found themselves facing bankruptcy.

But back to Harvey. If we were in a meeting and I started talking about something in the company that needed to be changed, modified, or fixed, Harvey would get bright red in the face. His whole body would literally start shaking. He would jump out of his chair and start to scream at me – yes, actually scream – with spit flying out of his mouth. He would scream about how they were not going to alter or adjust anything. "How dare you come in here and start trying to make changes to our operation!" he would yell.

I have always tried to be extremely calm and diplomatic when dealing with my team, including people at the companies we had just acquired. For Harvey, I would allow him some time to scream at me until he ran out of the room, jumped into his company Lexus, screeched out of the garage, and left for the day. Typically, he did not not return until sometime the following day, arriving in the office whenever he felt like it. He would usually head to the golf course, because that is what he did best – golf. The son of the previous owner of the company, who was also in our meetings, would always apologize for Harvey. He would explain that Harvey had a bad temper and did not like change. It was nice that he acknowledged Harvey's bad behavior, although it did not do much to make me feel better or to move the company forward.

I made many attempts to tell Dick that the atmosphere was not healthy or productive, and that I was not able to bring about change in an environment where people would not allow it. He would nod gratuitously to me in false agreement – and then do absolutely nothing. As hard as I tried to work with the people who ran their company into the ground in the first place, it was clear that they were not going to adapt, nor were they going to let me make changes to save their company.

So, I realized that we needed to change **them.** They needed to move on. *We need to give them retirement packages and let them leave gracefully,* I thought. But that idea also fell on deaf ears. Instead of listening to me, Dick promptly bought another broken company that was owned by another one of his old cronies.

When it came to firing people who really should have been removed from the company, Dick just would not do it – they were his people, from his old company, and he wanted to protect them even if they were driving the business into the ground. With the purchase of two flailing companies, he saved his friends, looked like a hero, and cultivated his own crew of cronies within ZVL.

As I said, prior to the purchases of those two companies, I was part of a team who performed considerable due diligence on mergers and acquisitions, including contract/deal review and forecasting. In these two acquisitions I found that Dick's friends had made many terrible decisions while running their companies, which is why one company was almost bankrupt and the other was heading down that path.

One bad deal in particular stood out; it was with a hotel in San Francisco. The structure of the deal was so badly constructed that it should have reversed our decision to acquire the company. It was evident that we would lose millions of dollars per year by taking on the company. When I brought the details of that particular deal to Dick's attention, I suggested that we either fix the deal – and a few other problematic deals that the company had executed – or walk away from the acquisition. Dick was set on purchasing the company, though, and would not listen to anything I said.

A man named Kevin was the director of operations at one of the firms we acquired. I went to his facilities and investigated the operations. I looked at the staffing structure, and reviewed the profit and loss statement and the contract. I then recommended improvements to make the operations profitable, and asked Kevin to implement them. He agreed; but when I came back to town several weeks later and checked on progress, nothing had been done. Everything was still running the way it always had. Despite my requests for change, nothing ever did.

It was a constant battle at ZVL, and it became exhausting. I would tell Dick, "You can't buy a broken company that is on the verge of bankruptcy without fixing what is broken." I was a fixer, and I was very good at fixing. For example, in my last position at Center Parking, I walked into a very broken region with no leadership that was losing $3 million per year. By the end of the first year, I brought that loss down to only $1 million; by the end of the second year, we were in the black, turning a profit. I did the same thing in other cities and regions throughout my career. I enjoyed fixing broken businesses. But Dick would just not allow me to effect change at ZVL; he wanted to protect his friends at all costs.

Dick finally did agree to remove Kevin from his position – he was not one of Dick's old cronies – since he was not working to fix things in the field. We worked with our legal and HR departments to put together a severance package and a plan for the termination. The plan was: Dick and I would meet with Kevin in New York where he was headquartered, and we would give him the news and the severance documents together. Our plan was in place, and the papers were drawn up.

I took a redeye to New York and Dick was supposed to fly in the next morning. By the time I landed in New York, my newly-hired regional manager for New York was calling me. He said that Dick had decided not to fire Kevin – instead, he was promoting Kevin to vice president of our hotel division. I thought, *What the F?! We had a plan. We all agreed to it. Kevin is bad for the company and bad for business. He has to go – we all agreed with that. Now at the last minute, not only are we not firing him – but we are promoting him and giving him more responsibility? More power to cause more damage?*

It made absolutely no sense. It was a disaster – and literally an insane reversal of what was supposed to take place. But that was Dick – he was very unstable, and unable to make decisions and stick with them. His erratic behavior drove the company further into the red.

Soon, we needed to hire new people for a few regions, because we were growing – from acquisitions and organically. I needed to build a strong team that could make an impact on the operations, the employees, and the clients, in order to improve morale, relationships, and the bottom line.

First, I needed a formidable leader in New York to oversee that region. I immediately thought of a terrific, talented guy who had worked for me in Chicago. We had become friends when we worked together, but we had lost touch. His name was Steve Dryer, and I knew that he would be perfect for the job. I called him up, explained my plans for the company and for the region, and asked, "Would you be interested in the position?" There was a pause on the line. Then he said, "I knew you'd come for me one day, sister." He agreed to work for ZVL Parking to run the New York region.

Then, when I needed someone for the West Coast, I thought of Jeff Lott, who had worked with me in Los Angeles once upon a time. I reached out to Jeff, and he also readily agreed to work with me at ZVL Parking. Lastly, as we were negotiating a deal to break into the European market, I brought in Calvin Davis. I had also worked with him in the past, and he was an excellent operator and dealmaker. Calvin said yes too, and would move to London to start up our new London and Berlin operations. Steve and Jeff were hugely instrumental in making considerable improvements in their regions, and Calvin was working hard with me to plan our kickoff in Europe.

But once Dick understood how tight we all were – all four of us having worked together in the past – he was not happy. He saw that the four of us were powerful and effective together as a team; and, in his mind, that was a direct threat to him. Also, like a typical narcissist, he was desperate to be liked – to be part of a group and be accepted – and that was not happening with Jeff, Calvin and Steve.

It did not take long for the three of them to see that Dick was not to be trusted, and that there were strange things happening at the corporate office. They started to steer clear of him as much as possible – they kept their heads down and did their jobs. Due to his feelings of being threatened and left out, Dick started to do everything he could to make us all very uncomfortable.

Things started to happen, like Dick blowing up our phones to find us if two or more of us were coincidentally out of the office at the same time. He was always demanding to know where we were and what we were doing; presumably, he thought that we might be off having fun without him, or talking about him and the shady goings-on. That was never the case, because we all took our positions seriously. There was no monkeying around for us – only very hard work to make sure that we were successful and that the company improved.

Dick would also ask Jeff, Steve, or Calvin for their opinions on something, and then delight in shooting down their ideas (as he had often done with me), mocking them with his cynical grin and cocky laugh.

He began to dig into their personal lives, asking inappropriate questions and making strange comments about things he saw on their social media accounts – things that were none of his business. This was before there were more effective ways to lock down one's social media, so it was not difficult for him to gain access to our accounts.

We did wonder why a busy CEO would waste his time cyberstalking his employees and making weird remarks about what he had viewed on their social media. For example, Dick would compliment my regional managers on their pretty girlfriends or wives, based on what he had seen on their accounts. We all knew we had not "friended" him on our accounts – it seemed clear that he was shadowing us online.

For Jeff, the final straw was when we found a listening device that Dick was using to monitor us in private conversation. It made Jeff so uncomfortable that he left ZVL Parking and went back to his old firm. It only took Dick about nine months to get him out.

Steve and Calvin were not going to leave so easily. But Dick manufactured a ridiculous story about missing money, implicating Steve, and used it as ammunition to try to fire him. The fact that he thought Steve had stolen money was utterly ridiculous. First, Steve did not operate at the level in the field to have access to cash. Second, I had known Steve for years – he was a very honest guy. He was not stealing money.

Dick did not have any proof whatsoever that tied any wrongdoing back to Steve, but he really thought his fabrication would hold water. In hindsight, knowing now about all the funny business that ZVL did with embezzlement and money laundering, it appears to me that Dick was trying to set up Steve. Dick was looking for someone to take the fall for some of his own underhanded activities.

Dick actually developed a severance package for Steve and planned a trip to New York to let him go. Literally right before his flight to New York, he decided not to, and allowed Steve to continue in his role. That was one way that he instilled fear in us and flaunted his power over us; it was his way of letting everyone know he was still the boss. Things were going to be done his way, no matter how bad it would be for the company – or for us.

Dick did, however, succeed in firing Calvin. I won't go into a lot of detail, but it was for a very ridiculous, manipulated reason. Calvin was a more recent hire without a role in the US, brought on board for our European operations. Unfortunately, those operations were falling apart due to unforeseen incidents with our would-be overseas clients. So, at that point, there was not much of a reason to keep Calvin – and I was tired of the fight. I knew it was better for Calvin to work somewhere else instead of at ZVL's three-ring circus.

When it came to making decisions for the company, Dick just did not make good ones. They were based on his narcissism, his ego. He always did what would make him look good to his friends in the two companies he bought, and what would make him appear powerful.

One seemingly good thing came out of working at ZVL – or at least I thought it was a good thing, until it was not. ZVL had sold a parking lot in downtown Chicago to a large international entertainment firm that wanted the lot for development. Not only did we earn a very pretty penny from the sale, but we also picked up contracts to run the parking and transportation for their arenas in London and Berlin. Those were the European operations that Calvin had been hired to run. I dove head-first into planning for the opening of the operations. I was very excited, because I had always wanted to work internationally; my former company, which had offices and operations in a dozen other countries, had refused to send a woman to work abroad.

The plan was for us to open the London operations in time for a series of 50 scheduled *This Is It* comeback concerts by Michael Jackson at the firm's arena in London. After that we would open operations in

Berlin. During the planning for the startup of operations, I was given a tour of the arena's back of the house and shown various areas and activities we would manage.

My guides showed me Michael Jackson's short path of travel to his dressing room, from the point where he would be dropped off by his limo. As I walked the arena hallway with several of the vice presidents of operations, we rounded a corner, and one of them commented that Michael's golf cart could barely make that turn. I stopped dead in my tracks, very confused. I said, "Golf cart?"

Their response was, "Yes, Michael doesn't walk anywhere."

Surprised, I said, "So you're telling me that you are expecting a guy who hasn't toured or performed to this level in years, and who is at least 50 himself, to do 50 concerts in a row, singing, with choreography and dancing – but he can't even walk to his dressing room?"

They looked at each other and then looked at me and just started laughing. It was not clear to me what was so funny; but we continued with our walk-through.

Tragically, just a month later, before any of the shows, Michael passed away. Our international deal that was contingent on kicking off with Michael's concert series fell apart. After the death of Michael, the entertainment company now had to deal with bigger issues than a parking contract.

At the same time that we were working on operations in Europe, I was trying to increase the revenue and profitability for the new acquisitions that had been purchased at Dick's insistence. One company was based out of Los Angeles and owned by an absolute ass named Moses. OK,

Moses was not his real name – but he had to be pushing 90 and he had no business running a company in his condition. Moses was as toxic as the other ol' boys. He also did not want any change – and he absolutely hated women. He would talk trash behind my back; and he would say to my face, "You're not doing anything to my company. You're not making any changes."

So, there I was, spending all my time battling former owners, presidents, and vice presidents in various regions from those two broken companies – always trying to stay calm, being the bigger person, and never allowing my emotions to show. Yet, I could not make changes. In other words, I could not do my job. The amount of unprofessionalism and harassment that I experienced at ZVL was something I had never encountered in the corporate world before. It was exhausting, to say the least.

As for Dick, he was in a torturous situation of his own making – he desperately needed me and our teams to run the companies, but he was not letting any real improvement happen. His motivation came from a mix of greed for power and psychotic emotions – never a positive combination.

Not long after we bought the two parking companies that were already in financial peril, the crash of 2008-2009 happened. ZVL's board, like every other corporate entity in the country, panicked about bleeding revenue and profit. They mostly blamed Dick, but they also blamed me, for acquiring companies that were total losers and that became even bigger losers after the crash.

Our board was made up of the heirs of the original founders, none of whom cared about the actual business of parking, or about our employees or clients. However, they definitely wanted the business to continue to be their cash cow.

One day, I was working at my desk, when Dick came in and said, "Listen, I've got a company coming in tonight to do a bug sweep of the office." I just looked at him, very confused. "What?" I responded. He says, "Well, we think that maybe two of the board members, Nancy and her son, put listening devices in the office. So, we're going to do a sweep tonight." I thought, *What the hell? What kind of company is this?*

This was horrible. *All I do is park cars. That is all I do. I just want to work and support myself, but this company is clearly screwed up.* The drama from the dive in the market, the crazy owners, and the battles between the owners of the companies we bought was too much! After adding the money laundering, embezzlement, politician and government employee payoffs, and other very shady business, it was like working in an insane asylum.

The next day, I noticed colored stickers on all the doorways to the offices on our executive side, and a few on the other side at the chief financial officer and controller offices. I did not really think much about it at that time. I realized later that they were not searching for bugs; they were installing them. I know that because I found several of them months later. But more on that shortly.

My relationship with Dick got stranger and more strained. I lost any shred of respect that I still had for him. He had sold me a bill of goods. I left a company where I was very well respected, and joined his company – where I was harassed, rendered powerless, and set up to fail. But that was only the beginning. I was "beaten up" all the time by a bunch of old cartoon-character white men who had let their businesses go down the drain, and were utterly disrespectful. It was becoming untenable.

It was not where I thought I would be at that stage in my career; but I tried to make the best of it. I kept plugging away, trying to make a difference where I could. I had been focusing on merging and improving the operations of our acquisitions, renegotiating existing contacts, and restructuring, but also focusing on growing our portfolios organically. I decided, however, that it would be better to really concentrate on new business growth for a while instead of continuing with the old drama.

I started encouraging managers in each city and each region to add new locations and bring in new high-profit properties. That would help offset the bad deals that were made even worse by the decline in the economy. I did everything I could to help my team members accomplish those goals whenever they wanted my help – from initial outreach and meetings with potential clients, to underwriting and finding improvements in potential deals, to making presentations on our services, and finally, to negotiating and closing the deals.

After spending a fair amount of energy and effort with my teams on new business growth over many, many months, I presented the results of the campaign to the ownership to explain what I had been working on with our regional teams. I also wanted to show the owners what the new growth was doing for our company's bottom line. We had added 86 new properties across the US and generated millions of dollars of new revenue through our laser-focused efforts – not bad for a somewhat small firm.

After my presentation, one of the board members, the aforementioned Nancy, looked around at all the other owners in bewilderment.

Then she looked at Dick and said, "This is incredible. Nothing like this has ever happened in this company. Dick, you never brought in that many new locations when you were EVP. Why haven't we been doing this all along?"

That was not the response I expected. I shrank in my seat, knowing that her question would anger Dick. I could see Dick's face literally change to several shades of red – he was furious that he was called out like that. What I had intended as a celebration of new, high-yield business turned into a disaster. I could tell that the incident made the downward spiral between Dick and me much worse.

All the drama was causing me to become increasingly stressed. My heart rate would escalate at times, beating very fast. I scheduled an appointment with a cardiologist to make sure my heart was not going to explode. (Sometimes, it felt like it would.) The doctor prescribed a beta-blocker for me to take when I felt my heart racing, which at that point was daily.

After my doctor's appointment, I went home to lie down for a little bit. However, almost immediately, my assistant called – she told me that Dick wanted to know where I was. I told her that – as she already knew – I had been at a doctor's appointment and would be back when I could. She apologized and said that Dick just wanted me in the office.

It was another example of his increasing need to feel in control. More and more, he wanted to keep track of where I was. He figured that if he knew where I was all the time, I could not do anything behind his back.

What exactly would I be doing behind his back? Make the company more money? But I later learned that he would go into panic mode if he could not hear me through the listening devices that had been planted in my office, car, and in other places. He would also be anxious if he could not see me in the monitoring system, through the cameras installed in the executive side of the offices.

Was he worried that I was talking to the police or FBI, ratting out the company's illegal practices? It occurred to me that when someone accuses you of bad behavior, it is likely they are doing that very thing themselves.

In my mind, Dick had established himself as a blatant and unrepentant liar. For example, in executive meetings, he would contradict and deny previous statements he had made in private to the executive committee. Why did he lie so much? We – his colleagues – all questioned it, and did not understand it. And we actually joked about it when he wasn't around.

Or so we thought he couldn't hear us joking about it. With the listening devices that were installed, and later discovered everywhere, he was most likely listening to the mockery. That, no doubt, only made things worse around the office. Nevertheless, whatever he was taking part in – the irregularities in the counting room, the questionable nature of the cash business, the backdoor deals – made Dick paranoid, and he could not keep his lies straight. We were all confused by his baffling, unstable behavior.

In a last-ditch effort to make me an ally – and most likely to ensure that I was not reporting illegal activities to the authorities – Dick hired a new assistant for me. He knew I was gay, and somehow knew that my girlfriends tended to be very pretty, very feminine Latinas (probably from stalking my social media – which I promptly shut down after learning what he was doing). The woman Dick hired for me fit the profile to a tee; and he openly gave me a winking, elbow to the ribs, as if to say, "See what I did for you?"

How was I supposed to respond to that as a woman? What would a guy do in that same situation?

My new assistant happened to be a lovely person. When I finally moved from San Francisco, to split my time between our headquarters in Chicago and our Los Angeles office – because the larger firm we acquired was based in LA – I needed a housekeeper. My assistant and Dick suggested her mom for the job. I thought that was a great idea, and I gave her mom the keys to my house.

As of that moment, she, and her daughter – my assistant – had full access to my life. As I later learned, so did Dick.

CHAPTER ELEVEN

HOLLYWOOD!

Oscar Wilde said, "Man is least himself when he talks in his own person. Give him a mask, and he will tell you the truth." It is a true and brilliant statement, meaning that if someone can conceal their real identity, they will let all of their worst impulses, thoughts, and beliefs run rampant.

The kind of people who Wilde was talking about were not mentally ill, deranged, or totally devoid of morals. He was talking about the general population, going on the assumption that most people do have a moral compass, and have the good sense to be ashamed of – and therefore would conceal – the ugliest parts of themselves.

Dick was not the type of person that Wilde was describing. Dick did not need a mask to display who he really was or what he wanted. He had no moral compass whatsoever. He openly fired anyone who displeased him and wantonly surrounded himself with yes-men and yes-women who did whatever he wanted – regardless of if it was wrong or if it made no sense. He gleefully undermined me and a few of my team members with obvious rancor and contempt, most likely because we were not the yes-woman and men he thought he had hired.

Dick craved power and money. When hurting someone is not necessarily the goal, but you do not mind hurting someone to get there, you are a sociopath. When you intentionally hurt someone to get what you want, and you enjoy hurting them, you are a psychopath. That is what Dick was. That is an important distinction that should not be forgotten as the rest of my story unfolds.

Dick hired me because he did not know very much about parking operations or running a parking company, other than working on contracts and legal negotiations. He needed someone to help him with day-to-day management, so he chose me. On paper, that must have been an attractive idea to him in the beginning; but in practice, it put me in a precarious situation of always having to provide insight to him. And that seemed to infuriate him. Apparently, his annoyance in that is why he always did the opposite of my and several of my team members' counsel – even when he was clearly wrong. He was like a child who wanted his own way, and he was not willing to take advice – even when he asked for it. I was in a no-win situation – and the severity of it was clearer with each successive, ridiculous incident.

By removing or trying to remove Steve, Jeff, and Calvin, he was getting rid of people who could help him do his job better. Keeping his cronies on board meant that he was retaining unproductive people; they would only do harm to the financial health of each of the ZVL subsidiary companies.

Those kinds of moves exemplified my struggle with Dick. He wanted excellence, but he created an environment where it was impossible for us to deliver it.

The CEO's job is to protect and foster the health of the company he or she serves. But Dick's interpretation of a CEO's job duties meant he could use ZVL Parking as his personal ATM, treat people horribly, and protect his cronies. As CEO of ZVL Parking, he had access to ridiculous amounts of cash, and he was burning through it at breakneck speed. He paid off city officials and politicians, only flew first class, and only stayed in the very best five-star hotels in the biggest suites. More chaos was added by the old guys – the cronies that Dick had bailed out – with their backbiting, jockeying for money, and efforts to blame everyone else for their companies' problems.

Why did I stay in such a toxic environment? The country had tumbled into a recession, and earning a living was far better than not earning a living, so I bit the bullet. I also figured that, while it was a work environment that could not get any worse, I was surviving. I would hang in there until a new opportunity presented itself.

Then, unbelievably, it got worse – so much worse. It got so bad that it almost killed me – literally.

A book like *The Firm,* or anything else by John Grisham, or Dean Koontz, or another author who writes in the thriller or suspense genres, is fun to read. Those books are fun to read because the characters and circumstances are often outrageous. The plot lines are frequently beyond the scope of any normal person's imagination. As you read about each twist and turn in any story about espionage, or murder, or corporate fraud, you think, *This couldn't possibly happen. Maybe the author got the idea from something in real life that just bears a passing resemblance to the plot; but this isn't like* Law & Order *on TV with its ripped-from-the-headlines storylines.*

Actually, yes. That kind of stuff really does happen – and for the worst reasons. And those activities are perpetrated by people you might personally loathe, but could not imagine to be insane.

The more I dug into existing deals, particularly the more lucrative ones that the company had in place for years, the more I began to see improprieties. Specifically, we were paying clients to give us their contracts. I had heard there had been some "pay to play," but I did not know how extensive it was until I had a run-in with a longtime client of ZVL Parking, who we will call Bill. Bill represented a county jurisdiction. In a meeting with me, Bill made it clear that if I wanted to keep the large, lucrative contract we had with the county, I needed to continue the very long-term payment arrangement that he had with us.

I was absolutely dumbfounded! Later, in my office, I joked with Jeff about it. I was laughing, telling Jeff what I was going to do to that guy and how I was going to call his bluff on it – just to scare him. We joked about the revenge we might take for such blatant illegal bribery. Mind you, both Jeff and I had come to ZVL from very upstanding companies, and neither of us had ever been put in that kind of immoral situation.

In the middle of our little mayhem of laughter and jokes, my office phone rang. It was Dick. He never called me anymore – ever. He had his hands full with the dive in the economy and the rambunctious owners, who took up much of his time. Plus, the more I resisted becoming a yes-woman, and the more I discovered the unsavory and illegal practices of the company, the less we interacted. I loathed him for so many reasons, so we barely spoke. Before this moment, he had not phoned me for months.

I picked up the phone and heard his voice, and was quite surprised. "Hey, what's going on?" he said, somewhat stumbling over his words. I was totally confused and definitely sounded it. "Not much, how about you?" I said. "Same – just checking in on you to say hello. Anything... happening?" he stammered, seemingly unprepared to talk to me. *Why in the world is he calling me if he does not have anything to say?* "Not really, just in my office figuring out what to do with our client, Bill, from the county," I responded. I went on to tell him what Bill had said to me. He quickly said, "Oh, don't worry, I'll handle him. I'll take care of it. You don't need to do anything at all," and he abruptly hung up.

What the hell? Why did he call me out of the blue at that exact moment? Was he nervous I was going to uncover more bribery? He had to have been listening in. Or, someone had been listening for him, and had alerted him to what Bill had told us.

This was not the first time that I had been suspicious about Dick possibly listening to me. For the last several months, I had noticed that he had started mentioning things to me that I had never told him or anyone else at the company. These items of conversation had been discussed only with my friends or my girlfriend in my home or car, when I assumed no one else was listening. I leaned back in my chair to again consider the possibility that Dick had bugged me, and the bizarre timing of his "check-in" phone call.

Because I had become suspicious of being listened to, I had been eyeballing this thing in the ceiling of my office that I had always presumed was something innocent, like a fire alarm. I had occasionally wondered if Dick could be listening, but I had always told myself I was crazy for thinking that way.

However, after that last call from Dick, I was even more suspicious. So, with Jeff still in my office, I got up on my chair, reached up to the fixture, and pulled off the cover. There were listening devices in it! I pointed to them, so Jeff could see. Jeff was shocked. He started yelling at me, "What kind of company is this? What kind of company did you bring me to? What the hell?" I was so horrified and pissed off that before I could give it a second thought, I ripped one of the devices out. That was probably a bad idea, because now Dick would know I was onto him.

I did not know what to do with the bug, but I also did not know what to do with my new, horrible revelation. I knew that the bugging of my office was a federal offense, but I also did not want to be a whistleblower. I knew that Dick could go to prison, but I did not want to be the one to make that happen, out of fear of the ramifications. I could not handle the inevitable drama and hassle that would come along with reporting him. So, I decided to stay quiet.

Besides that, the bugging was not the only illegal activity that I was aware of at ZVL Parking. Far from it. Dick was lining the pockets of government officials and politicians with large donations made by his executive team; he then reimbursed us with "bonuses." That kind of palm-greasing was bottom-of-the-barrel stuff, but it was not designed to hurt me personally.

Bugging my office definitely was intended to mess with me – so, of course, I wanted to do something about it. But when I weighed the pros and cons of becoming a whistleblower, I could not fill up the "pro" column sufficiently in my mind. After Camila, distancing myself from drama had become one of my priorities. Even though I knew I was already up to my neck in a different kind of drama – one that Dick had created – I was not inclined to add fuel to the fire. The revelation of the listening devices, however, was enough to make Jeff resign.

Although the situation at work was so far beyond weird that it almost defied description, my career and financial success were still the most important things to me. I was not going to just quit without securing a position somewhere else. And again, I was not emotionally ready or legally prepared to take the device to the police. I determined that all I could do was stay as cool as possible, and keep my eyes open, while performing my job to the best of my ability.

It was at that precise moment that fate decided to rain down another type of craziness on me. No one in their right mind could have possibly seen it coming.

At roughly the same time that I was realizing exactly how crooked Dick and ZVL Parking were, I decided to rent a house for a time in LA. Since I was spending much of my time in LA integrating one of the new companies we had acquired, I found a beautiful, small Spanish-style house in Hollywood. It was right off of the Sunset Strip, up against the Hollywood Hills. I would still keep a small apartment in Chicago, but by spending more time in LA, I could stay out of the way of the owners in the Chicago office. Unfortunately, I still had to deal with Dick because he spent a lot of time in the LA office as well.

From the day I moved in, I started to suspect that my neighbor in the house to the left of mine, Teddy, was a drug dealer. He had an area behind his house set up for styling hair, but it was clear that he was not much of a hairdresser because he hardly had any clients. As my movers were carrying boxes out of the truck, I stood outside watching, and directed them on where to put the boxes in my new house. During that short time, I saw about a dozen people visit Teddy, each staying for no more than five or ten minutes. Many of them were very pretty girls. So, at first, I thought, *Wow, did I pick the right house. My neighbor has hot friends!*

Teddy was definitely not doing much hair; but he was an OK guy. There was never any craziness or noise or obnoxious parties at his place, so I tried not to pay too much attention to what went on over there.

To the right of my house was Valerie's house. It was really gorgeous; Valerie had a backyard that was bursting with plants, trees, and flowers of all colors. The yard was beautifully tended and it was a great pleasure living next to it.

My backyard, while not as big as Valerie's, was also full of lush, colorful foliage and flowers. I felt so fortunate to find a beautiful house with such a lovely backyard right in the middle of Hollywood. I did not even need curtains on the Valerie side of my house, because the wonderful foliage created a divider between our homes. The sun was always shining into that side of the house every morning when I woke up. It was a lovely home.

Soon after I moved in, I ordered shipping containers to pack up the rest of Camila's things and ship them to her in Texas, where I had moved her some time before. While I was filling the pods, Teddy strolled over to the fence between our houses, pointed at Valerie's place, and said, "Hey, did they ever tell you what happened over there?" My stomach dropped, and I thought, *Oh, man. This doesn't sound like it is going to be a positive story, but now I have to know. Damn it!*

Teddy could tell that I did not know what happened, and opened his eyes really wide. "They didn't tell you what happened over there? I thought, by law, they had to tell you!" he said. I could see where he was going. I am not very impressionable, but I knew that whatever creepy shit Teddy was about to plant in my head probably was not going to make me love my new house any less. The backyard alone was so lush and peaceful that I would have moved in for only that.

I felt that not knowing the weirdness that had happened nearby would probably be worse than knowing. So, because my curiosity would have gnawed away at me, I gave Teddy the go-ahead for his story.

"OK, well, Valerie over there used to be a pretty famous photographer; maybe she still is a little, and she was married to a surgeon. And you see that house behind hers? A Hollywood screenwriter used to live there, but he was killed." My eyes widened.

This is not good, I thought.

He continued his story: "A guy who was higher than a kite broke into the screenwriter's house and murdered him. That's not the worst part," he said. "Then he cut off his head – actually decapitated the writer – and threw his head into Valerie's backyard."

WTF, I thought.

"Wait, it gets worse. I guess he decided that leaving a head lying around in someone else's backyard wasn't a good idea, so he climbed over the fence between the two houses to get the head back. Just as he was doing his recon in Valerie's backyard, he saw her husband through the window, sitting at a desk working on the computer. So, he broke into

Valerie's house and he killed him too, while Valerie was home. Before you ask, no, he didn't take his head off. This was eight or so years ago. So weird, right?"

Weird is an understatement for sure, I thought.

Setting aside the unnerving glee with which Teddy relayed the story (which he must have told countless times because he had it down), what gave me pause was the fact that Valerie still lived in the house. It was where the worst thing imaginable had happened to her, and of course to her husband, **while she was home.** How could she stay in a house that must have a gruesome vibe? Maybe she thought that her husband's spirit remained in or around the house, and that she could not abandon him? Or maybe she lost her marbles when he was killed, and just hunkered down with her memories in that house, like some kind of West Coast Grey Gardens? If any of what had happened to her had happened to me, I would have been out of there like my ass was on fire.

Teddy had moments of providing entertainment, but he was a sketchy dude. Not only did he have the hairdressing setup as a front for his drug deals, but he also had people hanging around his place that looked like Hollywood fringe. The scene was a mix of a David Lynch casting call and a Narcotics Anonymous meeting. Shockingly, Teddy had a girlfriend at the time. Even more shocking was the fact that she was gorgeous – blonde, tan, blue eyes, super sweet, an occasional model – and heiress to a family fortune.

Who knows why she decided to shack up with Teddy, but she did. The modeling gigs kept her traveling, so it was noticeable when she would arrive home. She and Teddy would hang out with friends, party, make a little noise – nothing outrageous. The girlfriend had a younger brother with whom she was obviously tight, because he was a regular at Teddy's place. He would join the parties with or without his sister. That always stuck with me, because I thought it was sweet. The brother's presence would make me think of my brother Frankie, which is always a good thing.

One night, while the girlfriend was on an extra-long trip away, I woke up around 2 or 3 a.m. Both my bedroom and my bathroom windows faced Teddy's house, divided only by a narrow driveway and fence. I was in the bathroom in the dark when I heard a very loud blood-curdling woman's scream come from Teddy's house, followed by a sickening thud. The noise seemed to come from the backyard, and it sounded like someone had fallen from a significant height. Teddy's house was a single-story structure. I could not imagine a place at the house where someone could have fallen from such a height to cause that awful, loud sound. I suppose they could have been up on the roof or could have been tackled to the ground.

I looked out my back windows, but could see nothing. I ran to the front of my house to see if someone had tried to climb over my high gate and had fallen onto the concrete – even though the sound had come from the back of Teddy's house. But no one was on the ground in my driveway.

That scream had been so violent and terrifying that it seemed like someone was being violently attacked or killed. I ran back to my bedroom, which was near Teddy's backyard, and I could now hear whispering coming from his backyard. I went to each of the windows on that side of the house hoping to see something that would help me understand what had happened. I started to see lights go out in his house from the back of the house moving to the front. So, I followed, moving toward the front of my house. I stopped at a window that looked directly into Teddy's living room.

As I stared at the house, I saw Teddy's girlfriend's brother appear in the living room, scurrying around. He was shutting off lights and closing curtains. I was standing in front of my guest bedroom window watching him, when suddenly he turned to the window facing me. He froze, curtains in hand, looking at me. I froze too, as we stared at each other for what seemed like an eternity – but was probably only a couple of seconds – until I came to my senses and dropped to the floor to hide. *Holy shit – he saw me! He knows that I know something happened. Do I call the police? Do I get the hell out of here? They know I am here and that I saw something. What if they come over to my place?*

To my infinite regret – even to this day – I did not call the police. I ran outside, got in my car, and headed to my friend Ann's house in West Hollywood, just a few minutes away. By the time I got to Ann's, I was in a state of sheer panic. I pounded on her door, but no one answered – except for her dog, who jumped up and down at the window, barking his head off. After what felt like an eternity of pounding, she woke up and let me in.

I told her everything, and she decided that we should go back to see what was happening. We used her car, which would be unidentifiable to Teddy, and drove the five minutes back to my house.

For whatever reason, Ann casually pulled into Teddy's driveway with her lights on, completely illuminating the front of his house. The curtains were drawn, but there was no way that Teddy and the girl-friend's brother could have missed that someone had just shown up. I begged Ann to pull out of their driveway. It was also disconcerting that there was a car in the driveway that I had never seen at Teddy's before; it was an old brown Subaru station wagon with Utah plates. Its incongruity made everything even more disorienting and frightening. I could not handle how stressed and terrified I was, and I demanded that we go back to Ann's – which we did. I stayed there overnight.

As I got out of my car the next morning when coming home from Ann's, Teddy intercepted me. He leaned over the fence and said to me, "Hey, I heard you leave in the middle of the night last night. Everything OK?" Teddy had never before tracked my whereabouts. I traveled out of town all the time for my job, leaving and returning at various times, but Teddy had never asked me that kind of question – ever. Knowing I needed to come up with something other than, "I heard you murder someone, so I ran for my life," I said, "Yes, a friend of mine was sick and I had to take her to the ER."

After inquiring about my middle-of-the-night departure, he suggested we hang out at my place that morning and "catch up over some wine." Now, Teddy and I had never hung out socially. We had never, ever had wine or cocktails together. I had let him highlight my hair a few times, but he was terrible at doing highlights – and that was the extent of our interaction.

I said I was busy, but he persisted. Teddy was nervous, jumpy, and kept repeating that he should come over to my house and hang out and have some wine. It was 9 in the morning – and he was talking about sharing a bottle of wine. I knew that it could only get worse. He said he had a client coming for a hair appointment, but we could hang after that. *Wine in the middle of the day,* I thought. *Yeah, right.*

I decided that I needed to do something that would show him I was not afraid of him – and hopefully, that would put his mind at ease. I told him I would come over and hang out in his salon while his client was there. That had to be safe, I thought – he would not dare try anything with his client there. I told him I needed to shower, and then I would come over.

The window in my shower faced Teddy's driveway. As I showered, I could see that he had his truck – a big black truck with a cover over the bed – backed up in the drive next to the side door of his house. The hard cover was lifted a little and the tailgate was down, so I could see what was resting on the tailgate and a few feet into the bed of the truck. It was filled with cleaning supplies. He had scrub brushes, bleach, industrial cleaners, rubber gloves, and trash bags. I could also see blue tarps, but could not see very far into the truck bed because of the cover. The tarps could have just been rolled up, or they could have been rolled around something – or someone.

Next to the truck on the grass was a huge, heavy, metal piece of machinery, possibly part of an engine. It had never been there before, and now it was getting loaded into the truck with the tarps and cleaning supplies. I pieced it all together: screaming woman, sickening thud, suspicious movement in the house, cleaning supplies, tarp, heavy weight. Now I am really scared.

After showering, I made my way to Teddy's salon in his backyard – sick to my stomach and very nervous – but determined to show him that I was not afraid. I hung out for a bit, talking to him and his client. I figured that hanging out with him while his client was there was the safest situation possible.

Teddy mentioned that he had been cleaning that morning, before his cleaning lady came over. I thought, *Sure you were. You were cleaning up whatever mess was made from your previous night's murder before the cleaning lady came over.* But I didn't say what I was thinking, and continued to make small talk.

After I felt like I had visited with him long enough to show that I was not afraid, which I hoped would put him at ease, I said I needed to head back home. He said that he would come over after he was finished with his client and would bring a bottle of wine to share. *Who drinks a bottle of wine at lunch time? Drug-dealing murderers, that's who!* Now he wanted to come to my house – he had never been inside since I had lived there. I figured that he had had time to think about it, and did not want another crime scene at his house. Did he plan to do whatever he wanted to do to me at my house?

After I returned home from his salon, I was trying to figure out if he had believed my nonchalance. Considering that he really still wanted to come over to my house, I decided he probably had not. About 15 minutes later, I heard his truck start. I peered out the curtain to see him pulling out of his driveway.

I knew that if I was going to leave, it had to be then or never. I packed two suitcases as fast as I could, changed clothes, closed up the house as if I were going on a long business trip, and loaded the suitcases into my car. I felt like I needed to get the hell out of there – and fast. His insistence on coming to my house with wine in the early afternoon was too scary for me to contemplate. *What would he do to me if I let him come over?* I was not about to find out.

I locked up the house, pulled out of my driveway, and was just heading down my street when I saw Teddy's big black truck coming down the street towards me. I wanted to keep driving past him, but he flashed his lights and waved his hand out of the window for me to stop.

Teddy asked where I was going. I told him I was going to get some food because I was hungry, and asked if he wanted any. I thought that might throw him off my track. He said, "No thanks," and I said, "OK. See you shortly."

As I drove away, I looked in my rearview mirror to see his truck slowly pulling away – and I could see that he was looking at me in his side mirror at the same time I was looking at him in my side mirror. Our eyes actually met in the mirrors and locked briefly. It was all so damned bizarre and scary that I never went back to that house, except to move out. A mysteriously murdered woman and obvious threats to my own safety were too much to take.

Yes, it took a lot for it to register with me that the energy there was exceptionally bad. But I thought about what had happened to the screenwriter, and Valerie's husband; and now I believed that some poor woman had clearly died at the hands of Teddy and his girlfriend's brother.

Was that just how Hollywood was? Was there a curse on the neighborhood? Yes, I continued to live there even after I saw that Teddy was a bit loony and a drug dealer. But the prospect of my own murder to add to the other three murders – within a three-house radius of my house – was enough to finally motivate me. I had to "get the hell out of Dodge."

On the day the moving truck came, Teddy asked where I was going. "New York," I lied. "My company is moving me to New York." For years,

Teddy continued to reach out to me a few times a year via phone calls and texts. I never answered or responded to his texts.

I was so wrapped up in my fear of being slaughtered by Teddy that I did not notice I was being stalked by killers of a much craftier and more insidious nature. Remember how in old horror movies, the scariest thing that could happen was when the main character would get a phone call, and then she would realize that **the call from the killer was coming from inside the house?** That is basically what happened to me. And the evil mastermind signed my paychecks.

CHAPTER TWELVE

PICK YOUR POISON CAREFULLY; IT JUST MIGHT KILL YOU

After fleeing the obvious danger of living next door to Teddy, I did not return home to LA for over a month and a half. I worked out of the corporate office in Chicago, stayed at my apartment in Chicago, and spent the rest of the time on the road for work. But I knew I needed to find another place in the LA area, away from Teddy. It was the only way I would feel safe. So, I started my search for a new home in Los Angeles.

One weekend, my girlfriend Tracy, her daughter, and I were driving to an open house in the hills of South Pasadena. Just as we approached the open house, the cover for the built-in car speaker for my cell phone fell off from above my head. It was dangling from wires, almost in front of my face. As I stopped the car, Tracy and I looked at each other. I made a sign to be quiet and not say anything. Right away, I thought of the listening device I found in my office, and quickly realized one must have been installed in my car as well. I felt up in the roof cavity and pulled out several strips of heavy-duty, double-sided tape. Obviously, that double-sided tape had been holding something up in there at some point, although it had been removed.

Interestingly, I was just weeks away from turning in that car because the lease was up. I had been talking to coworkers, Tracy, and my friends about the next car I would lease – so it was no secret in my circle that I would not have that car much longer. Now with the speaker cover falling off, I could only presume that there had been a listening device in my car – and when they realized I would be turning in the car soon, it was taken out.

How would they have access to my car, you ask? I parked my car using the valet service every day in the office garage, and my company ran both the parking garage and valet operations. I also valet-parked at an off-airport garage that ZVL owned, so the company had access to my car there as well. I was not surprised that they would put one in my car since they had installed one in my office.

Angry at being so violated, I put the cover back in place. It did not fall off again over the next few weeks – so obviously, whoever removed the bug had not done a good job of securing the cover. Tracy and I were both in shock, and we discussed it on our walk through of the open house.

The house turned out to be the one I decided to rent. It was a beautiful house that overlooked the rolling mountains near Pasadena. It had a stunning backyard with a pool. It was a cool, modern mid-century house – sunny and very private, because it sat atop a really steep hill. You could not see the home from the street – and the only way to approach the house was to go up a really steep driveway. It was like I had found a fortified castle; from that vantage point, I could see any new potential danger coming. It would have been even better if it had a moat, but that was a lot to ask in LA.

I had movers pack me up and move me from Hollywood to South Pasadena. While I was disappointed to leave the area of LA that I loved, I was happy to be moving away from Teddy and to a safer place – or so I thought.

There was a three-sided carport connected to my new house, convenient for parking my orange sports car – a Lotus. The car was named Orange Peel, because he was orange, and he peeled out. I loved that car. He was built as a race car; he was rare, as they only made about 500 street-legal versions each year.

There were not many orange cars of that make running around LA, or anywhere else for that matter. He was very distinctive. I bought a new cover for him, and wrapped him up nice and tight in my new home's carport. On one of the first weekends after I moved into the house, I went to Home Depot to pick up some things. While I was there, I saw Morgan Freeman. I thought, *This is one reason why I love LA. Where else can you just bump into Morgan Freeman at Home Depot?*

While I was musing over celebrities in big-box stores, my cell phone rang. It was my alarm company, and they said that there had been an attempted breach on the door leading into my house in the carport – and did I want them to go and check? I said, "Yes, of course." I quickly finished my errands and drove home, a little nervous at what I might find. I hoped it would be nothing more than a fault in the new alarm system I had installed.

Instead, when I arrived home, I found that someone had removed the cover on Orange Peel, and then had tried to break into my home through the door next to the car. Because they had set off my very loud alarm, they left. It freaked me out – big time. It was as if the intruder wanted to confirm that he had the right house by verifying the presence of my car. Thank goodness for my good security system. Was it a warning? Was it Teddy looking for me? Was it Dick or someone working for him? He knew that I knew that he was listening to me in my office and car and doing other illegal activities, so it very well could have been him. My fear was real – I just did not know where to place it.

I had been traveling a lot for work; but after the move, I stayed in LA and spent more time in that office. I got all settled in; I set up a normal, predictable, and seemingly regular routine.

And then I started feeling sick.

Of course I was sick! You know how your body adapts when you are in an extreme crisis in order to get through it? You are filled with extra adrenaline; and you are laser-focused in a way that you would never normally be. But then, the second that things return to non-crisis mode, you fall apart. All that adrenaline that was keeping you going has completely drained out of your system – and every virus or infection that can strike does exactly that.

There I was – ready to dig into my new, normal routine, and I was struck down by a nasty *thing*. But what was it? After a lifetime of winding up in various emergency rooms from many bizarre injuries – injuries that I had convinced myself were a punishment for causing my brother's death – I had a deep antipathy toward doctors. I also had an extremely high tolerance for pain. So, I decided to diagnose myself and deal with it accordingly.

The symptoms were terrible headaches, puffy eyes, sore throat, and a very raspy voice that made me sound pretty grim. I deduced that something associated with the new house had to be the cause, because my symptoms arrived just a few weeks after I moved in. I decided that there had to be some mold in the walls, or dust mites, or some other mega-strength allergen taking me down.

It frustrated me, but after more than a month and a half of trying to address the issue, I knew I had to move again. I could not tolerate being sick, and the house had to be the problem. So, just a few months after moving in, I paid the landlord a lot of money to break the lease. Dick offered to negotiate the transaction for me, since he was an attorney by trade. I paid movers to pack up all my stuff – again – and put it in storage.

I was able to move into an apartment that Dick helped me find on short notice. One of his best friends (Dick called everyone he knew his "best friend") owned a residential loft building and could get me an apartment right away. I took the bare minimum of furniture with me, because I only wanted to live there for a few months until I could find a new house. I felt that I needed to move to the apartment immediately, so I could rid myself of whatever had been affecting me at the house.

Tracy helped me out yet again with this move, including the difficult assembly of a new Ikea bed frame. Normally, it would not have been a big deal; but I still felt awful, and having an extra pair of hands to assist me was a blessing.

Unfortunately, none of the original symptoms dissipated after I left the house, and they were joined by a grab bag of new and hideous ailments. I started developing sores in my ears and down my throat – the right side of my face felt like it was on fire. My right eye was inflamed; it was extremely painful and swollen, and felt as if it was burning deep in its socket. The same burning sensation ran across the right side of my face and head. My joints hurt all the time, and I could not sleep. The horrible headaches got worse and my raspy voice became worse, and my skin turned a strange hue of gray.

Moreover, I had terrible brain fog, to the point that I would forget my destination while driving. I would have to pull over to check my phone to see where I was supposed to be going. The brain fog got so bad that I would zone out at my desk while working on my computer; 20 minutes or more would go by, and I would have no idea what I had been doing or where the time had gone. Why was this happening?

People at the office kept asking me what was wrong, and they told me I looked terrible. My friends were alarmed and begged me to see a doctor. I knew I should – something was me nagging me, poking at the back of my mind. I wanted to figure it out before I explained my problem to a doctor. I had noticed something, and I knew it was vital information. It came to me one weekend when I did not go into the office, and instead traveled to North Carolina to see Tracy. I realized that when I was in my office, I always felt horrible. All my symptoms were the very worst while in my office. When I had a meeting in a conference room, or if I went out to lunch, or if I did a bit of traveling, I did not feel as terrible as I did in my office.

I was also always uncomfortable in my office, because the company kept it overly air-conditioned. I had to go to the restroom or elsewhere in our vast offices just to warm up. It was freezing all the time. I bundled up when I was in my office with long sleeve shirts and sweaters; and I always had scarves wrapped around my neck. I even got a space heater to deal with the freezing cold in my office. I set it up under my desk so it could keep me warm, but not blast anyone who came in and sat in front of my desk.

When I returned from North Carolina and finally realized that sickness had to be caused by something in my office, I began looking in the vents. I thought that perhaps there was something in those vents that was making me sick – like mold or something. I am highly allergic to both mold and dust, but there was nothing in there.

Still, I just knew it had to be environmental; it had to be coming in through the vents or somewhere else in my office. And I realized I had gone to all the trouble and waste of money to break my lease on the new house I had rented, thinking it was the house that was making me sick. But it was my office, not the house. Nevertheless, I still could not figure out what in my office was making me sick.

Several weeks later, when my space heater conked out – possibly because I had it on constantly – I had to crawl under my very large desk to see what was wrong. While under there, I happened to look up at the bottom of my desk. Right there, glued above my head – on the underside of the desk and directly above where I had placed the space heater – were two large, commercial-size pesticide pods. I went numb.

What the **hell?!** I had no idea what was in them – but it was obviously some kind of chemical. Were they pesticides? Were they some other chemical? How did they get there?!

No matter what they were, I immediately realized that they had to be the reason why I was so sick. Their toxicity had been exacerbated by my space heater, which I had to use because ZVL always kept my office so damned cold. The way I often sat at my desk was with my right side against the main desk where the pods were, because I needed to turn to work at my computer station. Therefore, my right side received the brunt of the chemicals, which would explain why the right side of my face and head was always burning. My right eyeball always felt like it was going to burn right out of its socket – and I had lost the use of my right thumb several times when trying to text.

It all made sense. *Who the hell would do this?* I wondered. I panicked; I pulled one of the pods off with tissues so I would not touch it. I went downstairs and outside, to be away from the office and everyone in it. I assumed it was likely that I was still being monitored, and I did not want whoever had planted the bugs I had found earlier to know that I also knew about the pods.

I called the 1-800 number on the back of the pod. A woman answered. I explained the symptoms I had been having for some time and told her that I just found two of their pods stuck up under my desk. She told me that the pods could not make me sick like that. She said a dog could eat one of their pods and still be fine. I thought, *Seriously? These things kill bugs, but a dog can eat it?* It was clearly bull – but debating the issue with the random person who had the bad fortune to be working customer service that day would have been a waste of time.

It did not make sense; but since I was getting nowhere with her, I hung up and went upstairs to search the rest of my office.

One of the other symptoms of my illness was a constant thirst. By that, I mean that I felt completely parched, 24/7. I had a small refrigerator in my office that I kept well stocked with bottles of water; and because I was – yet again – terribly thirsty, the first thing I did when I got upstairs was get a bottle of water out of my fridge.

If someone wants to poison me, they would probably put these industrial-strength pesticide pods – filled with God knows what – wherever I am most likely to be, right? That is what sprang to mind as I stood there drinking my water. And yes, there it was! Another pod, affixed to the side of the refrigerator that was against the wall, near my desk. Once again, the obvious conclusion was that someone had put serious thought into how to expose me to the highest level of toxins. *Could the pesticide somehow seep into my water?* I had no idea. Nonetheless, there was the pod. That made a total of three in my office.

My office was huge. It had a couch, table and chairs, a refrigerator, and a credenza. If it had been necessary to put pesticide pods in my office to kill bugs, there were plenty of other places to put them other than under my desk – right by my ovaries. *This had to be intentional,* I thought. It seemed kind of ridiculous – overkill – to cover someone's private office with industrial pesticides, or whatever substance happened to be in the pods.

I remembered that before I started getting sick, I was walking down the hallway on the executive side of the company's headquarters when I noticed a disgusting roach on the floor ahead of me. I did not think twice; I was so grossed out that I just smashed it with my foot. Where the hell had it come from?

Prior to that, we never had any kind of bug or pest problem in what was an amazing Class A office building on a very high floor. The property was perfectly managed and always immaculate. I reported the roach to our office manager, who called the property management company. They then sent a pesticide guy to deal with the one lone roach sighting. I recall that when he arrived several days later, he asked me where I had seen the roach. I showed him; it was not near my office at all. I then went to the conference room for a meeting and forgot all about the incident.

Now I had to make sense of what was happening to me and my symptoms' possible connection to the pesticide pods. *Maybe the bug issue wasn't an isolated event,* I thought. *Maybe others reported roach sightings too.* But if there was a widespread bug problem that had been reported, there would be pesticide pods in other offices – right? Of course there would be! If there were pods elsewhere on the floor, then it would be evident that I had not been targeted, and it would mean that my imagination had simply gotten away from me.

I immediately took a pod to my assistant and showed her what I found. I had her help me search the entire rest of the office. We explored the whole half a floor we leased, including a large storage room, the kitchen, and restrooms. I was down on my knees looking everywhere, in every office, conference room and cubicle, under desks, chairs, shelves – you name it. We left no stone unturned in our huge office, and we found absolutely nothing – not one single pod. There were only the three that were in my office. Any hope that I had not been singled out was gone.

It was clearly intentional. The pods were a means to make me sick – or even kill me. *Who would do this, and why?* I was furious. I now knew that I had been breathing that toxic garbage every day. I also knew that the space heater had intensified the toxicity of the poison from the pods. Whoever had decided to make me ill – someone in authority at ZVL – must have realized that the heater would have that effect, because they intentionally kept the office freezing. The frigid temperature made it necessary for me to keep the heater on.

My right side had suffered the worst effects of the toxins. I realized that side had received the most exposure, because the pods had been placed next to my lap. Then I got very, very scared – and felt very, very sick to my stomach. I could not help but wonder: *Had Dick or one of the owners planted that roach to create a reason to install those pods?* Or maybe they had simply seized an opportunity to "fumigate" when I complained about the bug on the floor?

Either way, someone was trying to seriously harm me – and I had to get past the shock and try to figure out what to do. As it turned out, it would be only the first of many exposures to poisons, placed in various places, in an ongoing campaign to kill me. But more on that later.

I left my office and did not return for over a month. I went back to my apartment and packed my suitcase. I had to be in Florida for a conference, and then I was to go on to a meeting in New York City. After that, I planned to stay with Tracy in North Carolina for a bit. When I arrived in Florida, I was so sick from the poisons that I developed a high fever. I stayed in my room for several days. I debated going to the hospital because I felt so sick; but I did not have the strength to get out of bed. I finally forced myself to attend the last day of the conference.

From there, I was scheduled to fly to New York for meetings with Dick and our corporate attorney. We were meeting with financial institutions as possible partners for potential acquisition and infrastructure deals. It was difficult being in NYC with Dick, knowing that he was most likely involved in poisoning me. And obviously, I still felt very sick. After New York, I flew to North Carolina, and stayed at Tracy's house for over a week. I wanted to try and recover, and to hide out while I figured out my next steps.

While at Tracy's, I started doing investigative work on Dick. First, I found listening devices in my office, then evidence of a listening device in my car. Most recently, I had discovered poisons in my office. What was going on? What had I done to anyone to make Dick or anyone want to make me so sick, or kill me?

What I found on the internet was interesting. Prior to weaseling his way into his position as CEO at our company, Dick had seemingly performed some freelance legal work for a California biomedical company that was developing treatments for cancer. Specifically, the company focused on the types of cancer that women experience. It was not a crazy leap to conclude that someone who had spent time around scientists and medication patents would have access to information about what might cause the very cancers the company was trying to cure.

It was then I determined that Dick – and possibly some of the owners – were behind the pods. There was not any other possible explanation. Even so, I could not know whether it was actual pesticides in the pods or just some other chemical aimed at making me sick.

I believe firmly in the concept of Occam's razor, which is: the simplest explanation is usually the right one. Arthur Conan Doyle had based the entire psychology and methods of his alter-ego Sherlock Holmes on Occam's razor. And if it was good enough for Sherlock, it was good enough for me. A ticker tape scrolled through my mind: Dick knew people who knew what gave women cancer. Dick had access to my office. I was the only one with highly toxic material in my office. Both my office and my car had been bugged.

I needed to figure out what was happening. I was scared for my life. But the good news was: while away from the toxins, my symptoms were dissipating – albeit very slowly.

No matter what else has gone on in my life, one of the only things that has always kept me together and given me a sense of purpose is my work – and excelling at what I do. That sense of fulfillment, coupled with the calming influence of independence that my salary and savings give me, is what drives me. As crazy as it sounds, despite everything that was going on, I was still determined to stay at ZVL. I wanted to know why I was being targeted; and I wanted to leave on my own terms – not out of fear. So, I pulled my sick self together.

I had taken the pods with me on my trip. I had packaged them very carefully – encasing them in layers of foil, and then in baggie after baggie; then wrapping that bundle in plastic grocery bags; and finally, wrapping the whole thing in a garbage bag before placing it in my suitcase. I know it sounds insane, but I did not feel safe leaving the pods in my office or at home. I wanted to get those pods tested by a lab, so I would know what I had been exposed to. And I was convinced that if I had left any of the pod material behind, it could be seen as evidence, and Dick and his cronies would find a way to get rid of it.

From the safety of Tracy's house, I researched and found a lab; and I learned how to safely send one of the pods to the lab for analysis. I went to Home Depot, bought latex gloves, a mask, and material to wrap the pod. I assembled the package and included a handwritten note for the person at the lab who I had spoken to on the phone.

While I was writing the note, I used the pen to scratch an itch on my face. Later that day, I had a burn mark on my face where I had scratched myself with the pen. It was as if an open sore had burst out on my cheek without warning, and I knew it had to be because the pen had somehow touched the poison on the pod. From then on, it was confirmed to me that everything that was physically wrong with me was because of those pods. Tracy told me where to go to ship the package; I shipped it overnight to the lab and hoped a clear answer would be coming soon.

Two days later, I received a call from the lab tech. They had received the package and had questions. Could I please take the time to talk to them? Something in the way that the questions were asked made me feel nervous and suspicious. It seemed as though he had not read my explanatory note. I asked if the note I had sent along with the pods was in the package, and when the tech said no, I pressed further. I asked about the condition of the package when they received it. They said they had received a thick white envelope with "the materials" inside.

I had sent the pod in a brown cardboard box, not a white envelope. *What was going on?* The lab technician said, "I am looking at the packaging right now. It is for sure a white shipping envelope." How and why was the package different from what I had sent? Had they even received the correct pod? I started to panic again. If someone was conspiring against me, how would someone in North Carolina know to mess with my particular package?

I was shaking with anger and fear, and called the store where I had shipped the pod. The woman who answered the phone was the same woman who had helped me when I shipped it. She took an earful from me, and then put me on hold for a while. When she came back on the phone, her nervous response was, "It just wasn't in the right kind of packaging to ship it. I took everything out and put it in a different package." I went ballistic. I told her that tampering with my mail was illegal. Even worse, the contents of the package were highly toxic. I told her that I certainly hoped she had not touched the contents. I hung up when I realized I was not going to receive additional clarity from the woman.

I kept running over the situation in my mind. Who would tamper with my package? Who would not want me to get a lab's confirmation that someone might want to poison me? How could anyone know exactly where I was sending my package from – in North Carolina, of all places? The only person I could think of was Tracy. She was the one who told me where to go to ship the pod, and she was gone all that day while I was home alone. Could it have been her? But why?

I should back up a bit and tell you how I met Tracy. My former company, Center Parking, had scrubbed my computer after I left them for ZVL Parking. They found that I had sent myself a few documents from my company laptop to my personal email. It was only my annual bonus calculations because I knew I was leaving and wanted to have the records of it.

But after finding that information, Center Parking wanted to see if I had sent any other confidential documents to myself as I was leaving their firm – or so Dick claimed. He was the one who said that Center wanted to look through my emails. In hindsight, I am not sure if that was true. He said they wanted to dig into my personal Gmail account and go through all my emails. At the time, I was puzzled as to why they could not just check on what I had sent from my company laptop.

Because Dick helped me deal with the alleged Center Parking's claim (again, because he was an attorney by trade), I had to give him my username and password to my Gmail account. Perhaps Dick made all of it up so he could dig into my personal life – but I have no doubt that Dick snooped around in my Gmail account, just as he had in other ZVL employees' social media.

One of the things he would have seen in my emails was correspondence from a dating site I used to meet friends and perhaps a girl to date. A few months after we resolved the Center Parking issue, I received a "like" from a girl in North Carolina on the dating site. She was a pretty, sexy blonde who looked very straight. I like straight girls and have dated more than my share of them; it was always my preference to date a straight girl from out of town. But why would this girl all the way on the other side of the country be pinging me? We started talking, and eventually we met. It was Tracy.

On one of Tracy's early visits to meet me in Chicago, she confessed to me that she was a "kept woman." I was shocked. She said she used to be a dancer at a strip club and one of her rich, high-powered customers wanted to help her get out of that life. He had agreed to support her and send her to school. What I later learned from her was that this high-powered customer was supposedly a land-use attorney out of DC. I did wonder why a powerful, wealthy attorney from DC frequented a strip club in North Carolina.

Anyway, this attorney bought her a BMW, and rented a very nice house for her, her daughter, and her mother. He also paid for her school and gave her spending money. She insisted that she and the attorney did not sleep together, but she was expected to call him every day. It did not make sense to me, but I did not question her too much.

I gave her the benefit of the doubt; I accepted her story that she was not sleeping with him. And that seemed to be the case, because she was always available to see me anytime I wanted her to be with me in Chicago or LA, or anywhere else. And it was always no problem for me to spend time with her at her home in North Carolina. There was never a time she was not available. But I did accidentally hear her on the phone with the attorney a few times, although she always left the room for her daily call to him. The few times that I heard her on the phone with him, the conversations sounded very benign.

Now, almost a year later into our relationship, I began to question if the person "keeping" her was Dick or one of the other owners. I began to wonder if she had been introduced into my life as a way to keep tabs on me. But why? Why would anyone from ZVL need to keep tabs on me? Were they paranoid that I might tell the authorities about all of their illegal activities?

I only started questioning Tracy's existence in my life after the switch-up of the pod package; but then, several other red flags started nagging at me. On that same visit to Tracy's house, she could not find her check from her "sugar daddy," and started becoming anxious about it.

She seemed convinced that I had found the check; but the issue became more about not wanting me to see whose name was on the check rather than being concerned about losing it. I even asked her why it would matter if I knew his name. She said, "You just cannot know who he is."

Funny thing – if you were to conduct a search for Tracy online now, you would find that she does not exist. There is no evidence of her. Was our whole relationship a farce? Was her name fake? If so, why? In my opinion, my very wealthy and powerful employer took extreme measures to watch me. I believe that Tracy's daily calls to the attorney (who could have been Dick) were to fill him in on my whereabouts, my activities, and the things I told her about the company.

It made sense to me that Dick would want to get information out of Tracy and use her as a way to manipulate me. Particularly when I was driving in my car, she was the one I would call. I confided in her about what was going on at ZVL Parking and how much I hated it. I was candid with Tracy about all of the illegal activities. I told her about what appeared to be money laundering, the fraud, all the other shady business practices to benefit Dick's friends, as well as Dick's illegal political donation practice, the under-the-table payments in exchange for contracts, the listening devices, and the poison. She knew about all of it. Many of those conversations took place in my **bugged** car. I had certainly been vocal about my issues with the company to Dick. And he and ZVL had surely learned even more about my disdain for them and the company when I spoke to people in my car – when I thought I was having private conversations. There was much for them to be concerned about. And when you are doing illegal things because you are a part of a mafioso-type organization, you will go to any lengths to not be found out.

I know it seems far-fetched that they would hire a girl to pretend to be my girlfriend to monitor me, but it simply added up. The entire situation, from nearly my first day at the company, had been insane – so why not?

If you are thinking, *Oh man, she's really off her rocker now*, you are not wrong. But you are not right either. Once you have been in a situation that is so incomprehensible, so unbelievable – your internal gyroscope gets broken. Nothing is believable; yet, at the same time, everything is believable. You trust no one. You just cannot rule out anything that seems crazy, because crazy has become the norm.

The idea that I could look at someone's incomprehensible, bizarre behavior – and make sense of it so well that I could trust my conclusion – was absurd. But my suspicions about Tracy only intensified when I observed some new, odd habits – like suddenly washing her hands constantly, and brushing her teeth with scalding hot water – all after I had discovered the poison. Who does that all of a sudden? She said it was something her dentist recommended for tooth sensitivity. Come on. Using hot water like that would make sense if you had handled something that might be contaminated or toxic – but simply because "your dentist told you?"

Nothing made sense after the package-tampering incident; I didn't even know if the pod that had been poisoning me even made it to the lab. I seriously doubted it. The longer I stayed in North Carolina, the more my anxiety and distrust grew. I decided to leave and head for our New York office. I did not go back to Chicago or LA for over a month.

But when I did get back to Chicago and LA, more eerie stuff started happening.

I went back to the Chicago office after five or six weeks. I had taken time to think through things and decide my plan of action. I went to our vice president for Human Resources, Sarah, who I used to work with at Center Parking. She actually had initially recommended me to Dick. I felt like I should start with someone I trusted, and I felt that I could trust her. I told her all about the poisons – how I found them, and how they had made me so sick. And I told her that I knew it had to be Dick and the owners.

Sarah asked how I would know that, and I told her I had found a listening device in my office and remnants of one in my car. I relayed information from people who had shared their involvement in some of the illegal activities. I also told her that several reputable people within the company – and with companies we had acquired – had told me that ZVL Parking was being investigated by the FBI.

She cried after I confided in her. I am not sure if it was because she thought I was crazy – or if she knew that what I had said was true. Perhaps she felt bad about bringing me into the company. Regardless of the reason, she said I needed to confront Dick with the information. She said that I needed to tell him about the poisons and how sick I had been. I did not love that idea – but I also thought that if I saw his face and his reaction, it might give me some sign that he was involved. He had not been very stealth-like up to that point, so it was worth a try.

So, I sat down with Dick and repeated what I had told Sarah. Specifically, I informed him that I had discovered the poison pods in my office. Amazingly, the first thing out of his mouth was not, "That can't be," or "That couldn't have happened in this office; you must be mistaken." Instead, he said, "Who do you think did it? Do you think it was Nancy, one of the owners and Joel, her son?"

That hit me like a ton of bricks. He did not try to deny it or change my thought process regarding what had happened. Instead, he immediately tried to redirect the blame to others in the office. I told him that did not make sense about Nancy or her son. I pointed out that even though she was still on the board of directors (and an owner), due to the infighting among the owners, she and her son were no longer employees of the company. Therefore, they were not allowed in the office and could not have installed the pods. That was the only discussion I had with Dick over the pods in my office. There was no offer from him to help me, or to investigate further. He only tried to place blame elsewhere.

When I finally went back to LA and walked through the front door of my apartment, I discovered several small roaches right inside the front door. They were similar to the one I had seen in the office. *What the hell?* I had never, ever lived anywhere that had roaches. And this was a very nice, new building, so it did not make sense.

I immediately called the management office to tell them; but they blamed me, and said I must have brought them with me. They had never had any roaches, they said. I knew it was impossible that I had brought them with me – I had never had roaches, and had not left any food in that apartment whatsoever to attract them. These roaches, I later figured out, were another plant so that more poisonous chemicals could be introduced into my apartment.

Someone was sent to my apartment when I was not there, and literally flooded my entire apartment with liquid chemicals in the name of killing the roaches. It was as if they poured it all around my apartment, directly from the bottle. There were puddles of pesticide all around my apartment. I could not stay there; I had to get a hotel room. I stayed away for several days and then finally went back in – with a mask, goggles, and gloves – to clean. It took a long time to clean up the disgusting mess; there were many dried puddles of toxins. I left for a few more days, afraid of the residue.

Then, other scary things started happening in my apartment. It became clear to me that someone was coming into my apartment when I was not there. I found small, telltale hints, like the toilet seat left up in my bathroom – as if a man had used the toilet. I do not pee standing up, and I never had any men over to visit – or anyone else, other than Tracy a few times. *Who used my bathroom and left it like that?* Then, I found a cigarette stubbed out on the floor of the kitchen. I do not smoke, and never let anyone else smoke in my home. Another time, after being gone for several days, I came home to find every single piece of my framed art hanging askew on the walls. I checked to see if there had been an earthquake – there had not been a single tremor while I was away.

I was still feeling sick through all of those discoveries, but I was not totally debilitated. Thankfully, I was no longer sitting at my desk with pesticides hidden underneath, and with a heater blowing toxins up into my face and lap. Sleeping was difficult, though, and I could not get comfortable in my bed – no matter what I did.

When I had first moved into that apartment in LA, Tracy helped me put my bed together. It was one of those beds where you click connected slats into slots on the bed frame to make a platform bed. When I finally lifted the mattress to look underneath and see what might be making me uncomfortable, all the slats were completely out of place. Now I had to worry if someone might have put something in my mattresses!

I was scared because someone was coming into my apartment to screw with me – so one day I set a trap before I left on a trip out of town. I went to the sporting goods store and bought clear fishing line. At home, I built a pile of dishes on the kitchen counter – the kitchen is the first area anyone would encounter when they walked into my apartment – and I ran the fishing line through all the dishes. I then ran it down along the ground – in effect, setting a trip wire. I put the line far enough into the room that someone would have to be well into the apartment before hitting it. As I left for my trip, I thought to myself, *You are insane, Kendra. No one is going to set that trap off and you are going to feel like an idiot.*

However, the exact opposite happened. When I returned home, the dishes were broken all over the floor, and the fishing line had been pulled away from where it was taped. Clearly, someone had come into my place and tripped my trap. I became emotional. I was over it.

I also started having issues with my dry cleaning. I used a dry cleaner in our office building, as some of my colleagues at ZVL did. This dry cleaner also did the cleaning for our employees' uniforms. I began to notice that there were days that my arms would start burning and aching – down to the bone – after I would put on a dry-cleaned dress shirt. It would hurt so bad I had to go home and change shirts. That happened on numerous occasions. Had I become allergic to dry cleaning chemicals? If so, would such an allergy hurt and burn just my arms that severely?

I had always left my shirts in the plastic wrap that came from the dry cleaners until I was ready to wear them. But after about four or five times of feeling burned by my shirt, I started investigating my dry cleaning. I found that many of the plastic bags had slits running down the sides. I thought, *holy shit, are they now putting poison on my dry cleaning?* Tampering with my clothes using chemicals would explain the slits down the sides of the plastic bags, not to mention the horrible pain I felt on my arms. Was it happening at the dry cleaner or in my apartment? It was all too much to get my head around.

Another way they poisoned me was through the beta-blocker prescription I was taking daily. I do not know how long someone had been "dosing" my prescription with poison, or how long I had been ingesting it, but one day I opened the bottle – which I kept in my briefcase in my office – and the stench of chemicals was so strong it almost knocked me out. I thought, *They will try anything to kill me.* Because the smell was so toxic, I did not take any more pills from that bottle. I also stopped putting any personal things in my briefcase.

At least one of my cars was used to poison me. I had turned in my leased sport utility vehicle because the lease was up. I did not lease another one right away; I drove my other car (not Orange Peel) for a while. I soon noticed that when I drove it, I would get headaches and a burning sensation in my eyes and on my head. I was suspicious, but could not find anything in the car. One day, after the car had sat for about a week while I was on a trip, I climbed inside and the chemical smell was very strong. Because the car had been closed up for so long, it was obvious. I thought, *Dick is an idiot and not very stealthy at trying to kill someone.* I tried to clean the car as best I could, out of fear of the poisons. I rarely drove it after that.

I began to take evasive action. I stopped parking at our off-airport parking facility when I traveled for work; and I stopped parking at my office for work, since ZVL ran that parking as well. I started paying for parking elsewhere, so no one would have access to my car.

One day, I came home to find yet another roach by my front door. Another call had to be placed to the management in the building, and I had to go through the entire fumigation process again. I could not take it anymore; I knew I was not safe in that apartment.

I left and checked into a series of hotels for several months – hopping from hotel to hotel, using laundromats to wash my clothes. I would only occasionally stop at the apartment to unpack and repack my suitcase. I never let anyone know where I was staying.

Tracy knew that I was switching hotels every few days, and badgered me for information each night about where I was. That raised more suspicion in my mind. She did not know any hotels in LA; and since she lived in North Carolina, she certainly was not going to just pop in for a visit. Again, my fear of her connection to all the insanity was ebbing and flowing in my head – I started speaking in a more guarded way when I was on the phone with her.

It was during all of this absurdity, when – out of the blue – Dick asked me to lunch when we were both in LA. It had been months since we had spoken at any length of time or had spent any one-on-one time together, other than when I told him what I found in my office. The trust between us had been severely damaged when I found the listening devices. Our relationship had become even more strained after all of my discoveries and his attempt to place the blame on someone else. But off we went to lunch, under the guise that he just wanted to "catch up."

During lunch, I fielded an uncomfortable series of silly questions and made light conversation. There was no real discussion about the company, work, or anything of importance. I let him lead the conversation, since he was the CEO. He fidgeted and stammered, and kept looking at his watch and the clock on his cell phone. When we were done, he looked at his phone again, and suddenly insisted that I order dessert. It was then that I knew he was stalling. I had suspected it throughout the lunch because of his suspicious behavior, but after his insistence that I order dessert, I knew he was simply trying to keep me from going back to the office.

Finally, after dessert, we headed back. When the elevator door opened to our floor and we started to step out, we were practically run over. A clean-cut, professional looking, handsome, muscular man was trying to run into the elevator we had just vacated. He reminded me of Tom Cruise in *Mission Impossible.* He had on a dark suit, with a black turtleneck.

He seemed shocked to see us – and instead of getting on our elevator as he had started to, he abruptly turned around when he saw us. He then ran through a door in the elevator lobby that led to the back hallway of the entire length of our offices. Mind you, half of the entire floor was ours, and the other half was allegedly empty. No one had a reason to be on that floor unless they had business with ZVL Parking.

So why was this unknown man running out of our offices? Why did he not get on the elevator as he had clearly intended to, and why did he disappear down the back hallway after he saw us? I was infuriated. I realized that Dick wanted to take me to lunch for no other reason than to get me out of the office. It was why he kept stalling before we returned.

Did that man go through my office and laptop? Did he plant more poisons? Another listening device? Or was he with the FBI, since I kept hearing that they were investigating the company? Was Dick trying to set me up, so he could point the finger at me? Who the hell knew? But I was not going to stand for it!

I made a comment to Dick about what had just happened with the man running down the back hallway; but Dick made a flippant comment, saying perhaps the man was a job applicant or a delivery man. Seriously? I took off and ran after the man, through the door to the back hall, but he was gone. I went up and down the hall, opening every door and looking everywhere. I even went into the women's and men's rooms to see if he was there. He had disappeared into thin air.

I was furious. I was exhausted with ZVL's bullshit and shenanigans. I had been trying to figure out my exit strategy from the firm, and every successive incident just fueled my desire to get away.

Living in a series of hotel rooms is not a sustainable lifestyle, particularly when you are sick. It is even worse when you are traveling for work and leaving hotel room A for hotel room B, and then coming "home" to hotel room C. I felt like I was constantly on the run, living in fear, and running for my life. Those people had poisoned me. When I found the poisons in my office, they started invading my residence and doing things to scare me. Because of all of that craziness, I felt like I did not have a center. I could not focus. Moreover, after many months of being sick, my symptoms were changing to a different set of symptoms. I needed to find a real home.

I found a beautiful house right outside of the community of Silver Lake, and I was excited to leave the hotels and the unsafe apartment behind. I felt sick, but not as sick as before, and I no longer had sores in my mouth and ears. I could speak, I could eat, – and those were improvements. My skin was still gray, and I had constant headaches and pain; but I felt that I was moving in the right direction.

When it came time to pack up my apartment, I began removing all the scarves from my coat rack so I could box them up. I had many scarves – I wore a scarf every day to the office, because it was so damned cold there all the time. But when I got down to the last layer of scarves, my stomach dropped to my knees. An enormous adrenaline rush shivered through me – and nearly knocked me off my feet.

Every single hook on the rack was filled with small pesticide pods. They were little, tiny versions of the big ones I had found in my office. So – every day, I had been wrapping a contaminated, toxic scarf around my neck and had been breathing in whatever the poison was. The toxins had been soaking into my neck and thyroid. No wonder I had developed a raspy voice. I also had packed some of those scarves with me when I went on business trips and when I stayed incognito in hotels.

It seemed that no matter what I did to try to get away from Dick, he and his toxicity followed me. He had found ways to poison me without being anywhere near me. I am not a crier – like, not at all! But in that moment I lost it. I sat on the floor and cried hysterically until I had exhausted myself. What I had known finally hit me in a visceral and sickening way – these f*#king people really were 100 percent, positively, trying to kill me!

CHAPTER THIRTEEN

I CAN'T BELIEVE I'M NOT DEAD

If you think that knowing people are trying to murder you is bad, I assure you it is even worse when you are not entirely clear about why they would want you dead. Part of the reason it had been difficult to acknowledge that I was unknowingly listened to, recorded, trespassed on, put under surveillance, and poisoned, is because I could not fathom why anyone would want to do me harm. For God's sake, I was an employee in a relatively small business! It was a family business – actually, to be precise, it was families who hated each other. Their constant battling with one another was something I could not understand, and I had never experienced such a negative work environment. But it made sense, since they were participating in so many illegal activities.

One thing they all did seem to agree on was continuing the illegal practices of skimming, laundering money, and hiding revenue to evade paying taxes. This was in addition to the company's under-the-table campaign contributions in exchange for new deals, more under-the-table payments to municipal officials and other clients for maintaining the status quo, and the practice of forcing ZVL executives to make campaign donations.

Evidently, they also had no problem with planting listening devices to eavesdrop on their employees' conversations in the office, their cars, and their homes. And now it appeared that even murder – or at least attempted murder – was within their scope.

I do not think that ZVL's action against me was their entree to murder or attempted murder; I am sure there were others who had crossed their path who had met unfortunate endings. After all, when you are part of a mafia, you do not just start poisoning and murdering people – it is part of the family business. These families – owners of the company – fought among themselves and tried to cheat one another out of profits. These families kept tabs on the people closest to them, **just in case.**

Oh, dear Lord, why was I working for an organized crime family? I asked myself, *How did this happen?* Had I been working so hard all those years to build my career just to line the pockets of career criminals who considered murder an easy answer to a minor problem? Were they willing to murder simply on a **suspicion** of a problem? It made as much sense as anything else. I tried to think of what I could have done to qualify as a potential minor-to-medium-sized problem.

The list I came up with was brief – but damning. Here is what I concluded:

1. I was a very senior member of the executive leadership, but an outsider. I was not part of the family – neither figuratively nor literally. I was new; and was, therefore, automatically not to be trusted by the inner circle.

2. I am smart and have the capacity to put clues together and reach a sane conclusion. Even so, it would not take a genius to see that the back-room cash-counting, along with a staunch refusal to automate customer payment transactions, meant that a lot of untraceable cash was hanging around. This cash was likely hanging around in the pockets of the owners – and that was just the beginning.

3. Due to Dick's sloppiness, he made it possible for me to figure out that he knew things about my conversations that he should not have known. When I realized that, it led me to look for – and find – the illegal listening devices.

4. I was terribly, horribly sick. Toxic chemical pods had been hidden all over my office, as well as in my car and home. The poison had been on the clothes that I wore every day, and in the prescription that I ingested every day. Anyone with half a functioning brain would conclude that the person (or persons) who could be harmed by my knowledge would want me out of the way.

Once I had it all out on paper, I was able to fathom why someone who was the perfect mixture of psychopath, narcissist, and dumb ass would try to kill me. Since I am a reasonable person, the next few things I did were part of what would become a long-haul plan to not end up dead.

The first order of business was to get away from any place where the toxic poisons had been. I removed them from my office, my house, my car – all the various places that Dick and his minions had stuck them. I also removed myself from the apartment where I had been living.

My symptoms started to dissipate once I was not around the poisons anymore. They did not go away instantly; it was a process. But as those symptoms cleared up, new problems appeared about four months later.

My immune system had been so zapped by the constant exposure to toxic chemicals that I could not fight off even the most minor infection. That period of my life while I was purposefully poisoned – and even afterward – was a blur of sickness and chaos, with constant infections. I had sinus infections, bladder infections, urinary tract infections, chest infections, and even staph infections. One morning, I was in a rush and cut my leg while shaving. It was just a scratch – nothing you would ever think twice about. But it developed into a staph infection that spread all over the back of my leg. It was so painful that sitting down became an ordeal. So many infections, one after another, meant many trips to the ER.

After about four months, many of the chemical exposure issues had died down, and I made the incredible mistake of thinking that life might be returning to normal – or at least an acceptable new kind of normal. I was wrong again. Out of nowhere, I suddenly started losing weight at an insanely fast pace. I lost nearly 20 pounds in a matter of six weeks, leveling out for a while at 92 pounds. At the same time, half of my hair fell out, my vision failed, my hands shook uncontrollably, I experienced worsening heart palpitations, and had bouts of searing joint and skin pain. I thought, *This has to be the end of it... there can't be anything left to go wrong... I'm going to get a break.*

Once again, I was wrong. A lot of my eyelashes and the outer half of my eyebrows started to fall out, leaving me looking like an emaciated lab rabbit. *What the hell?* What had I done to deserve this? I knew that having my immune system compromised could leave me open to all kinds of opportunistic diseases; but was I going to get **all** of them? I began to check my body multiple times a day for anything new and unusually alarming, like bruises, open lesions, or sudden hemorrhaging. I started to assume that anything that could go wrong definitely would.

By the time I got to the doctor, I looked like death. My eyes had sunk deep into my skull; my skin was a papery, sallow mess. I gave my doctor the full history of what had happened, including all of my illnesses and the symptoms from the chemical exposure. Then I told him about the new symptoms that I had recently developed. I told him what I firmly believed – no, **knew** – had caused it: the poisons.

He did a battery of tests and sent me to another specialist who ran tests, who then sent me to another specialist – and so on, until it was finally determined that I had Graves' disease. That diagnosis was nightmarish; but, in some ways, it was also a way for me to confirm that I was not insane. The diagnosis proved that I had, in fact, imagined nothing about the damage that Dick had done to me.

Graves' disease is an autoimmune disease that affects the thyroid, which is a gland located in one's neck. The thyroid's job is to create and release hormones into your body. Graves' disease causes an overproduction of thyroid hormones. That leads to a lot of seriously painful and intrusive symptoms. I learned that all of the illnesses and debilitations I had experienced recently were typical symptoms of the disease. Some of the symptoms that my doctor identified for me were: weight loss, intense fatigue, heart palpitations, sallow complexion, hair loss, pain and grittiness in the eyes, double vision, and light sensitivity. It all added up.

The worst part about being diagnosed with Graves' disease was learning that the disease is not curable. Even if the disease went into remission, which would mean taking medication, at any point in my life the symptoms could reoccur.

Yes, the disease could come out of remission, and it actually happened all too often during the next decade. Those recurrences would always remind me of Dick, and what he put me through – correction: what he put me through for no reason except that he and his bosses were sick individuals. The more I thought about it, the more enraged I became.

One question materialized out of all that rumination; and I still do not have the answer. I wondered, *Why the hell didn't Dick, or one of his henchmen, just confront me?* They could have asked what I knew. Surely, they found out from listening to me – through the bugs they placed in my office, my car, and probably in my home – that I was not talking to the FBI. According to the owners of both of the companies we had acquired, the FBI was investigating us. But I did not ask specifically what it was that the FBI was investigating, and they did not say. The less I knew, the better.

At that time, there were multiple investigations occurring in New York, LA, Chicago, Cleveland and other cities in which we operated, because city officials and employees had been taking bribes in exchange for contracts. I knew that ZVL Parking had done plenty of that kind of 'business' in their time. However, since we had just bought two companies based out of those cities and we did not have operations there before, I doubted that anything would happen to the owners of my company.

Even if the company had participated in those particular bribes that were a part of the investigation, no one goes straight to killing a theoretical threat on a hunch! Hadn't these idiots watched even a single Martin Scorcese movie? For God's sake, I had kept my mouth shut.

I never even reported the poisoning to the police out of fear of ZVL doing something even more severe to me. That is what happened to Jack, who was the CEO before Dick took his job. He was found "swimming with the fishes." That occurred after Dick was fired, and after Jack came back as the CEO; I had left the company by then. Jack's murder created a lot of speculation – and it was definitely murder. And while I am not aware if anyone has ever been charged, it is quite obvious to me that the murder was related to the company's criminal activity. Other people in my industry who know about the people who own ZVL agree with me.

I would never have left Center Parking to work for ZVL if I had known what I would go through for three years. I battled many health issues – which were a result of the company's attempts to kill me – for more than a decade after I left ZVL. I spent years looking over my shoulder, in fear for my life. I was always afraid that "they" were coming for me, so I kept hiding and staying under the radar, so as to not pose a threat to them.

However, there was nothing I could do to change what had already happened. I had to look to the future and figure out how to play the hand I had been dealt. I began to concentrate on finding a new job, because I knew I had to leave ZVL before I was killed. I broke up with Tracy because I did not trust her. And I started to focus on my health, and my physical and mental well-being.

For the next decade, I would fight to keep my Graves' disease in remission. It was very difficult, and I slipped out of remission often. When I was out of remission, my symptoms would include terrible body pain in my muscles and joints, muscle weakness, digestion issues, and allergic reactions to fabric softener. Dealing with Graves' disease was particularly challenging, especially considering that I stay in hotels during my travel for work. All hotels use fabric softener in their laundering of sheets and towels.

I have also struggled with insomnia, shaky vision and loss of vision, loss of eyebrows on the edges, muscle atrophy in my forehead and around my eyes, and eyelid edema. I developed a horrible constant ringing in my ears, which continues to this day. I have experienced heart palpitations, brain fog and forgetfulness, extreme and constant – and I mean constant – fatigue and exhaustion, hand tremors, anxiety, and a very swollen thyroid. To top it all off, I have had a very weak immune system due to it all.

Because of the muscle atrophy in my forehead and the eyelid edema, I eventually had to have an invasive surgery that resulted in about 70 stitches on the inside of my eyes and on my forehead. But after that surgery, I started to grow very coarse, thick eyelashes on the edges of my eyelids, which would grow directly into my eyes. I would have to wait for the eyelashes to grow out enough so that I could pull them out with tweezers. In the meantime, they would scratch the hell out of my eyes, which was extremely painful. I dealt with that for years, before an eye doctor finally told me that he could cauterize them so they would not grow back. Oh, happy, happy day when I got that done!

For over a decade, I was constantly in and out of doctor's offices and emergency rooms for infections and other related issues. I had constant medical challenges as a result of Graves' disease and my weakened immune system. And it was all due to the poisons.

It was only when I finally had my thyroid removed – a decade after the poisoning – that a few of the symptoms dissipated. However, a whole new issue arose – hypothyroidism, which can develop if you do not have a thyroid. Many of the symptoms that one would have with hyperthyroid disease also surface with hypothyroidism. (But more on that shortly.)

Little did I know back then that Graves' was the least of the illnesses that came from the poisoning. Now, with hypothyroidism, I continue to deal with many other symptoms.

Like any other autoimmune disease, Graves' disease can go in and out of remission; and if left untreated, it can kill you. My doctor told me that you can be genetically predisposed to Graves' disease; but if you do not have the genetic markers for Graves' – which I did not – you can still get it if you experience a triggering event.

When I was first diagnosed, I went home, sat at my desk, turned on my laptop, and said a silent prayer of thanks to the internet gods for the astounding amount of medical information online. I set about researching the disease. My diagnosis with Graves' was the result of Dick's insanity, but I needed to confirm the facts for the sake of my own sanity.

My investigation confirmed what my doctor had told me. Major hospitals, research centers, academic abstracts all said the same thing: Graves' can be triggered by various environmental events. I kept reading, and found that since 2002, there have been scores of university-backed studies researching the connection between environmental toxins and Graves' disease. As I suspected, they found that exposure to industrial chemicals, pesticides, herbicides, toxins, and heavy metals all contribute significantly to the incidence of thyroid disease in people who are not genetically predisposed to it. Guess what else? Heavy metals are frequently used in pesticides and herbicides. I had been exposed to at least three of the contributing factors that can create a lifelong autoimmune disease. Great going, Dick! That bastard did not manage to kill me, but he did manage to screw me up royally.

There it was. I knew what he did to me; I knew I was not crazy. I had been exposed to chemicals – breathing, wearing, and ingesting them – that made me sick. I also now knew why my symptoms and illness had shifted from chemical exposure symptoms to the Graves' disease symptoms.

I knew I had to get as far away from Dick, that company, and their mafioso practices, as quickly as I could – which I did. It took about nine months to transition out of my job at ZVL; but I did get out.

The CEO of one of our competitors had asked me, each time I saw him, when I was going to join his firm. I had never really considered joining his company until I knew I had to make a change to save my life. Joining this new company would require me to take a step down from the rung I had finally reached on the corporate ladder in my industry, as well as a very large pay cut. But I knew I needed to leave ZVL, so the negotiations with this CEO commenced.

Nine months were spent negotiating the best package I could possibly receive from the new company. In addition, I had to have some assurance that there would include a way for me to grow in my new role. In the end, I accepted the title that I had previously at Center Parking but making much less money than I had at Center or ZVL. I knew I had to make the change for my life's sake; so, I took the position with the new firm, grateful to get away from ZVL.

While transitioning out of ZVL, I also consulted several attorneys. I had thought about bringing a civil suit against Dick and ZVL for poisoning me. I had saved the pods. I had my diaries that detailed everything that happened. I had all the information I had gathered about the listening devices that Dick had planted; and I had the actual listening device. I felt I was well prepared for a fight.

Each attorney I spoke with did not seem surprised by my story. They said that this type of corporate sabotage and attempted murder is not all that uncommon. One attorney, who I met after I started my new job, asked me to bring the pods to his office to show him. Wearing gloves, goggles and a mask, I packed them in foil; then, in baggie after baggie and in plastic bag after plastic bag. Finally, I put the package in a garbage bag and then in a zippered handbag. I took the handbag to my office to take to my meeting with the attorney later that day.

But while I was working, my right eye started to burn profusely, as did the right side of my head. My throat and lungs started hurting, I developed a bad headache, and my gums started to ache and burn. I had forgotten briefly that I had brought the pods to my office; but when I made the connection with how badly I was feeling to what was in the bag, fear and panic came rushing over me. It had been about a year and a half since I found the toxins in my office; yet, even after all that time – and wrapped up so carefully – they still made me sick.

I did end up hiring that particular attorney to help me sort through things and get the two years of bonuses that ZVL owed me. ZVL had refused to pay me my bonus because of the "decline in the economy." The unpaid bonuses were equal to over $600,000. Mind you, they withheld my bonus while they were still making tens of millions of dollars in profit on their cash-cow business. But screwing people over was just their way – whether it was employees, or vendors, or sometimes even clients.

During the process of dealing with ZVL, my attorney also pushed them for answers about the poison pods; but of course, they claimed they had no answer, and that they had nothing to do with the poisoning. ZVL never said that it did not happen; they just said they did not know how the pods were planted.

We used an arbitrator to negotiate the bonus settlement. My attorney pushed me to agree to their condition that I drop the poison case in order to settle the bonus issue. My attorney said that I just did not have enough evidence to connect Dick or the company to the poisons. He said that without having a witness to testify to the placement of the poisons under Dick's direction, or a video showing who planted the pods, it would be impossible to prove that Dick did it.

I could have pushed ahead with the suit, but I had to face the fact that it would be incredibly expensive to do so. I could have been embroiled in the suit for years, which would have kept me tied to the nightmare of ZVL long after I had left the company. And – bottom line – why would I want to antagonize such horrific people who were completely absent of any moral or ethical code? Talk about stirring the pot! That was really the deciding factor; I had to move on. I could not live with this guy or this company in my head for another day.

I know that it would be amazing if I had an Erin Brockovich-type story to tell – where I found a plucky lawyer who had my back and vanquished the evildoers. It would have been so incredibly satisfying if that lawyer and I could have caused those bastards to suffer the loss of their money, their business, their reputations, and potentially their families. But, as I had learned in all the previous phases of my life, stories generally do not have fairy-tale endings. If anything good was going to happen, it was going to happen because I would create it on my own. So, I agreed to settle for most of my bonus money, and I dropped the poison piece of the case. I was sick and tired, and just wanted to be done.

But, looking back, I often wonder about my attorney – he was so eager to drop the poison piece of the case. When it was all over, and I asked him for all the evidence back, it took months to finally receive some of the items. He never did send back my coat rack, which was filled with dozens of pods. I wondered: did Dick and ZVL get to him? Did they pay him off, like they did with so many other people? I guess I will never know. And all I could do on my own at that point was move on, focus on my health and healing, and continue to try and rebuild my career.

The next 12-plus years were spent healing my body and my mind. Being constantly sick with Graves' disease – and then an even more serious illness caused by the poisons and their aftermath – took a tremendous toll. I struggled with severe fatigue and incredible body pain. The pain was so bad it was difficult to even walk at times. On top of that, my mental state was fragile. I lived in fear – always looking over my shoulder – not allowing people into my home for many years.

I installed the best alarm systems and cameras that money could buy. I always locked my doors and set my security alarm when I was home, no matter what. I never left my windows or doors open for fresh air. I kept my blinds closed all the time. I would lock my bedroom door at night, and sometimes I put furniture in front of the door if I was particularly unnerved. I slept with weapons that could protect me. And I got into the habit of locking my car doors as soon as I got into my car.

Always, always, I stayed aware of my surroundings when I was out and about. Finally, I shunned social media or anything that could put attention on me. I was fearful of anyone – suspicious of everyone – and I trusted no one.

I stopped socializing; I stopped entertaining in my home and throwing parties, which I loved to do. I just basically shut down. I always checked the rearview mirror in my car when I raised the garage door to make sure no one was there. I often searched my entire home when I arrived back from a trip to make sure nothing had been moved or touched, and to confirm that no one was in the house. I could not let go of that fear for a very long time.

To this day, I do not allow anyone into my home if I do not accompany them. Cleaning ladies or service people do not access my home without me there. No one has a key to my home, and no one knows the alarm code – period. No one is allowed to be in my home alone except my family, or occasionally a very close friend.

I joined the other parking firm upon leaving ZVL; but as I said, I had to take a step back in position and in pay. My new company would not hire me at the same level that I was at ZVL; I had to prove myself. I was back to overseeing a territory, making considerably less than I had in almost a decade. It was a huge blow to my psyche after working so hard for many years to become successful and well respected in my industry.

But I decided it was the best choice for me. So, I joined the new firm, and I worked my butt off – trying to get back to where I had been for so long, both financially and positionally. I worked hard while being very sick; but I did not let my illness slow my perseverance. I worked for this new firm in two different roles simultaneously for a number of years in order to make it happen. Working hard to prove myself was exhausting and trying, but I kept at it. All the while, I continued to deal with the mentality that permeates the male-dominated industry in which I chose to work. But that topic is perhaps for another book – another day. I kept my head down and stayed focused. I delivered results – and lots of them – along with a lot of profit.

By opening new markets and new business segments, I was allowed to move into a more suitable position and a better financial package. I dealt with all of the challenges and did what I do best – I pushed the physical and emotional stuff aside and down, and just kept going. I was happy and fortunate to be gainfully employed; and I knew I was so much better off than many people in the world. That knowledge kept me focused and grateful.

Here is another nod to Erin Brockovich: she made it very clear to the company that was pumping toxins into her clients' land that there was a direct connection between their waste and the cancer that was killing those clients. Her investigation also made it clear that there is a seven-to-eight-year gestation period for cancers that are caused by exposure to toxic chemicals. Thanks to Erin, that information is readily available, and it shined a very bright light on the fact that Dick was – like herpes – the worst gift that kept on giving. Exactly seven and a half years after I was surrounded by those chemicals, I was diagnosed with breast cancer; and it was growing aggressively on my right breast – on the side where the poisons were most of the time.

I had left ZVL Parking years before; but when I was diagnosed with cancer, I felt like I had been sucked back in time. I was right back in the reality where I had been poisoned and I would have to deal with what it had done to me.

Earlier, in the immediate aftermath of the exposure to the poisons, I had remarked that if I was ever diagnosed with cancer, it would be because of those poisons. I had even forgotten that I had made that remark, but it came back to me. I was horrified and terrified at the diagnosis; but I kept reminding myself that there was no way I was going to let that bizarre and destructive experience with ZVL dictate the rest of my life.

I wasted no time consulting the best doctors I could find, and I put my treatment plan into action. It was important to me to use both modern, western medicine as well as homeopathic methods in my treatments. My cancer was growing three times faster than what was typically seen for my type of breast cancer. I felt that it was necessary to attack the cancer from all sides.

There are a lot of books out there about people's experiences with cancer. This is not one of those books. My cancer experience was not a journey or opportunity to explore religion; it was not a time to explore my soul, my motivations, or my relationships; it was not a time to realize my oneness with the universe. My cancer diagnosis, and the hell of fighting to recover from it for almost six years can – even now – be summed up in one word: RAGE. I thought, *How **dare** Dick come back over seven years after he planted those chemicals, and devastate me again? How **dare** he still have an impact on my life? How **dare** he give me **two** devastating diseases?*

Why was he allowed to do this by the universe – or whatever god or gods exist – and go on living? I was always a good person. I never acted out of ill-will or spite, even when I was put-upon and victimized by the people around me repeatedly. I had never, ever tried to exact revenge.

I had always believed that the key to survival was to keep "my side of the street" clean and look after my own interests, because no one else was going to be as good and kind and generous a person as I was. I strongly believed that I had to live according to an extreme moral and ethical code of doing the right thing – treating others well, and always being the better person by taking the high road. If there was one good thing that came out of being raised in a religious cult, it was that. It was, and still is, something I firmly believe.

What did being such an upstanding person get me? What was the point of working hard to rise above all the shit I had been through in my life? Why were my acts of kindness and fairness rewarded with physical and emotional suffering, the near collapse of my career, an autoimmune disease, and now – **CANCER?!!**

The only answer I could conjure up was: the constant fight to move forward, to move beyond my brother's death, to cope with my mother's existence, to deal with my father leaving, to handle the challenges from Terrie, Camila, Dick, and everyone like them, was – in itself – the lesson

I was supposed to learn. The same universe, fate, or God that had let Dick slide by, unscathed and unpunished, had conspired to teach me how to fight and survive and thrive. And I have done exactly that. I am one of the most mentally and physically strong people I know. My will to not just survive, but to also thrive, is unparalleled – and I am proud of that.

I am also incredibly lucky, simply because I am one of the women in this country to survive breast cancer. My story is not that different from any other woman who has faced this disease and done her best to wrestle it to the ground; although, the way I came to have breast cancer is quite unusual.

I had a double mastectomy and several lymph nodes removed, with all the horror that goes with that incredibly atrocious procedure. I had pain, lots of pain, lots of stitches that turned into ugly scars, drainage tubes, expanders for five months, rebuilding, more surgery, implants, and then more severe pain. The healing process from the surgery was awful; and the chemo added even more pain to what I had to endure. I lost my hair again – all of it this time, which was another grim reminder that someone had poisoned me. I felt like I was experiencing a double whammy of depression.

I went through all the nightmares that go along with chemotherapy including pain, insomnia, and exhaustion. Although it seemed beside the point considering all of the other symptoms, my libido disappeared, which added to my general sense of depression and malaise. I was a bald-headed, sad, and very broken person.

Even so, my life up to that point had taught me that brokenness does not have to be the end of the story. Broken is not the same thing as dead. I never stopped working during any of the treatments. I even continued to travel for work, although I did cut back on the amount of travel. I gave presentations bald-headed – making jokes that I had lost a bet and had to shave my head – to try to diffuse the awkwardness in the room.

To this day, more than six years after cancer, I fight severe fatigue and body pain as a result of the poisons, the thyroid disease and cancer. I have had multiple surgeries, and many treatments to try to fix the damage that the chemo and the poisons did to me. I continued for years to live with so many painful and inconvenient health-related issues – trouble walking, severe insomnia, brain fog, and memory loss. I have also experienced a loss of testosterone, so I have had to take testosterone shots and creams – which made me lose some of my hair again.

I still cannot lay face down because of the lingering pain from the double mastectomy. I have had continuous infections, such as sinus issues and UTIs, because of my low immune system. The sinus infections are also related to the broken noses Camila gave me, but were exacerbated by the chemo breaking down my immune system. I had carpal tunnel surgery on my hand, and received multiple epidural steroid shots in my spine, neck and feet to try to alleviate the pain – all due to the poisons and chemo.

My thyroid was also severely impacted by the Graves' and then the ravages of chemo. I am a back sleeper, and my thyroid had grown so large that it was literally choking me in my sleep. I had difficulty swallowing, and I put up with laryngitis for months.

The thyroid had developed multiple tumors with blood flow in them, which the doctor said could indicate cancer. So, I had another cancer scare to deal with until we could do a needle biopsy. Thank God it was benign, but the doctor – with his terrible bedside manner – reminded me that there were a million places that cancer could be hiding in the thyroid. The needle biopsy only tested four areas, he said. So, until I was able to have the thyroid removed and thoroughly tested, I agonized over the fear of having cancer again.

When I finally had my thyroid removed the surgeon said he needed to make a much larger incision than normal to get it out (yet another ugly scar), because it was three times the normal size. He said he had difficulty removing it because of the size, and because the tumors had attached themselves to other areas inside my neck.

The surgery itself severely damaged my vocal cords when he removed the thyroid. I could not talk – only whisper – for well over a month after the surgery, and then I had a very weak and raspy voice for about half a year afterwards. Even now, my voice is very different than it was before – deeper and somewhat scratchy. I also lost my ability to sing because of the surgery – something I had enjoyed and was actually quite good at. I am crushed by the fact that I am totally unable to sing anymore.

After the surgery, I was kept overnight in the hospital with a drain in my throat. I had thought I would never have to deal with drains again; but thanks to Dick, there I was. I had a thin tube inserted in my neck just above my clavicle. When I was ready to be released from the hospital, the surgeon came and removed the tube. It was inserted much deeper than I thought, and he kept pulling and pulling. I almost threw up. It was disgusting. When it was out, he put a small Band-Aid over the hole. I said, "All I need is a Band-Aid?" He said, "Yes, that usually does the trick."

My friend Carla caught a flight to come take care of me through the surgery and was an angel. She made sure I had good care; she even stayed the night in the hospital with me. She drove me home upon my release, and I immediately headed to bed.

I went to sleep sitting up in bed and woke up coughing – my shirt was soaking wet. I got up and looked in the mirror – my shirt and bra were completely soaked in blood. I pulled back the Band-Aid, and the hole in my neck was literally squirting blood like a gunshot wound. It was unbelievable! I started applying pressure with tissues. After going through about half the box of tissue with no improvement I went downstairs and told Carla there was a problem. I removed the tissue, and it was still gushing blood. She freaked out; I freaked out. We kept compressing the wound, and Carla called the surgeon who did not answer. Then she called the hospital, and they told us to go to the ER.

At the ER, the bleeding was finally stopped. When I saw my surgeon a few days after, I told him about what happened. He said that had never happened to one of his patients; but he speculated that he must have cut an artery during surgery, because a vein would not cause such overt bleeding. It was one more event to add to the litany of bizarre stories and events in my life. Now I have to take daily hormones since I do not have a thyroid. And almost three years after having it removed, I struggle to keep my hormone levels balanced. I have also had two heat strokes due to my difficulty staying hydrated and keeping minerals in proper balance. I had one heat stroke during chemo and the other several years later, which landed me in the ER yet again.

A month and a half after I had my thyroid removed, I had my nose rebuilt from the inside. I needed to have the work done due to the multiple broken noses Camila had given me. I had a lot of trouble breathing through my nose; one of my nostrils had completely collapsed during one of Camila's beatings. The surgeon said that my septum was not just deviated, it was completely crushed. My nose was slightly crooked, and it actually had a dent in it.

After the procedure, the doctor told me that it took a lot of work to rebuild my nose. He had to use cartilage that was not mine (I did not want to ask where it came from), and that he really had to work hard to correct the issues in my nose. He said that I needed to be very careful, so I did not mess up his work. Never mind the possibility of messing up his work – I did not want to screw up my nose!

My trials and challenges from autoimmune diseases and cancer continued. I had severe foot pain that was getting worse, and the shots for the pain did not provide relief for very long. I began limping badly because it felt like there were knives in both of my feet. I started leaning on people when walking; and when choosing a route on foot, I would calculate the path with the fewest steps.

When I traveled for work, there were times I did not think I could make it to the gate at the airport. I frequently thought that I might have to get a wheelchair. The pain went on for months; I tried everything to get some relief. At one point, I thought, *If this is my life, I cannot continue to live it.* The pain was unbearable; so, I finally had foot surgery on both feet to help alleviate the pain. I had to wear big boots for over a month as I recovered, which was just ridiculous.

At the same time, I was still battling considerable pain elsewhere in my body. After seeing many doctors and trying many things to help with the pain, I decided to have a food allergy test. I would cut out all foods on the list in the hopes that it would help; I had exhausted so many other avenues to try to get relief. While I was working on that, my oncologist called me with some blood test results.

He told me I was in vitamin D toxicity, and that I needed to stop taking vitamin D. Some background: when I was first diagnosed with Graves' disease, I had almost no vitamin D in my body. I was put on an emergency vitamin D replacement program as part of my treatment. Since then, I have had trouble keeping my vitamin D level balanced. It is often either too high or too low. My dosage of vitamin D is a constant balancing act, similar to what I go through with my Graves' disease medicine and my thyroid medication.

So, I stopped taking vitamin D and cut out all the food on the allergen list. My feeling about cutting out food to which I was allergic (or just sensitive to) was, *Why would I put things in my body that my body has to fight?* My body has already had to fight sickness and toxins; it just made no sense to intentionally make it fight even harder and further wear down my immune system.

Within days, I stopped limping and the inflammation in my body started decreasing. It took several more months for the pain to dissipate to about 75- 80 percent – but I was happy to be on the right path to becoming pain-free.

I developed kidney stones on a business trip to San Francisco. I had to go to the ER for treatment because the stones were so painful. I passed them right after I left the ER, which scared me to death because I bled considerably. I have since had another bout with kidney stones, and both incidents were caused by the chemo. Speaking of chemo – my teeth chipped and became brittle from it. And since my thyroid was removed, I have struggled with some weight fluctuations.

Due to the effects of the illnesses caused by the poisons, I had to have yet another surgery to have my piriformis muscle removed due to very bad sciatica. A lot of my pain had gotten better as a result from the many other treatments I had tried: acupuncture, cupping, muscle trauma massage, active muscle release technique, steroid shots, chiropractic care, herbal and nutritional supplements, vitamin IVs, saunas, chelation, cryotherapy, laser therapy, and the list goes on and on – all on my own dollar. The two things I refused were prescription drugs for the pain and sleeping aids for my insomnia.

I tried to address my sciatic pain with all the therapies I mentioned, as well as stretching programs, yoga, and other ways – but it was all to no avail. The excruciating pain continued.

I have incredible inner strength. I can, and have, taken on more physical pain than most – but I could not continue to take this level of pain. I had to find a solution. I could not sit in a car and drive for even five minutes, or work out at the gym for very long, before the pain would send me over the edge. It ran all the way down my leg into my foot. Finally, I found a surgeon who could remove the piriformis muscle that sat on my sciatic nerve. I thought, *This is my last hope, because I am back to limping at times due to the pain.*

The surgery was quite invasive and made sitting extremely painful for some time. It also left a huge scar on my buttocks. It took some time for things to calm down around my sciatic nerve, but the procedure did eliminate the pain running down my leg into my foot. The surgery relieved the sciatic pain itself by about 75 percent – so it was well worth it. I sometimes still have pain in that area of the sciatic nerve; but it does not shoot down my leg anymore and is not as intense.

The effects of Graves' disease and cancer have been devastating. It has ravaged my body, my mental well-being, and even my ability to truly be myself. I completely lost my sense of humor – I was a pretty funny person before all of the sabotage and illness. I lost my passion, and occasionally even my will to fight for life – although that was always very short-lived. My powerful inner strength would always kick in; and my fury at what Dick had done to me would drive me to keep trying to heal myself. I knew that I had to keep fighting and not let him win.

As if I hadn't endured enough, I decided to have another surgery, to transfer some of my own fat over my breast implants. I hated seeing all the ripples from the implants. No, this particular surgery was not necessary – and yes, it was about vanity. But after all I had been through, looking in the mirror – and hating what I saw – just brought me down even more. So, I decided to do something about it, on my own dollar – just like I had with so many of my other treatments and procedures.

I am pleased with the results of all the procedures I have had in order to heal from Graves' and cancer. I call it **chasing the pain.** The last 12 years have been me chasing the pain and constantly fighting to find ways to improve my health. Many things have helped me, but perseverance has definitely been the key. And while I am not 100 percent,

I am far, far better than I have been over the last dozen years – and I am so thankful for that.

If I have learned anything about medical care and healing, it is that you cannot allow your doctors to manage everything and make all the decisions for you. You have to take responsibility for your own well-being and health. I have focused on self-education, lots of research, and second and third opinions. I have sought help from homeopathic doctors while still consulting western medical doctors. I am willing to try new things to help myself; and I believe that was critical in discovering what would make me better. Chasing the pain, answers and solutions for my health works for me.

Now, if Dick ever reads this book, I am sure he and the owners at ZVL will take great pleasure in knowing about the suffering and damage they have caused me. But, I take great pleasure in knowing that I beat them. I am still alive – and I am not just alive – I am thriving and have become healthy. I won. I will be damned if I let Dick or any other person like him write the end of my story.

I get up every day and perform better than any healthy person does. I drive myself extremely hard and focus on winning in my life. I am winning in regard to my health and my body's physical well-being – winning at love and friendship – and winning at being an honest, kind, compassionate and generous person. And those are not empty words thrown in a book – for me, those are my life's true focuses. If all that I have been through has taught me anything, it is to be grateful for my life, to be thankful for the love of my family and friends, and to always try to pay it forward.

CHAPTER FOURTEEN

SURVIVING AND THRIVING!

Not only did Dick **not** get the opportunity to write the end of my story – he was unsuccessful at killing me – he also did not get to define how that **chapter** of my life would end. I was certain that the only way for me to get past what I had been through was to see it as a distinct set of experiences. And then I would need to view what was to come in the future the same way. I needed to make an unmistakable division between what came before and during my stay in Dicktown, and everything that was to come next.

I tried to psych myself into that head space over and over again, but I could not get past the trauma brought on by so many years of violence, illness, and mistreatment. I just could not let go. First of all, I could not let go of my guilt about Kent Jr., which had not left me for a single moment after he died. I felt responsible for his death; I felt so responsible that it transcended feeling and became absolute truth.

The guilt that came with reliving the circumstances of my brother's death left me with two thoughts that circled endlessly in my mind: Why had I not made the choice to run toward Kent Jr., instead of hesitating on that awful day that he lost his life? As a result of my terrible inaction, was I destined to be stuck in a loop of pain, bizarreness and abuse forever? These thoughts chased each other in my head for decades, like two single-minded goldfish in a painfully small fishbowl.

I shifted my approach to life. After evaluating the many unfathomable events and injuries that had happened to me for no explainable reason, I became a much more conservative person when it came to choosing my activities. I had often just been at the wrong place at the wrong time.

There are so many other stories of ridiculous things that have happened to me – like the time when my girlfriend and I were almost murdered in Jamaica because we were gay.

There was the time as a senior in high school when I had a stalker, who would wait for me after school at the entrance to my father's neighborhood. He would race on his bike to corner me in my garage, where he would try to talk to me. Then he would try to follow me into the house, while no one was home. So, I started speeding home and getting in the garage as fast as I could. I would close the garage door behind me, but he would go to every single door and window, peering in them and trying to open them (I often wonder what he would have done if he had found a door or window open). That occurred several times a week, for several months, before my father stepped in to help me. Still, after that, he would just sit outside the house on his bike, patting the knife that he carried on his waist – watching the house and waiting for me to leave.

Or there was the time I got my ass kicked by three large Dutch dykes in Amsterdam at the Gay Pride festival because they were bullying everyone, and I was the one person who refused to be bullied. And there was the time that a stingray took a huge chunk out of my heel with its stinger, in Hawaii, on the very same day I had to shave my head due to chemo. Or the time a shower door broke just as I stepped out of the shower, and shattered into a million pieces? I had puncture wounds and cuts all over me and glass came out of my scalp for over a month.

One last story – of the many I could offer – is the time I took a path on a ski trail in a canyon, reaching the top of the trail at full speed only to find no snow there. I wiped out royally, and ended up breaking my hand and requiring hip surgery. The only positive thing that came out of that experience was that I had my physical therapy alongside John Madden, who was quite entertaining and funny.

Those are only a few of the crazy events that left me – and my friends – questioning, "Why Kendra?" I began to feel like I needed to proactively protect myself from activities that could result in debilitating – or even catastrophic – injuries. I decided that I should not participate in activities like bungee jumping, paragliding, scuba diving, or parachuting from a plane. And I avoided other adrenaline-filled adventures that I would have absolutely loved. Because I became convinced that history would continue to repeat itself, and that one day I could end up injured beyond repair. And with over 80 visits to doctors and the ER – for stitches, broken bones, concussions and even things lodged in my eye – I felt protecting myself was for good reason.

I had even shut myself away from my family. I did not go back to Oklahoma much after I left for New York City – not for many years. I needed to heal – and it was very hard to see my mother and be around things that brought back horrible memories. The few times I did go back during the next 15 years, I would become depressed and could not wait to leave.

I never went back for Christmas, except for that first year after I left. I spent three and a half decades away from my family at Christmas because of my guilt and pain over the death of my brother Kent Jr., who was born on Christmas Day. It was just too much for me; it made me sick to my stomach when his name would come up on that holiday – because I knew the truth of what happened the day he died. My solution was to avoid traveling to Oklahoma for Christmas.

As part of my healing, however, I finally went back for Christmas in 2021. It was wonderful to see my family and be with them for the holiday. It was still tough, though, knowing it was my brother's birthday.

The other thought that occurred to me was, *I'm a good person. I always try to do the right thing; I'm driven to do the right thing for other people all the time. Do I really deserve the pain I've suffered? Awful people don't suffer as much as I do; where's the sense in that?* I tried and tried to puzzle it out. No amount of religion, philosophy, faith, methodical thought process, or optimism provided the answer. The only thing I could come up with was that **if** the universe does indeed have some order – which is a concept I have always clung to, despite the chaos in my life – then I simply **did** deserve all of it. That was a very depressing thought. It was that thought that would drag me back down every time I felt like I might come up for air.

Finally, after living in that quandary for years – not understanding why bizarre things happened to me the way they did – I simply decided that I had had enough! I had just gone through one more bad breakup with a woman – I was actually engaged to her – and I had had enough toxicity, darkness, and mistreatment in my life. I decided that I was no longer going to allow people to treat me badly or hurt me. The damage others had done to me and my body had been insurmountable. It had been a lifetime of suffering, and I was just done with it! I decided that I **did** deserve to be happy and safe and healthy – and whatever curse or karmic bullshit that kept me in a spiral of bizarreness had to end. I was going to stop living in fear.

I knew that I deserved better! I deserved peace and health and happiness, and I was going to make it happen! So, at the end of 2018, I made the decision that 2019 would be my **YEAR OF CHANGE!**

I made a resolution to take ownership of my destiny. I threw a huge New Year's Eve party at my house to welcome 2019, and my Year of Change. People flew and drove in from all over to attend the party – my dad and his wife even came. I had not had a party or let people into my home since the ZVL Parking catastrophe. But it was time for that to change.

There were over 80 people at the party. It was catered – and I had music, cocktails, and party favors. I even hired some fire breathers and fire dancers to perform. We watched fireworks from my rooftop deck – even though it was freezing – and we danced until 4 a.m.

I decided that I had lived in isolation and fear for too long. It was time to start opening my heart, my home, and my mind, and to stop living in so much fear. The party was my coming-out event. It was such a success that since then, I have hosted smaller New Year's and 4th of July parties every year, as well as smaller gatherings. Letting people back into my home was a huge step for me.

I put a plan into action for that Year of Change. I decided to work on changing my thought processes and to eliminate negative energies around me. Although I had always been very conscious of, and grateful for, the wonderful life that I had built for myself, I began practicing gratitude more fervently. I began to express gratitude for all the good in my life. Even though I had many crazy experiences, my adult life had also been full of adventure, travel, and a rewarding career. I was focused on shifting my mindset to heal my soul.

In that Year of Change, I not only dabbled in social media, but also got my first tattoo. I had "Lucky" inscribed on my left palm, as a daily reminder to me that I am lucky to be alive, and lucky for the life I have lived.

I worked hard during the Year of Change to make sure it was positive and effective for me. And I made many changes. One of the biggest decisions was to take the time to write my story. When I first started writing, I had zero plans to publish. The intention of writing was simply to document my bizarre life, and hopefully bring some healing. I feel that the book did become a vessel for healing and truth. It has helped to cleanse me of many things I had been holding on to, and to start living more freely. To be sure, this book was never written with the intention to "out" "Dick" and "ZVL." Who these people are will go with me to my grave. That kind of revenge is not within me – and for my own safety, it is the best path. But writing about it has been part of the healing process.

As 2020 approached, I was proud and happy of the positive changes I had made over the previous year, and I wanted to continue with more healing. I decided to name 2020 **The Big Year.** I just knew that big things were going to happen – and I was going to make them happen for me. I wanted to finish writing my story, and I wanted to start focusing not just on my physical and mental health, but also on strengthening my body. So, I started scrambling and bouldering, which are forms of rock climbing. It was something I had never done before. I was ready and excited for 2020, **The Big Year.** Little did I know it would be a big year for the entire world – and not in a good way whatsoever.

As COVID reared its ugly head, the focus for the year shifted to survival for the whole world. It was a terrible year for everyone, and very difficult. Even after the end of the year, and into 2021, there was not much relief from COVID. So many of my plans were put on hold, just like those of so many other people around the world. Everyone was focused on the task at hand – getting through COVID safely.

After the COVID lockdowns lifted in the summer of 2020, one of my best friends on earth, Gretchen – who knows my full range of good, bad, and ugly – wanted to travel. She suggested we go on vacation together, as we had done before over the years. But there was not any international travel happening at that time. Gretchen is very into New Age stuff, so I suggested that we go to Sedona, Arizona.

I have never been intrigued by spiritualism, crystals, energy transfers, necromancy, astral projection, or anything else along that category. It just seemed too far out for me. I could barely believe what goes on in the immediate physical world – what we all deal with every day. Contemplating multiple spheres of existence was just too much for me.

Engaging with the outer limits of spiritualism was beyond my capacity. New Age topics had always reminded me of the cult of my growing-up years – so I had readily shunned those activities. Nonetheless, when Gretchen suggested we visit a community of psychics, seers, and healers in Sedona, I agreed.

I would have agreed to almost anything that Gretchen proposed for the trip, if for no other reason than we always had a terrific time together. But she asked at exactly the right moment of blending my Year of Change with my Big Year. I gave her a more enthusiastic "yes" than I expected.

When we agreed to the journey to the "great beyond" in Sedona, I did not have an action plan for the trip – just the intent to continue my healing and growing process. I figured that a trip to Sedona was as good an idea as any. Even if I ended up deciding that Gretchen's New Age practice was not for me, at least I would feel like I went outside my comfort zone. A few weeks later, in August, Gretchen flew in from Atlanta. We packed up my car and hit the road to what I hoped would be enlightenment, but suspected would turn out to be merely an entertaining week with my best friend.

Later that day, we rolled into what some people consider to be one of the most spiritual and beautiful places on Earth – or at least in the United States. Sedona boasts the highest population of mediums, psychics, and other vessels of the metaphysical. It also has what is fabled to be the thinnest of veils between our world and the supernatural.

It is a place of incredible beauty, with lots of hiking trails and climbing locales through the stunning, orange-colored mountains and vistas. Gretchen had planned a whole week of metaphysical, spiritual, and healing activities for us; and surprisingly, I was excited. It was the first vacation in a decade that I would not receive or make work calls unless it was an emergency. Nor would I do any work or crack open my laptop, although I did check emails from my phone.

Gretchen even scheduled us to meet with a psychic, and said that if we wanted to, we could talk to dead people. I was not interested in that at all. In fact, I told Gretchen that I specifically did **not** want to talk to any dead people. The idea of it was creepy to start; but the possibility of communicating with Kent Jr. – on the off chance that spiritualism was not total nonsense – was too much for me. I was not ready, and probably never would be.

I decided that all I could hope to learn from the psychic was to know why my life had been so full of tragedy and trauma, and what I could do to change that. Maybe I could get some insight to ensure that I would have a peaceful, healthy, and happy life for my days left on this Earth. Gretchen had made the appropriate appointments for us before we left for the trip, so we spent our first night in Sedona hanging out, eating well, and wondering what the next day would hold.

On our first day, we planned an early hike to Devil's Bridge. In fact, we had to get up every day at 5 a.m. to make sure we were on the trails early and then done with our hike by 10 a.m. Otherwise, it would be way too hot to continue to hike. After hiking each day, we spent the remaining hours of our days keeping all the appointments that Gretchen had planned for us.

The next day, we went on a tour of several vortexes. It was incredible – and you really could feel the Earth's push and pull in those vortexes. As the week went on, our time was filled with incredible hikes and enlightening, spiritual events. Of course, there was also plenty of delicious eating and drinking, and shopping in Sedona's many amazing galleries.

Towards the end of the week, we each had our auras photographed and interpreted, and then individually met with a psychic who did past-life regressions. This was in a complex with many spiritual healers, psychics, energy therapists, and all other kinds of New Age practitioners dedicated to enhancing their clients' self-actualization.

While total self-actualization would have been fantastic, I was willing to set the bar far lower to begin my explorations. I really wanted to discover why my life had followed certain traumatic patterns – patterns that I fervently desired to break. It seemed like a simple enough mission, given the amazing claims made by so many of Sedona's resident practitioners of the spiritual arts. In my opinion, setting the bar low has always been a good way to avoid disappointment and frustration. Big Year or not, it was not a strategy I was ready to abandon.

I had never heard of aura photography, and it was very different than I expected. The photographer takes your photo with a camera that reads energy through your hands. Your energy shows up in the form of colored washes of light that constitute your aura, which is made up of your energy, personality, potential, and strengths. Red, orange, blue, indigo, yellow, green, and violet are, respectively, active, happy, peaceful, imaginative, friendly, healing, and mystical. If a white orb shows up in your photo, those are supposedly your spirit guides. Should you choose to subscribe to the discipline of aura photography, it is pretty straightforward.

We went in together for our photos and aura readings, so we could hear about each other's interpretations. Gretchen went first and turned out to be a healer, through and through. Her photograph was as blue as blue gets. Gretchen is a nurturing person who was laser-focused on helping to heal people from toxic mold poisoning. She had been through that herself, and had worked for several years to heal her brain and body from the mold. So, it was not much of a surprise – at least not to me – to learn how very true blue she was. The reader was so excited by Gretchen's blue aura that they talked for a very long time about it. The reader told Gretchen that she should be in Sedona working at the reader's New Age center, which she owned with her mother.

Then, as it was my turn, the reader then turned to me and said, "I am so sorry. That is going to be impossible to follow because it was so amazing and pure. Hopefully you won't be disappointed." *Wow*, I thought. *Way to pave the way for disappointment.* But when my photo was revealed, the reader was amazed and could not get over what she saw.

Unlike 99 percent of the photos she takes, which usually have three or maybe four colors, mine had every single color, along with three white orbs or spheres floating in the aurora borealis. She said, "You are literally two people." Apparently, that means that I am as fully left-brained as I am right-brained. According to the reading, I am rational and logical in my thinking with a sharp intellect; and I am simultaneously very spiritual – a teacher, a counselor, and an empath, as well as a very creative person.

Those three floating white orbs in the photo were identified as my protector spirits, one of whom I now believe is my brother. Did I unquestioningly believe what was revealed that day? Not 100 percent –

although I did always know myself to be a strong mix of left and right brain. I also knew that I was an empath with some low-level predictive abilities, and I had seen my share of dead people – or spirits, if you will. But now I had a new lens to look through for assessing myself. I could think about who I am, versus who I want to be.

Like most people, I wanted to believe – and still do – that what the reader said was the undeniable truth. But my natural skepticism – bred from years of distancing myself from organized religion and blind belief, particularly my mother's version of it – has made it difficult to accept anything at face value. Don't get me wrong. I liked the possibility that I could be the human embodiment of the convergence of many human qualities and potentials – and so said the reader! The experience also opened me to seriously consider the spectral realm and what else it could teach me. So, I happened to become more receptive to metaphysical communication just in time for my session with the psychic, who turned out to be just as much a therapist as a psychic.

A brief aside about therapists: I am not a fan of them and have never been treated by one at any point in my life, other than the 6 weeks with Jody. How can someone who knows nothing about my life, my family, or my background – and has not lived through my situations and emotions – effectively guide me to some epiphany about myself? How is a completely uninitiated stranger able to decode the layers of complexity and craziness that I have dealt with my whole life?

And – I have spent decades building protective layers around the bits and pieces of my heart and psyche. I have been damaged by the events of my life: Kent Jr.'s death, abuse from my mother and Camila, and so much more. The idea of some random person picking at those layers and possibly destroying them was frightening.

A past-life regression therapist, on the other hand, was not going to ask me much about myself. She was going to **tell** me about myself, I reasoned – and I would be able to choose what I wanted to do (or not) with her wisdom. All of this is to say that when I walked into her office – and it looked like I had imagined a psychotherapist's office would – it did not faze me.

Now, I am not saying that therapy does not work for others; I know many people who have been helped tremendously by therapy. And I encourage it for any friends or family who are hurting or need help. It just was never for me.

I was shown into the psychic's room; it featured the usual desk, two chairs, a couch, and a few decorations, including the standard-issue Sedona dream catchers and crystals. The woman who was doing my reading was a thin blonde, roughly 65 years old with a slight southern drawl, and with a warm, kindly manner. I sat with her for 10 minutes or so to give her some background on why I was there, and what I wanted to learn. I mentioned my brother's death, but not in detail; I talked about my bizarre work experience as well as my sickness and injuries, and I described some of the other events that I had survived.

The overview of my life was intended to make it clear what I was hoping to achieve in the session. I told the therapist that I wanted off the insane merry-go-round of pain, struggle, and trauma that I had experienced from the time of my earliest memories. All I wanted was peace, I told her. I wanted to move past the patterns that I had lived with for so long – and had grown to hate. I settled back in my chair, waiting for the healer to begin.

She allowed me to record her, so I could always refer back to our session. She closed her eyes for a while and seemed to be channeling a message. She then said, "You are one of the most powerful people I have ever met." That surprised me. I knew I was strong; but to hear her share that with me really caught me off guard. It made me feel a little uncomfortable.

But she went on to share more encouraging words: "If you allow it to be, this moment could be the turning point in your current incarnation. This is a profound moment where your awareness is going to be shifted – about who you are and why you're here. There's no accident that you landed here today to hear this message. This is going to be a huge unburdening and an awakening to new possibilities." "Unburdening" sounded spot on. I settled in, a little more relaxed, as she continued with information about who I had been in my past lives, and how those events and any trauma caused by them carried into my present-day.

She went on to say, "In your past lives, you were in very responsible leadership roles. You were a leader of leaders, responsible for many people. You're the one everyone came to for advice and inspiration. You were the one in the castle; you came from a lineage of royalty. But before that, you were an amazing warrior and hero in your country, in multiple lives. The bravest, strongest, smartest; warrior of warriors. Over and over, you proved your commitment to bravery, integrity and truth. You were unwavering. The spirit guides are showing me a scenario where you're in England, Scotland, or Ireland. I see rain, rocks, horses, armor. You're in the front of an army of people who are defending their homeland. This is the place where you were being confronted by another army that you saw coming at you, flowing over the hillside on the horizon. You knew you were outnumbered."

She broke out of her monologue and asked me what I would have done in that situation. I explained that I would have wanted my people to be safe. I would have wanted to save them. "Which is what you did," she replied. "You fought. You turned around to everyone following you, knowing what was coming and you said, 'Follow me, we're going in,' and you went in. You were knocked down. You were one of the first to go down this time, which inspired your followers to fight even harder. And they won. You gave them the courage and inspiration they needed to carry on with a vengeance, because of what had happened to you. The foe left. The conflict ended with your people holding steady. You were revered as a hero. Your name carried through history."

I did not ask what my name was, or anything about who I was specifically. It was not that I did not want to know; but it was overwhelming to hear a story that so immediately touched on some of the key emotions that had brought me there in the first place. There was not anything tangible about what she was saying that I would be able to research later – but a feeling of possible truth was there. Maybe I just wanted it to be true.

She continued, "Now you're coming into a new lifetime, passing out of being that warrior, dying many times on the battlefield through your lives, and into being the leader I described earlier. Now you can be a leader without being on the battlefield. Your last life before this one, I see you in a castle. You're the one your people come to for leadership and inspiration. Do you know anything about Oliver

Cromwell and England? That's the era, the 17th century. Cromwell was unstoppable in his fight against Charles I. He led the armies of Parliament in the English Civil War and ruled England for five years before he died. He destroyed towns, castles, and leaders all over England; and you and your people were one of his targets – among many. You felt overwhelming guilt because there was nothing you could do to protect your loved ones and your people. You couldn't stop him. Your castle was attacked and demolished. You and everyone you cared about – or were responsible for – lost everything."

Again, nothing specific was given in her narrative about which castle, which leader, or which part of England she was referring to; but it did not matter. That feeling of total loss, and the futility of my efforts to make things right for the people I loved, hit my core like a well-placed punch. It made perfect sense to me in that moment that there was a continuing line of exactly how I had always felt, straight into the past. It was a line of emotion that extended as far back as I could imagine – and as far forward as the moment before I stepped into that room with that woman. The context of the same pain repeating itself down through the centuries gave what I had endured in my present-day life a sense of meaning. The sense of randomness – which has always made the terrible things that have happened to me even more frightening – dissipated as she spoke.

"Now you're in a new incarnation. You don't want to fight. You want a peaceful life without conflict. That's where you are now. We're in your present. But the pattern and energy that you were accustomed to on the battlefield is fighting to come back over and over again, so you have to defend yourself and survive. Now is the time for you to take control and break the pattern by making different choices."

She continued. "I want to talk about the central pain for you – your brother's death. Your brother was a beautiful soul; but his path was very different from yours. His soul was dedicated to a volunteer life, unlike your warrior life. His role was to help you see that it's not necessary to continually manifest as a warrior. You couldn't have done all the things you did on your own in your previous karmic life. He was there with you. Your brother was always your defender in days gone by. He sacrificed himself for you before, and did it in this life too. That sacrifice is something his soul has to work through. He thought he could defend you and protect you; but he couldn't, so he sacrificed himself for you."

She then went on to evidently channel my brother, which is not what I wanted. "He says, 'I'm just about as OK as you are.' He's got guilt and shame for not being able to protect you. It's not your fault that he chose to protect you. It was his choice to do this. He was the older sibling. You were a little girl. It was a poor decision on his part."

I bristled at the implication that Kent Jr. was to blame for anything. That is not how I have ever seen things, and it sat like a fat, squat, toad on my chest – ugly and uncomfortable. The healer must have seen it on my face.

"You are doing as well as you're doing in this lifetime because you're a fighter. But your spiritual guides are asking you to release this pattern of self-loathing and self-sacrifice. It's time to consciously bring that to completion. Remember that you're not here to be a martyr. You're here to have a beautiful, joyful, loving life. You have free will. The spirits are giving you a choice to release the horror and the pain; but it's your choice to do it – your choice to move on and live a different kind of life. You don't have to live with all this disharmony, pain and discord. You have to reframe your story. Your brother's death wasn't your fault. It was his poor decision. You were an innocent bystander for something he chose, and he feels guilt and regret that you suffer. Shift your focus to gratitude. Shift from pain."

Her words were still angering me. It sounded like a criticism of Kent Jr., which was the last thing I wanted to hear or could accept. I also never considered myself a martyr or a victim – ever. I actually always fought against any kind of notion or suggestion that I was ever a victim. I was just someone who was often in the wrong place at the wrong time. But the rest of what she said made sense. Was it specific information about me? I had no idea; but I knew that wherever the advice was coming from, it did apply to me. It made sense to let go of the pain – the question was, how to do it? The answer came from her quite quickly, on the heels of my question.

"You have to learn to connect to people heart-to-heart, not mind-to-mind. But first, you must clear yourself so you can move forward and help other people. You've been engrossed in work so you can run away from feelings. But you won't heal until you feel. The more you can allow for heart-to-heart connection, the happier you'll be. Self-respect, self-love will be restored. Release all that is not love. Release the baggage you've been carrying around."

Once again, the question I had was, "How?" She went on to say, "There are three steps to do this. They are:
1. Forgive (yourself – and other people, their limitations and imperfections, and any intended harm that has come your way),

2. Release (the negative vibrations from your field, bad energy of all kinds),

3. Gratitude (for all you've been through, because it's allowed you to become the beautiful being that you are)."

She continued: "Use what you've dealt with and learned to go forward and be of service. Go forth and inspire others."

Now we were getting somewhere. I already kept a gratitude journal, so I understood the power of acknowledging what is good in one's life. I understand that focusing on those positive things will color the way you approach everything you encounter – good or bad. I had already dabbled in forgiveness by forgiving Camila for all she had done to me; but no doubt, there was so much more I could do.

Yet, forgiving myself hinged on letting Kent Jr. carry the responsibility for his actions. I did not know if that was something I could ever do; but at least I understood the premise of what she was saying.

Release was also something I had started practicing in my Year of Change. I had started disconnecting from people who carried negative energy or created drama. I had been trying to surround myself with positive, loving people with good energy. But I knew I could do more than that – particularly, releasing any negative energy inside of me from the anger I had kept, but shoved deep down inside, for so many years. To be sure, the practice of release would take concerted effort and focus.

After a brief pause, I heard myself saying, "I feel that by surviving all that I have, I should – and can – help people. About two years ago, I started writing down all the things that had happened to me, just to document all the bizarre experiences I have had. I did it for myself, and maybe – eventually – for a family member or two to read. I had no intention to share it more widely than that. But as the process of documenting my life has gone on, I think that maybe it is something I should consider sharing by publishing it. Maybe other people who have been through similar experiences and trauma in their life can learn something by reading about the extreme life I've led. Maybe they can come away with something that, at the very least, can comfort them. They can know they're not alone if bad things happen to them, and that they aren't broken or evil or rotten when they have to deal with bad things. I don't know exactly what my lesson or message is, other than that I'm a survivor; but I'm honing that message and trying to understand it more and more. Let me amend that. I'm not just a survivor. I'm finding ways to thrive, and to create a life I'll love in the wake of my own survival."

She contemplated what I said for a moment. "Okay, here's the key. The more you can do your own work, the clearer your message will be. You will be of great influence – of great service – but this time without having to sacrifice yourself or having so much pain."

The session ended and I walked into the Sedona sunshine, blinking after sitting in the shade of the psychic's office, and in the obscurity of my own thoughts for the previous hour and a half. I waited outside for Gretchen, who was shopping inside the building, and reflected on the last thing the healer said to me. "Do your work and your message will be clear. You can help others." Once again, as a very black-and-white person, that was not the most tailor-made answer for me personally. But frankly, it was solid advice for anyone. The mission is not to just do the work; the mission is to also have clarity about what and who you are, and about what you want to say to anyone who will hear you.

We all have something to share. And if you believe in past lives and energy, you believe that we are all connected through space, time and energy, and by the constantly intertwining stories that make us who we are. Even if there is no such thing as a past life, we are still connected in this life. That connection makes every story, from every person, relevant. It makes us all responsible to one another in whatever way we are capable. My story is relevant simply by virtue of my existence – as is your story, and as are the stories of everyone we know.

I do not yet have a conclusion to my story, because my story is still in process. My story is not over; it is a part of the continuum of our shared humanity, the same as yours. My story – as I have lived it in this life – has been about not just surviving, but thriving. All the crazy things that have happened to me aside, I have built an incredible life for myself. I have been fortunate, blessed, and lucky to have lived such an incredible adult life. And I will continue to have amazing experiences and a wonderful life.

My traumas and tragedies do not define me. I define myself, and I use my experiences to build, grow, learn, and become stronger. And even as I write this, my story is shifting into one of reflection – which, if the healer in Sedona is to be believed, is the gateway to even more thriving. I was told that my version of thriving is to be of service and influence – to step outside the boundaries of my own existence, and to try to connect with other people who can benefit from my experiences.

So here we are. You and me. You have heard my story. And if you have suffered and cannot see how to persevere, I hope this book is of service to you. If you have been born into – or are trapped in – a situation that is destroying you, or could destroy you, you **can** move beyond your circumstances. You can do it, no matter how horrific or difficult that departure may be. I hope I can influence you to think beyond the confines of your current situation.

This is how we start. For myself, I am going to keep hammering away at forgiveness and release – and I will continue practicing gratitude. Imagine me holding your hand as you do the same. We will find strength in surviving our experiences, trials and traumas; we will find peace and happiness and thriving. I will check in again, and I hope you do, too – in this life, and in all the others we might live together.

Journey on in love and pure joy,
Kendra

ACKNOWLEDGMENTS

I would, first and foremost, like to thank and honor my brother Kent Jr.; without him, I would not be here to write this book. I love you, cherish you, and miss you.

To my father – thank you for your love, humor, and affection; and for bringing so much fun and laughter to our lives. You are the foundation and the glue for our family. I love you very much.

To my brother Frankie – you are my "ride or die"; you are an incredible man, and I am so lucky to have you as my brother. To my brother Clint – you are such an amazing man, and I am thankful you are my brother. I love you both to the ends of the earth.

Rosie, thank you for loving my father, and for your love and friendship.

Thank you to all my Okie and Texas cousins, aunts, uncles, nieces, nephews, and sisters-in-laws, for all your endearing love. And, a very, very special thanks to my cousins Sheila, Donna, Shonna and Tawnya for giving me so much support, love and laughter over the years – and for letting me be the fifth sister.

Gretchen, my dear, dear friend – thank you for your encouragement and love. Our shared adventures and the hilarity (so much hilarity) we have experienced throughout our many years in each other's lives have been absolutely priceless. I am so grateful for you.

To Ronnie, Michelle, Tammy, Yvonne, Mark, and Megan – I am fortunate to have you as my siblings. I love you all. To the Lezzie Vibe Tribe – you ALL are the best; I love you!! K-Pop :)

To ALL my friends – and there are so, so many around the world – I thank you for your eternal solidarity, devotion and benevolence. I am extremely privileged to have such remarkable friends who fill my life with light and joy.

To those family members and friends who helped me through some of the very difficult times and assisted in caring for me when I was injured or ill – I thank you so much for your devotion and care.

Amber, thank you for your helping hand in the design of the book cover; I also truly appreciate your sweet support and excellent ideas as I headed into the homestretch with this book. xox

Mary, thank you for your friendship and for all your help in reviewing the book, as well as your valuable feedback and assistance with submissions to publishers. You rock!

Jessica J., without you, this book would not have come to fruition. It took us years of very difficult conversations, exceptionally challenging work, considerable collaboration and so much writing to get here. You pushed me hard and helped make this an amazing – and sometimes painful – ride. Through the process, I have found a forever friend. Thank you for introducing me to my publisher April.

Thank you to the whole O'Leary Publishing team for the roles that each of you played in creating and launching this book. You are so very talented, and an excellent team! To my publisher April, you have been a wonderful mentor and guide, and are now a friend. You were full of exceptional ideas that helped refine this book into a work of which I am so proud. I am honored to have partnered with you and your entire team. I am ready for the next book!

Heather, as head editor, you worked so hard throughout this process; and you were incredibly supportive, kind, and full of such fantastic ideas. I thank you. Kat and Boris, your work in editing the book was hands-down exceptional. Jessica A., the cover and interior design of this book are more amazing than I could have imagined. Dustin, thank you for designing a wonderful website and for supporting this book launch process.

To all those that have harmed me – without you, this book would not be possible. To all those that have loved me – without you, this book would not be possible. To any I may have hurt along the way – I am truly sorry.

This book was many years in the making and was a project of love and hate. Love – because I am able to share my story and growth with you. I hope that you find comfort and a path to healing through the words in this book. Love – because writing this book helped me find an avenue toward healing for myself. Hate – because writing forced me to think and talk about horrific experiences that I never talk about and try hard not to ever think about (not very successfully). But in the end, it was the talking, the thinking, and the writing that helped me on my way to finding peace, joy and happiness.

ABOUT THE AUTHOR

Kendra was born on a family farm in Oklahoma. Her father, Kendra, and the rest of the family, left the farm, so he could pursue his career dream – which was not farming. However, the farm has stayed in the family to this day and is an important part of the family's history.

Kendra and her family moved around Oklahoma, Texas, and Arkansas, settling in Lawton, Oklahoma. She was raised in a very strict bubble of God and worship. As a teenager she was not allowed to socialize in the secular world at all because her family became part of a religious cult.

Before graduating high school, Kendra served as a missionary in Haiti, which was an incredible experience for her. That experience taught her resolve and independence, and it showed her how much inner strength she actually had. It also made her extremely grateful for what she had in her own life, after seeing so much poverty.

After high school, Kendra left Oklahoma and the religious cult behind. In order to pursue her dreams and build a career, she relocated to New York City. During her eight years there, she attended and graduated from college and entered the world of fashion. But soon, she longed for a career change and a new city, and so she left New York and the fashion industry and moved to Los Angeles.

In LA, Kendra started a decades-long career in the parking and transportation industry. She moved 13 times during her career; in order to climb the corporate ladder. Over the course of her career, she has overseen operations in more than 180 cities in North America. Moving up through the ranks, she eventually became an executive vice president at two different firms.

Kendra understood all too well the challenges of succeeding in a male-dominated industry. Still, she was determined. She came to love working on mergers and acquisitions and using her skills as a powerful negotiator and dealmaker. She also became a dynamic public speaker and presenter.

Kendra enjoys bouldering, scrambling and off-roading. She also loves spending time with her family and friends, and traveling.

Made in the USA
Middletown, DE
21 April 2024

53294522R00199